# On the Warpath: My Battles with Indians, Pretendians, and Woke Warriors

## Elizabeth Weiss

# On the Warpath: My Battles with Indians, Pretendians, and Woke Warriors

**Elizabeth Weiss**

Academica Press
Washington~London

Library of Congress Cataloging-in-Publication Data

Names: Weiss, Elizabeth (author)
Title: On the warpath : my battles with indians, pretendians, and woke
warriors | Weiss, Elizabeth.
Description: Washington : Academica Press, 2024. | Includes references.
Identifiers: LCCN 2024937593 | ISBN  9781680533323 (hardcover) |
9781680533330 (paperback) | 9781680533347 (e-book)

# Contents

# List of Figures:

# Acknowledgements

There are so many people who I am grateful to; so many wonderful, sensible, and funny people reached out to me after having read about my case. Some were academics; others were bookstore owners, musicians, lawyers, medical doctors, librarians, and more. They came from all over: from as close as the Bay Area, to as far away as New Zealand. What they had in common was a love of anthropology and science, and sincere concerns about censorious actions. They ranged from Liberal to Conservative; religious to atheist; young to old! It warmed my heart to receive the many emails of support and I spent many evenings reading these to my parents.

I'd also like to thank the lawyers, Daniel Ortner, Ethan Blevins, David Hoffa, and Wilson Freeman, at Pacific Legal Foundation who took up my case. And, the four anthropologists, Marshall Becker, Bruce Bourque, Della Cook, and Douglas Owsley, who wrote affidavits on my behalf. There were also those who dared to post a positive review of *Repatriation and Erasing the Past* – Geoffrey Clark (who has written one of the all-time best criticisms of NAGPRA in his "NAGPRA, Science, and the Demon-Haunted World" essay), J. Kenneth Smail, and Glynn Custred (who has become a good friend to me – I always learn something when I talk to Glynn).

When *Repatriation and Erasing the Past* was under attack, I couldn't have asked for a better co-author than Jim Springer. Jim is the epitome of cool, calm, and collected; his excellent reasoning skills and detailed legal knowledge made *Repatriation and Erasing the Past* a far better book than I could have written alone.

I also want to thank the many others who have helped me along the way: Peter Wood, president of National Association of Scholars, for giving me a platform to fight back against the many false allegations of racism that Jim and I faced; Juliana Geran Pilon, who encouraged me to submit my manuscript to Academica Press; Michael Shermer, editor of *Skeptic Magazine*, who gave me my first big audience through his podcast; Michael Regnier and John Tomasi, both at Heterodox Academy, who saved the cancelled American Anthropological Association panel on biological sex, and many others!

Keeping my sense of humor was made far easier since my family – my mother Gisela, my father David, and my siblings Katherine, Alex, and Chris – were supportive throughout these many cancel culture attacks. And, I cannot forget to mention my husband Nick. Not only did he proofread the manuscript – though any remaining errors are my fault – but his humor and his reassurance that we'd be alright even if I lost my job made taking all this in my stride easier.

I also want to thank Paul du Quenoy, President and Publisher of Academica Press, and the entire team at Academica Press. I first became aware of them when they saved Jim Flynn's last book, and I'm proud to be published by them!

Finally, I want to thank all those who are fighting the good fight to save free speech, academic freedom, open inquiry, and the search for the truth. There are those who've experienced their own cancel culture attacks – Charles Negy, Amy Wax, Frances Widdowson, Philip Carl Salzman, Bruce Gilley, Carole Hooven, Kathleen Lowrey, Matthew Garrett, Jordan Peterson, and many more – who have provided support, advice, and, perhaps most importantly of all, humor.

# Introduction

*Figure 1: Holding Skulls: Then & Now*

These two photos tell a story: The photo on the left is one that was taken a few years ago and was used by my University for promotional purposes, which I also used for the title slide when I gave my August 2019 Warburton award speech – the Warburton award is the highest research award given in the College of Social Sciences at San José State University (SJSU), which is where I taught and researched since 2004. This photo was on multiple University websites until a cancel culture mob decided that all photos of bones needed to be removed from the University's webpage. The image on the right was taken in September 2021 after we returned from COVID closures – it's a photo showing my sincere joy to be back doing what I loved most – examining the past through the study of human skeletal remains and curating the precious research collections housed at SJSU. The image on the right became an international news story and was also used as an excuse to lock me out of the curation facility, remove me from curation duties, withhold funding from me, change the accepted protocols for handling skeletal remains, plan to burn x-rays, and more. It's the photo that the University used to attempt to silence me and led to the administrators' retaliatory actions that prompted me to file a lawsuit against my own University.

Let me take a step back and explain my love for skeletal collections, my desire to fight against the loss of these collections, and how my pro-research perspective – once tolerated and actively debated to reach a compromise in the reburial versus curate and study issue – is no longer a topic that can be discussed. Only one perspective, the pro-repatriation of remains and artifacts view, is tolerated now, and anyone who disagrees shall be ostracized, ridiculed, and cancelled – derailing one's ability to conduct research that can help present day people in so many ways.

My appreciation of the beauty of skeletal anatomy started at a very young age. As a child, my favorite toys were anatomical models that I had to build up like a 3-dimensional puzzle. One involved putting together an enlarged plastic eye in its plastic bony socket. Later on, my study of anatomy taught me the form and function of the skeleton, allowed me to grasp the evolutionary links between humans and other animals, and provided a key to reconstructing the past lives of people who lived in times before writing could capture their humanity and their stories. I learned something that the models could not teach me—the incredible variation in skeletal anatomy parallels the variation we see in the external appearance of humans.

Anthropologists have shown that cranial modification can be accomplished by shaping the malleable heads of young people; and even nowadays, doctors use helmets to shape the heads of children who have been deformed by too much time on their backs or from various illnesses. Practical applications of skeletal knowledge can also help to prevent misclassification of crimes. CSI and other TV shows that involve forensics have been extremely popular recently; forensic anthropologists are key to solving crimes because they can identify sex, age, and cause of death from victims who have been found as skeletons.

Over the years at SJSU, I took time to revisit the large skeletal collection of prehistoric and pre-contact Californian Native Americans that I curated. I spent over fifteen years with these individuals and with each visit, there was never a time when something new didn't catch my eye. And, I am grateful that I was able to spend time with this magnificent skeletal collection, before a cancel culture campaign resulted in the removal of my access to the curation facility.

I've conducted research at the Canadian Museum of Civilization on prehistoric British Columbian natives and on 18th century European-Canadian Quebec prisoners-of-war. I've traveled to New Mexico to examine European-American 20th century suburbanites, and to Cleveland to look at the largest donated body collection in the US. I've collected data on Amerindians from pre-contact California both during my years at Sacramento State University and during my time at SJSU. I examined the CT-scans of Kennewick Man, the nearly 9,000-year-old Washington skeleton that made headlines when Jim Chatters – initially called in to identify the "homicide victim" – realized that the weapon was an obsidian arrowhead from thousands of years ago.

In all cases, my research involved answering questions using bones to reconstruct the past, understand diseases, determine biological relatedness, and look at bone biology. My research methods included x-rays, CT-scans, metric analyses, and non-metric examinations. I will talk about three of my favorite studies.

One of my favorite studies includes a comparative study, that I undertook with the help of anthropologists Jeremy DeSilva and Bernhard Zipfel, of foot bone growth patterns that looked at a nearly 2-million-year-old foot from an early human ancestor compared to a forensic collection from South Africa and the prehistoric California collection housed at SJSU. This three-way comparison – looking at x-rays of foot bones – allowed us to conclude that "ghost lines" (which are remnants of fusion that occurred at growth plates seen in x-rays) cannot be used to estimate age, as previously thought. Some 20-year-olds have ghost lines and so do some 80-year-olds. This led us to conclude that the early human was not a juvenile as previously thought, but an adult. But, more importantly, it also helped us to let forensic anthropologists know that seeing a ghost line isn't evidence of youth and should not be used to determine a victim's age.

Another study I conducted, with the help of anthropologist Gary Heathcote, looked at a single individual with a large bump on the back of his skull. This bony protrusion was about the size of a half golf ball. At first, Gary and I thought it may have been an inflamed muscle marker from overuse of the muscle or even a pulled muscle, but upon closer inspection we saw that the asymmetry of the skull made this hypothesis very unlikely. So, we thought it may be a tumor. Malignant tumors have a hair-on-end appearance in x-rays; non-malignant tumors have a marbled appearance; this bony bump displayed neither pattern. Upon looking at the skull in an x-ray, we could see a hairline fracture on the bottom of the bump, which led us to further investigate the etiology by examining medical x-rays of cranial trauma. It appeared that this bump – on this nearly 2000-year-old skull – was the result of being hit on the head. It was what is called a ballooned osteoma. The injury caused hyper bone growth and, thus, instead of the usual depression fracture, the individual got a large bony bump. This individual came from a pre-contact Bay Area California collection with lots of evidence of violence – broken noses, cranial depressions, arrowheads embedded in bone. And, the collection also was not of one people, but showed evidence through nonmetric cranial studies of replacement, with invasions coming from the tribes located to the southeast of them – a conclusion that the present-day local tribe fought against, since they claim to have been in the region since time immemorial.

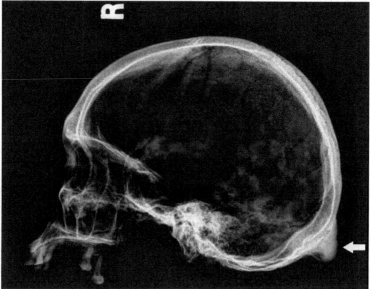

*Figure 2: Bump on a Skull: Evidence of Violence in Prehistoric California*

The final study I want to mention is a sex study. Anthropologists early on realized that there were differences between male and female hip bones (or pelves) due to childbirth requirements. Simply put, the pelvic gap in females is wider. The traits on the pelvis used to make sex determinations are universal – they can be used in forensics, prehistoric studies, and on historic samples. The same traits are used for human remains from Native American, European, African, and Asian populations. Early in my career, I was looking at ways to reconstruct activity patterns – what people were doing – by looking at muscle markers, which are areas where muscles attach on bones. For the most part, reconstructions prior to my research emphasized the labor of males and the overall delicate nature of females, to argue that males were doing heavier labor, walking more, and working harder. This conclusion may also have been helped along by the 1980s studies that showed hunter-gatherers had more leisure time than previously expected – especially for the female gatherers. Not satisfied with these conclusions, I decided to see if females were getting unfairly drawn as lazier than males! What I found is that when looking at muscle markers from populations of different times, places, and cultures, male bones were nearly always more robust than female bones. The majority of this difference is confounded by body size and if you control for body size, then the difference between the sexes is much smaller. But, hormones also drive the difference; mainly in that testosterone results in bone being deposited on the external bone circumference – the periosteum, which results in larger bone diameters and more pronounced muscle markings. Female bone, on the other hand, is laid down on the inner bone circumference – the endosteum, a result of estrogen, which results in smaller and smoother bones. It is driven by sex hormones, which demonstrates that sex affects the entire skeleton – not just the pelvis.

I would have been happy to continue such studies and I had planned to investigate malnutrition and neglect in child bones using crania and shin bone x-rays in a manner that I had hoped could also be applied in forensic settings to understand child neglect. But, these plans got derailed due to an intolerance of viewpoint diversity regarding the issues of repatriation and reburial.

In 1990, the federal law NAGPRA, which stands for the Native American Graves Protection and Repatriation Act, was passed. It requires museums and universities to repatriate (or give back) human remains, sacred objects, and funeral goods to culturally affiliated tribes. Affiliation, unfortunately, can be "determined" with the use of tribal oral history and myths (including creation myths). As a result of this law, many research collections have been lost to science. Now, NAGPRA and other repatriation laws are targeting unaffiliated collections and teaching collections for repatriation.

In 2018, with the 30-year anniversary of NAGPRA coming up, I decided to write a book criticizing NAGPRA and repatriation ideology – an ideology that places who tells the story above scientific evidence. It is a postmodern ideology where there is no truth and where victims' narratives – in this case Native American repatriation activists – are favored over scientific evidence to make claims of connections between past peoples and present tribes. My co-author Jim Springer, a now-retired attorney, wrote about the legal aspects with a focus on how repatriation laws violate the First Amendment's Establishment Clause – an important part of the separation of church and state. Since the law requires committees to include Native American traditional Indian religious leaders, it is favoring a specific religion. Also, since animistic creation myths are allowed as evidence, it supports one religious tale over others (and over science). We argued further that repatriation laws have stifled research because anthropologists fear upsetting tribes and, thus, losing access to collections when collaboration ceases. Our book – *Repatriation and Erasing the Past* – came out in September 2020; by December a vicious cancellation campaign had begun with an open letter asking for my book to be de-published and removed from libraries. Nearly a thousand academics signed the open letter, including half of my department and all the grad students!

This book and the campaign against it, coupled with an op-ed I wrote that criticized California's state law called CalNAGPRA (which I describe as NAGPRA on steroids), led to a series of events in which the University would remove me from my position of curator, lock me out of all collections – literally changing the locks – and try to take actions to prevent me from future research, including research on non-Native American collections. Collusion with tribes led to the removal of x-ray access and plans to burn the x-rays. My University tried to make this about the photo on the right, arguing that my smile, my lack of gloves, and the comment that these remains were "old friends" were disgusting. Yet, it wasn't the photo that caused the backlash – previously similar photos had never caused an issue; the provost who wrote a lengthy letter expressing his "shock and disgust" at the right side photo was even at my award talk in which I started with the photo on my left. Such photos are commonplace in anthropology (rather like a doctor being photographed with a stethoscope) – what caused the backlash was a change in the field, that does not now allow for any other opinion than that bones should be reburied.

In less than a year, I went from being celebrated to being the villain. At one time, not long ago, my University praised my different perspective; they heralded my scholarship as evidence that they were open to diverse viewpoints and welcomed strong debate.

As my chair, the same one who held a workshop on me called "what to do when a tenured professor is branded a racist," wrote in his approval of my request for leave to write *Repatriation and Erasing the Past*:

> Dr. Weiss's proposed project is likely to benefit the anthropology department in multiple ways…In the past her NAGPRA work has been cited in a wide range of public venues, including National Public Radio and Native American Times…since Dr. Weiss holds a controversial position on NAGPRA – focusing upon the ways in which the interpretation and implementation of repatriation and reburial laws may impede intellectual inquiry – her new project is likely to spark lively discussions among various stakeholders. Consequently, her book might potentially boost the department's national reputation as a center that fosters creative and unorthodox viewpoints on important public issues.

They also saw no problem with my photos prior, even funding a project that was based around the use of photos to highlight human diversity, and consistently used photos of me and others with bones to promote the department, college and University.

The difference between 2019 and 2020 was astounding. The difference is that cancellation became acceptable and even lauded. Some professors even put their efforts to cancel me, such as when they called for the Society for American Archaeology to deplatform my talk on repatriation and creation myths, on their résumés or CVs! Intolerance is seen as needed, to "decolonize" the field and atone for past 'sins,' including the 'sin' of being white. Repatriation activists will not be satisfied until everything is reburied, repatriated, or destroyed. But I think anthropology and its collections are worth saving, and that's why I'm telling this story.

# Chapter 1:

## Landing My Dream Job

In 2004, I was interviewed for my dream job at San José State University (SJSU): a tenure-track position as a physical anthropologist at a California university that also held a large prehistoric skeletal collection. The job would enable me to have an active research agenda – looking at bone biology and using the remains to reconstruct past people's lives. I would be curating the Ryan Mound Collection, the largest, prehistoric, single site, and – at that time presumed single population – collection west of the Mississippi River. As the only full-time physical anthropologist (anthropologists who study the biological aspect of humans through primate research, fossils, bones, or DNA) in a department with several cultural anthropologists (anthropologists who study living people) and one to two archaeologists (anthropologists who study the things people left behind, e.g., stone tools), I would not be competing for access to the collection, for funds to improve the curation of the collection, or for research tools to study the remains.

At SJSU, I would also have a busy teaching schedule in which I covered general education courses, such as Introduction to Human Evolution, the graduate statistics course, and all the physical anthropology courses – Mummies; Human Osteology (a course to teach students bone identification); Monkeys, Apes, and Humans; Bioarchaeology (a course on skeletal remains in the archaeological record); Human Origins (a course on fossils); and, Modernity and Disease.

It wasn't a done-deal that I would get the job – I missed the time slot for my phone interview and it had to be rescheduled; my teaching experience was exceedingly scant – I had undertaken a post-doctoral position at the Canadian Museum of Civilization, where I had collected data for my PhD, that was purely research-based; and, during the on-campus visit, we had technical difficulties before my lunchtime talk. Nevertheless, I moved from thirteenth position to second place after the on-campus interview; the first place candidate didn't take the job and so I was offered it.

Years later, the first place candidate would visit SJSU to study the Ryan Mound Collection since the skeletal collections at his University were off-limits to researchers – they had been removed from the care of anthropologists to the Native American Studies department, an activist department with professors whose interests are in decolonizing the university rather than learning about past peoples' lives. It is a common misunderstanding to think that all skeletal collections are available for research until they are repatriated or reburied – Sacramento State University, where I did my Master's degree, had made collections off-limits for research for years, even though there were no repatriations (in anthropology this is the term used to indicate that skeletal remains and artifacts are being given to an affiliated tribe, but in actuality, often the materials are given to an unrelated tribe, based purely on geography) or reburials planned. Some of their students, thus, came to SJSU to collect data, but others would need to go to Europe to finish their degrees, extending the time needed to complete the usual two-year degree and, likely, adding unnecessary student debt.

I was exceedingly happy to have landed the SJSU position. After all, I had applied for dozens of professor jobs. One rejection letter was misaddressed to someone else and when I reached out to clarify whether the rejection was meant for me, I was told it was, and that even if I was the last anthropologist on Earth, they wouldn't hire me! This may have been due to my early stance against repatriation and reburial of skeletal remains. I've always been against the reburial of human remains; I thought – and still do – that NAGPRA would ruin physical anthropology and archaeology. I've also held the position that the law is a violation of the US Constitution's First Amendment.

I completed my PhD in 2001 and my Master's ran from 1996 to 1998; thus, I grew into an academic during a contentious time when NAGPRA was not even a decade old, but when there was already a push to loosen regulations to increase repatriations and burials. The most famous example is Kennewick Man, a Paleoindian dating to around 9,000-years-old, that was first examined by Jim Chatters when the remains were found eroding out of a riverbed in Kennewick, Washington in 1996. Jim Chatters, a forensic anthropologist (which is an anthropologist who examines human remains in criminal or legal settings, such as in homicide cases), first thought that Kennewick Man might be a recent homicide victim. The unusual features of the skull led Chatters to question the race of the remains and he didn't initially think that the remains belonged to a Native American. Yet, a gleam from an obsidian arrowhead in the hip bone led to a closer investigation and the decision to date the remains. Upon the discovery that Kennewick Man was one of the oldest finds in North America, Native American tribes in the region started to make claims for the bones using their religious beliefs. According to tribes' (such as the Colville and the Umatilla of the northwest region) creation myths, they had always been in the region since time immemorial when their creator created them! A typical response given by Native Americans in regards to questions of migration from other places can be found with Armand Minthorn, a tribal councilman and spiritual leader for the Confederated Tribes of the Umatilla Reservation in northeast Oregon, when he said, "We didn't come across no land bridge. We have always been here."[1] Before the Army Corps of Engineers could hand over the remains to Native American tribes, but not before the Corps destroyed the Kennewick Man site by dumping 500 tons of rock and dirt on the site – an endeavor that the government spent $160,000[2] on – seven anthropologists (C. Loring Brace, George W. Gill, C. Vance Haynes, Jr., Richard L. Jantz, Douglas W. Owsley, Dennis J. Stanford, and D. Gentry Steele), helped by attorney Robson Bonnichsen, filed a lawsuit to gain access to the remains for research. The scientists would eventually win their case, and the right to study the skeletal remains. But, prior to that, the government chose a group of scientists, which included Jerome Rose of the University of Arkansas (where I was doing my PhD at the time), to examine Kennewick Man to determine his connection to modern day tribes. Rose provided me with CT-scans of Kennewick Man's leg bones and the raw data of his leg bone measurements; I examined these data and found that Kennewick Man was exceptionally strong-boned, especially for a man in his forties as was assessed by other skeletal features, such as the wear of his teeth and the changes in his pelvic bones. His lower limb measurements showed that his strength was on par with Neanderthals. This was not just from heavy activity during hunting – it must have been in part genetic, and it is distinct from the gracility of more recent remains found in the Americas.

In the end, Kennewick Man was said to resemble and be linked to early South American indigenous peoples; DNA evidence showed the same result.[3] However, due to a similarity between Kennewick Man's DNA and a local tribe, the Colville, President Obama issued an executive order, and the remains were turned over to the tribe and buried – gone forever! What was not considered is that *everyone's* DNA is linked together and the absence of a DNA database with many tribes leads to our inability to determine whose remains are closest to who; after all, these links may just be a result of a shared evolutionary link with *all* humans – we all share a common ancestor if you go back far enough. Kennewick Man should not have been turned over to a tribe that is less related to him than indigenous populations from South America – this was a travesty. But it was an early clue that worse was to come, despite NAGPRA having been touted as a compromise between science and reburial.

Kennewick Man; the presence of eminent anthropologists from institutions like the Smithsonian fighting for access and willing to sue the US government for the sake of science; even-handed coverage in mainstream media, such as *The New York Times* article *"Indian Tribes' Creationists Thwart Archeologists;"* and scientific articles from established paleoanthropologists (who study human origins using fossils), like Arizona State University's Geoffrey Clark who wrote "NAGPRA, Science, and the Demon-Haunted World," helped me articulate my position on repatriation and reburial laws. My pro-science and anti-repatriation perspective has not changed, even though the even-handed reporting by mainstream media has disappeared, and most of the anthropological community has abandoned science in favor of identity politics and postmodernism kowtowing to indigenous creationists.

Yet, it may be that the previously-mentioned rejection had nothing to do with my anti-repatriation stance – as I point out, this stance was not as uncommon in the late 1990s and early 2000s as it is now. Others were still writing on these topics in a critical manner, and I also had research articles, such as the ones stemming from my MA, PhD, and post-doc data. I even had articles in the top peer-reviewed journal of our field, the *American Journal of Physical Anthropology*, and I had won one of the top student prizes for my PhD work: the Mildred Trotter Prize at the annual conference of the American Association of Physical Anthropologists. There was another possible reason – a skeleton in my closet, so to speak!

Another possibility is that many of the rejections I received were a result of my marriage to Phil Rushton. At one point, I was asked in an interview for a post-doc position whether Phil would be moving to the region with me if I got the job. John Philippe Rushton was a controversial evolutionary psychology professor whose book, *Race, Evolution, and Behavior: A Life History Perspective* had caused an early cancel culture attack in the late 1980s. He appeared on talk shows, like the widely-popular Phil Donahue Show and Geraldo. And, he had been taken out of the classroom due to fears of harm – at one time even wearing bulletproof vests for protection. But, Phil remained a professor at the University of Western Ontario in London, Canada – researching and writing up his controversial conclusions – when I met him in 1997 at the Human Behavior and Evolution Society (HBES) conference that was held in Tucson, Arizona. We kept in touch throughout the year and re-connected in 1998 at the HBES conference that was held in Davis, California. We felt an immediate attraction between us. We were attracted to each other physically – Phil was 30 years older than me, but I still considered him physically my perfect type. More importantly, we were attracted to each other intellectually: thinking of big ideas that help to explain the world around us, focused on how evolution can explain human variation, and unafraid to speak up about our findings. On New Year's Eve, 1999, Phil proposed to me, and we got married in 2000, the day his divorce was finalized.

Unfortunately, Phil and I were incompatible in other ways; both of us were stubborn, never letting go of an argument. Phil also had a past filled with baggage that I had a difficult time overlooking – he had three children from three women; two of his children were born out of wedlock and one had been adopted when her likely drug-addicted mother lost custody. His youngest child was a mixed-race child from a black woman who was married – the child, when he entered into his early teens, Phil had told me, had behavioral issues. I only met his oldest son, who was a professor, but also deeply religious and prone to falling in with cult or cult-like organizations. Before I met Phil's son, he had married two sisters sequentially, since the first marriage didn't work out, but Phil's son planned to stay in the cult-like religion. Then, later, he joined Kairos Foundation's Life Training (now called More to Life), which is a self-help spiritual-coaching group, sometimes called "large group awareness training," which has been described as a cult by some. Phil's son spent an inordinate amount of money on such rubbish and had asked Phil for more money to spend. All of this, coupled with Phil's draconian control over finances, our inability to start a family (even after trying fertility treatments), my suspicions that he may have cheated on me, and his unwillingness to leave Canada, led to our divorce. Phil died on October 2nd, 2012; but, even with these faults, I have many fond memories – we'd spend our evenings reading popular science books to each other, like Lee Berger's *In the Footsteps of Eve*, about human origins research in South Africa; he had an undeniable charm with a mischievous twinkle in his eyes, and he helped me stay fearless in opposition – never shirking from controversy.

People sometimes ask me if Phil was a racist, since his work revolved around race research and his conclusions were that blacks were less intelligent than whites, who were less intelligent than Asians – a conclusion that he mainly attributed to evolution and climate-related natural selection. During my six years with Phil, he never displayed racist behavior. He was exceedingly polite and fair to everyone he encountered. He also wished young scholars the best, regardless of their race or sex. And, he spoke of the importance of treating people as individuals, even if group differences are present. Phil also allowed that some of the differences were related to nutrition, poverty, and other environmental factors – more so than I think that they are. But nutritional deficiencies can lead to poor outcomes in behavior and intelligence. These deficiencies can even be transgenerational, since a mother can pass on her poor choices to her offspring and small, undernourished females often have insufficiently formed uteri to carry well-developed babies to term. These female offspring grow up also to have smaller wombs and, thus, the cycle perpetuates. Furthermore, Phil believed strongly in the influence of TV and media; he had concerns over violence in cartoons influencing children's behavior, for example. And, he held strong views on the importance of altruism and modeling altruism (through behaviors such as blood donations), which he believed could be passed down to future generations.

When I left Phil, I continued to look for jobs and it isn't clear to me whether being back in the US or being away from Phil enabled me to land an academic job in a way that I maybe wouldn't have otherwise.

When I got the SJSU job, I dove right into teaching and research. Teaching didn't come naturally to me. Although I love to talk and write about physical anthropology, students in the large (around 120 students) general education class seemed for the most part uninterested. I couldn't understand this; during my years at University of California at Santa Cruz (UCSC) as an undergraduate, I loved nearly all of my classes. UCSC, likely the most liberal college in California (if not the nation), may have seemed an odd choice for me, but the beauty of the campus, the resident deer population, the absence of sports, and the pass-fail system led me to attend UCSC. I wasn't worried about grades – I had always done well in school – but I wanted a scholarly experience that just focused on learning without thinking about grades. However, in all honesty, this system (which has now been replaced with normal grades) was often just grades in a written form: "Weiss scored a 90 out of 100 on her midterm." UCSC, as it was then, would now perhaps be considered center-left. In one of my classes on the history of evolutionary theory, for instance, one student was admonished when she cried over the revelation that Charles Darwin was a sexist by our standards – the professor told her that presentism (i.e., judging past peoples by today's standards) is an unscholarly way to view the past. Today, presentism is alive and well in our finest publications coming from Ivy League professors, such as when *Science* magazine published an article in 2021 by Princeton professor Agustín Fuentes on Charles Darwin's "racist and sexist beliefs." Fuentes argues that students should learn that "Darwin as an English man with injurious and unfounded prejudices that warped his view of data and experience." Going back to my own experiences at UCSC, not all professors were as sensible as the one teaching the history of evolutionary theory course. One professor, teaching a course on the culture of communist China, was quite upset when I spoke of the similarities in electrified acupuncture used on the temples to treat mental illness and electroshock therapy – it was abhorrent for me to malign traditional Chinese medicine with Western psychology.

I spent my final year as an undergraduate in Egypt. Living in Egypt was eye-opening; I saw the Third World firsthand. Although Egyptians I knew claimed that Cairo, which is where I lived, had no homeless people (unlike the infidel US), the large number of families living in cardboard boxes, even on rooftops, belied that assertion. And, women were treated as second-class citizens; in Alexandria, I was flashed multiple times in a single day! I was also sexually harassed when a cab driver tried to grab my breast during Ramadan when no one was out and cabs were hard to come by. A fellow student who had a clear Israeli Jewish name had to leave early, because he could not find a place to rent. My own landlord was a Coptic Christian and, thus, I was never asked about my name's origins. Weiss, however, was unlikely to raise an issue, as it was viewed as a German name as opposed to a Jewish one. In fact, my mother is German, and my father is ethnically Jewish.

Before returning to the States to do my Master's degree, I spent two months in Kenya at the Koobi Fora Field School, run at that time by Harvard University. The experience, excavating in the hot Kenyan sun, finding little of anthropological interest, and living communally, made me realize that fieldwork was not for me. I loved the nature – seeing baboons in the wild, coming across water buffalo, spotting a rhino in the distance, and viewing the beauty of the giraffe herds – and the heat. But, indoor plumbing and a modicum of privacy are very important to me. In Kenya, I also noticed the extreme poverty, where a used battery could be bargained for handmade goods, such as carvings and jewelry. I ended up leaving many of my material goods, such as my tent, flashlight and water bottle to Kenyan students, with no bargaining involved. Some of the US students chose to go native, trying, for example, to enlarge their pierced earlobes with sticks, and swooning over the Turkana (the tall nomadic people of northern Kenya) who came around to the camp. But, it was clear to me that these people had ailments related to poverty, such as anemia and parasites, exposed by the children's extended bellies and the adults' skin sores that we don't see in the US.

Getting back to SJSU, it occurred to me that I would have to let students get to know me, to improve their attentiveness – and improve my student evaluations! So, I'd begin the semester with a photo of me as a child sleeping on a stuffed gorilla with a stuffed chimp in my arms – displaying my early love of primates. Then, I'd tell them of my love of anatomy, which is why I fell in love with anthropology. As a child, I'd put together model eyes, hearts that pumped, and plastic skeletons. Anatomy, especially skeletal anatomy, is also the clearest evidence of the evolutionary ties we have to other animals. There is a beauty in the imperfect form and function of a skeleton, such as the slight changes in the backbones of humans compared to our chimpanzee cousins that illustrate our shared past and also the human changes related to bipedality, i.e. walking erect on two hindlegs – an interesting example of evolutionary trade-offs, in that despite the advantages of bipedality this transition is the cause of much human back pain. And, of course, skulls are fascinating in so many ways. Changes in the skull that allowed room for our big brains are a key part of understanding our own species' skeletal anatomy – the knock-on effects altered our entire skeleton, such as smaller jaws, smaller teeth, smoother brows, and – in the end – a more gracile form. And, the reason we can identify a skeleton's sex by looking at the pelvis is because large-brained newborns led to selection for wider and larger pelvic outlets in females, but not in males. This basic concept is now under attack by trans ideologists and allied anthropologists who wish to argue that there is no such thing as binary sex – it's all on a spectrum and men can have babies! More about this issue and the cancellation of a panel on sex differences later!

Skeletal anatomy was also why being a professor of physical anthropology at SJSU was my dream job – the Ryan Mound Collection, that large skeletal collection of prehistoric indigenous remains that I mentioned earlier, is beautifully preserved with many individuals having nearly all of their 206 bones present. There are children and adults; males and females; and, a bevy of interesting individuals in the sample. This collection, which I spent years caring for and thousands of hours studying became like an old friend, a term which would later be intentionally misunderstood and used to keep me away from bones. Nevertheless, I am grateful that I was able to study these remains and reconstruct these people's lives.

And, as I grew into a competent (hopefully!) professor, I also grew my publication record with research done at practically no extra expense to the University. I achieved full professor status two years early and was granted the College of Social Sciences highest research award, the Warburton Award, right before the tables turned as a result of my spineless colleagues, when a cancel culture attack brought on by woke social justice warriors attempted to ban my book, *Repatriation and Erasing the Past.*

---

[1]Muska, D. Dowd. 1998. "Scalping Science: Sensitivity Run Amok May Silence the Spirit Cave Mummy Forever." Nevada Journal 98 (2).

[2]Lasswell, Mark. (1999, January 8). The 9,400-year-old Man. *Wall Street Journal, Eastern Edition.*

[3]Rasmussen, Morten, Martin Sikora, Anders Albrechtsen, Thorfinn Sand Korneliussen, J. Victor Moreno-Mayar, G. David Poznik, Christoph PE Zollikofer, et al. 2015. "The Ancestry and Affiliations of Kennewick Man." *Nature* 523 (7561): 455–58.

# Chapter 2:

## Scholarly Endeavors and High Praise

Although my student evaluations weren't always stellar, and the University had decided against the continuation of the large general education Introduction to Human Evolution class that I taught because of the high failure rate, my productivity in research was never in question. My ability to publish in peer-reviewed journals in my field, like the *Journal of Archaeological Science*, the *American Journal of Physical Anthropology*, the *International Journal of Osteoarchaeology*, and extend my research into medical journals, such as *The Foot* and *Rheumatology,* led the then-chair of my department to suggest that I file for promotion to full professor two years earlier than usual. Thus, I became a full professor at age 40, after only 10 years at SJSU. I believe at the time I was the youngest full professor in the whole University.

My robust research agenda and, thus, publication record was made possible as a result of the Ryan Mound Collection. This collection, as I mentioned previously, contains over 300 individuals, many with nearly complete skeletons. The remains come from a single site that was excavated on-and-off from about 1935 to 1971 – the majority of the remains come from a collaborative effort of SJSU and Stanford University anthropology departments. My predecessor, Bob Jurmain, used the collection for his research from the early 1980s until his retirement in 2004. A collection like the Ryan Mound Collection can be used for generations. Questions about these past peoples' lives can be answered. Bone biology can be examined by looking at the remains. The collection is a useful comparative sample for research that looks at multiple populations. And, it is even useful for forensic anthropology, as I mentioned in my introduction. By 2018, over 200 studies had used the Ryan Mound Collection for research.

The Ryan Mound Collection, which dates from about 200 BC to 1800 AD (spanning about 2,000 years), is all pre-contact – these individuals had not yet met Europeans. The artifacts illustrate that these individuals lived a stone age culture (even as late as 1800 AD) where the most sophisticated artifacts were mortars and pestles, and obsidian arrowheads. For a long time, there was a presumption that the collection belonged to one people due to the similarity in artifacts over the long time span – thus, it was said that there was biological continuity through time. This continuity was also used as evidence to argue that the present tribes in the San Francisco Bay Area, where the mound is located, were connected to these past people.

One may wonder why the remains hadn't been repatriated to the Bay Area tribe, who call themselves the Muwekma Ohlone, who claim they are descendants of the Ryan Mound people. Stanford University, unfortunately, repatriated their portion of the collection to the Muwekma Ohlone even before NAGPRA was passed – if they hadn't jumped the gun, the collection would have been twice the size! The reason for SJSU's ability to continue to curate the collection lies in the details of NAGPRA. NAGPRA initially only allowed for the repatriation of collections that could be culturally affiliated (in other words be ancestral to) to a federally recognized tribe. There are about 500 federally recognized tribes, but the Muwekma Ohlone aren't among them!

The reason why the Bay Area tribes (such as the Muwekma Ohlone) are not federally recognized is in part a result of University of California, Berkeley's first anthropology professor, Alfred L. Kroeber, who in the 1920s declared that the Bay Area tribes were extinct. Kroeber put forth that the Costanoans (the name then used for the San Francisco Bay Area tribes) no longer exist as a result of the extensive interbreeding with Spaniards and their adoption of the Spanish culture. The Muwekma Ohlone have been trying to reverse this decision and gain federal recognition for years now. I initially thought that the Muwekma Ohlone were correct in their assessment that Kroeber was wrong and that – in their parlance – they're "still here," but I now realize that Kroeber was right all along. DNA studies show that the Muwekma Ohlone are essentially biologically identical to Los Angeles Mexicans.

The examination of skeletal remains using nonmetric traits, such as the presence or absence of metopic sutures, that are inherited, made me conclude that there is good evidence that the oldest portion of the site is from a distinct people than the later portion – likely as a result of invasions from the south and inland. Ironically, some relatives of the Muwekma Ohlone have even questioned the term "Muwekma," claiming that Rosemary Cambra, the previous tribal chief, made up the name in recent times. As reported in *Anthropology Now* in 2016, in an article written by Peter W. Colby, although the Muwekma Ohlone have claimed to represent all Ohlone (a catchall term used for Native Americans in the San Francisco Bay Area), not everyone agrees with this claim. Relatives of Rosemary Cambra, Ramona Garibay and Ruth Orta "'by no means consider themselves to be Muwekma Ohlone, which they refer to as 'Rosemary's group' — they suspect that Cambra "made the name 'Muwekma' up herself.'" Other tribes in the Bay Area, such as the Tamien Nation and the Amah Mutsun Ohlone, are also now claiming affiliation with the Ryan Mound peoples, which may prevent a quick repatriation of the collection – however, it will not mean that the collection is available to study. Such infighting between tribes is common and one of the many reasons repatriation takes longer than activists hope for. Unfortunately, during this modern tribal warfare, many collections just sit on the shelves, unavailable to researchers.

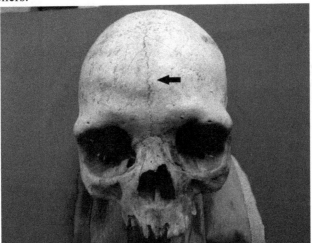

*Figure 3: Metopic Suture: Biological Trait*

In short, the lack of federal recognition enabled SJSU to curate the Ryan Mound Collection. New California laws threaten this collection – and all archaeological collections – because not only do tribes not need federal recognition, but also, tribal knowledge supersedes any other evidence. If a scientist discovers that the remains are not affiliated with a tribe claiming a connection, the tribe's word is given deference. Tribal elders are even considered expert witnesses, but ones who cannot be questioned. And, tribes can claim that their conclusions are based on secret knowledge that they mustn't divulge to non-Native Americans, i.e., white people! These are issues that I will return to later. The changes and additions to CalNAGPRA (as the California laws are referred to) are what led me to write an op-ed for *The Mercury News*, the Bay Area's mainstream newspaper, calling CalNAGPRA "NAGPRA on steroids."

Prior to the recent changes to NAGPRA, which allow non-federally recognized tribes to collaborate with federally recognized tribes for repatriation, there had also been concerns that repatriation to a non-federally recognized tribe may be breaking federal law. These complications, coupled with a lack of funding to implement CalNAGPRA, allowed for the Ryan Mound Collection to remain available for research until 2021, when the woke warriors and Pretendians (a term used to describe those who falsely claim Native American heritage) with recently made up tribal names, such as Muwekma Ohlone, came after me, and the then University president, Mary Papazian, shut down access to the curation facility that holds the collection.

Nevertheless, from 2004 to 2019 I conducted research on the collection nearly continuously. No matter how many times I looked at the individuals of the Ryan Mound Collection, I always saw something new and interesting. In the introduction, I highlighted some of my research. However, that was just a sliver of my work. Overall, I wrote two dozen articles using data from the Ryan Mound Collection. Nearly all of them single-authored and published in peer-reviewed journals. My research on the Ryan Mound Collection spanned from investigating causes of calcaneal osteophytes (also known as heel spurs) to looking at broken noses! I sometimes used the data to reconstruct past people's lives, such as when I looked at a male with a bony protraction on the bottom of his skull that we call a paracondylar process, and this was coupled with severe cervical (or neck) arthritis – an anatomical location where arthritis is uncommon, to conclude that his anomalous growth on the bottom of his skull, which also formed a false joint called a pseudarthrosis, would have led to a life of pain. In another study, I examined facial trauma and tied patterns that I noticed in the Ryan Mound Collection to universal trends. Males were more likely to be hit in the front – aggressor to aggressor. Females were hit on the back of the head (aggressor and victim). Fortunately, there was little evidence of trauma on children; thus, they may have been protected. The high level of violence found at the Ryan Mound makes sense when you view the collection as multiple peoples who were replacing each other through invasions, as I concluded in a 2018 study in the *American Journal of Physical Anthropology*. But such conclusions are likely not popular with virtue-signaling, indigenous groupies who push a romantic narrative of noble, wise, environmentally-aware and peaceful Native Americans, living in harmony with each other and with nature. The racism of this 'noble savage' false narrative is subtle, but should not be ignored. In reality, of course, Native Americans are like any other people in human history: sometimes they fight other peoples, and sometimes they fight amongst themselves.

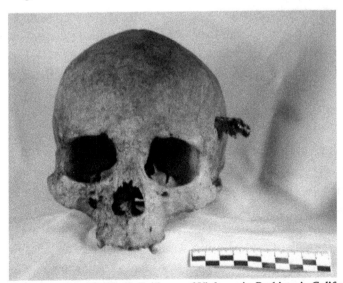

*Figure 4: Arrowhead in Skull: Evidence of Violence in Prehistoric California*

Other research centered around bone biology. It appears to me that anthropologists often attribute bony differences to culture and activity rather than biology and anatomical variation. In looking at stress fractures called spondylolysis, I confirmed that the high rate of these fractures (which can cause pain at the time of the fracture, but usually not after the pseudarthroses are done forming) in males compared to females is due in large part to anatomical differences in the lower back and pelvis. This is a trend found across populations, over different time periods. It seems to me, regardless of the bony trait, when patterns are so universal, then the difference is likely biological and not cultural. I wrote a book on this topic called *Reading the Bones: Activity, Biology and Culture,* which came out in 2017.

In *Reading the Bones,* I reviewed the literature on "activity markers" from stress fractures to entheses (which are sometimes referred to as muscle markers), and I assessed my own research on these markers – most of it completed on the Ryan Mound Collection – to determine how much of the skeletal variation is based on what we do, versus who we are biologically. What I found was a biological component is present in nearly all activity markers. This helps us understand ailments, such as heel spurs – it may be that the spurs are not related to long marches or running, but one may be prone genetically to getting the spurs. Interestingly, plantar spurs (on the bottom of the foot) are more painful than dorsal spurs, and in past populations plantar spurs were less common than dorsal spurs. This may still be the case, but clinical records show a higher rate of plantar spurs than dorsal spurs; could this be because people with asymptomatic spurs don't go to the doctor to get them looked at? Such issues illustrate how the study of a collection is not just knowledge for the sake of knowledge (not that there's anything wrong with that!), but can have tangible, real-world benefits, such as here where anthropological research can help inform medical doctors. This is why I'm pleased to have been published in medical journals.

Yet, some things are activity related. Much of my research revolves around the study of osteoarthritis, which is sometimes called degenerative joint disease. I was even asked to do an encyclopedia entry for degenerative joint disease. And, one of my most frequently-cited articles is one that I co-authored with Bob Jurmain, that discusses the etiology (i.e., the cause of) osteoarthritis. In past populations, upper limb osteoarthritis (such as that of the elbow and shoulder) was far more common than nowadays. It seems that upper limb osteoarthritis may be related to throwing spears in hunting and warfare. Osteoarthritis in other joints, like the lower back joints, is tightly related to aging. In the prehistoric past, people got osteoarthritis earlier than in modern populations and so we still see much lower back osteoarthritis in past people who rarely lived past 40 years of age. This is why I've previously said that osteoarthritis is not only an old-age disease, but also an age-old disease!

Going back to the elbow and shoulder osteoarthritis, males are more often affected than females in hunter-gatherer populations. Good evidence suggests that this is activity related and linked to spear throwing, since the sex difference is not universal.

Currently, there's been a push to argue that females are better built for hunting than males. The argument has been part that estrogen "increases endurance," that "the wider pelvis may be more efficient for carrying hip-placed loads," and that the extra fat increases energy availability.[1] Yet, a look at the skeleton reveals otherwise; longer limbs in males mean a longer stride and walking further with less energy; robust arm bones and muscle markers reveal the upper body strength needed to bring down large animals. Perhaps most importantly of all, females were (and still are) required for childrearing, which would preclude them from going on hunts in which the child may be put in danger.

Research on sex differences in anthropology has taken a decidedly strange turn recently. There seem to be two acceptable types of sex research: the type mentioned above where previously determined sex differences are now considered wrong and where it is now believed that females were doing the male activities. This type of research is often coupled with a type of feminism that argues women are better than men. In the hunting example, the researchers clearly argue that female bodies are better than males for hunting, but they ignore the decades of research that shows males have superior spatial awareness, a key component to hunting; that males have greater upper body strength; and, that in most cultures males undertake the hunting. They also fail to take into account pregnancy, breastfeeding and childcare as hinderances to chasing big game animals down. Injuries related to hunting, too, have been widely documented (mainly in males) from Neanderthals to modern hunter-gatherers! All this looks like conclusion-led research; some people want to portray women as hunters, which ignores the fundamental truth that men are generally bigger, stronger, and faster than women – and thus were almost always the hunters.

Another example of this feminine research includes the woman warrior phenomenon; whenever a skeleton is found with "warrior artifacts," the conclusion used to be that women were "respected" and perhaps "feared" warriors too. And, I don't doubt that some women were warriors (and, for that matter, hunters), but I think that the vast majority were males. It could be that the artifacts don't represent a person's past activities, but rather were a gift from a living male – perhaps one who was grieving, even! A once common principle in anthropology is that if the bones indicate one sex and the artifacts seem to be incongruent with this, then it isn't the bones that are wrong, but rather that the culture didn't practice a burial with grave goods tightly linked to one's sex or one's activity.

Now, the woman warrior tale takes another bizarre twist. Woman warrior cases are sometimes argued as evidence that these individuals were nonbinary or trans! In a Viking example from Finland, anthropologists published that the warrior that appeared to have been a male, with both male and female artifacts, may have been nonbinary; DNA evidence showed instead that the remains belonged to male who may have had Klinefelter syndrome, which occurs when the male has an extra X chromosome in the 23$^{rd}$ pair.[2] This anomaly is not the same as being nonbinary; Klinefelter syndrome individuals are male – I'll return to this issue a little later.

In another case, which was included in the "Written In Bone" exhibit, in 2017, at the Museum of London, lead anthropologist Rebecca Redfern noted that an individual dating between 50 and 70 AD seemed to display evidence of being nonbinary. This early Roman person found in London had grave goods that seemed to belong to a female and the skeletal anatomy looked to be female, but the DNA taken from a molar tooth seemed to suggest otherwise. So, they concluded that these remains were of a nonbinary person; however, a few years later, in 2021, a reexamination of the body with a better DNA technique applied revealed that all three lines of evidence matched up. The body belonged to a female! I find this woke obsession with the trans craze deeply offensive. The line seems to be that if evidence is found of a strong women (e.g., a woman buried with weapons), she must be trans! Can't she just be a strong woman?

Woke anthropologists have been pushing the trans agenda for years. There are anthropologists who claim that sex is not binary (i.e., male and female), but rather it is on a spectrum. And, it was the evil white colonialists who decided that there are only two sexes – men and women. Native American activists claim that indigenous people always had a concept of two-spirited people – people who were both male and female, and it was the Europeans who forced them to adopt the sex binary. Ironically the term "two-spirit" was coined in 1990 by Myra Laramy at the Third Annual Inter-tribal Native American, First Nations, Gay and Lesbian American Conference in Winnipeg. It is a completely modern and utterly fabricated invention!

Recently the British Museum has decided that the Roman emperor Elagabalus was trans, although historians state that documents using female pronouns for the emperor were products of competitors who wished to dethrone him – it was an insult and not his personal identity![3]

In order to tear down the binary sex reality, biological anthropologists are pointing to genetic abnormalities as evidence that sex is on a spectrum. One such example is Turner syndrome, in which some females have only one X chromosome in the sex chromosomes. Another is Klinefelter syndrome, where males have an extra X chromosome (XXY) in the sex chromosomes. These deviations from the normal configurations of XX, associated with females, and XY, associated with males, are called syndromes because they cause multiple effects on the person's anatomy and health. Females with Turner syndrome often have a severely shortened stature, scoliosis, a webbed neck, kidney problems, heart defects, and infertility. Males with Klinefelter syndrome often are infertile and have severe cognitive disabilities. These chromosomal abnormalities are not equal to nonbinary or trans individuals. Turner syndrome people are still females and Klinefelter syndrome people are still males. Sex is based on whether someone produces sperm or ova. Furthermore, disorders of sexual development – as in these chromosomal abnormalities – often result in infertility or sterility. To equate this with normal variation is a form of pseudoscience, and is clearly designed to promote a political, social justice agenda.

Normal variation of all sorts does exist; I've written about the variation I've seen in the Ryan Mound Collection – extra lumbar (lower back) bones, metopic sutures, bifurcated upper ribs and more. Skeletons show a great amount of normal variation, which has no disadvantage to the affected individual; but, abnormal changes belong in disease or pathology studies – in archaeology, we call this paleopathology. I wrote a book called *Paleopathology in Perspective: Bone Health and Disease through Time*, which touched on many of these issues.

Pathology research aims to try to understand the causes of the diseases, how the individuals can be treated, and how to prevent further cases. Polydactyly, i.e. extra fingers or toes, is a good example. We wouldn't conclude that the normal hand has between five and seven fingers because some people have extra fingers, which is often linked to inbreeding (as in cousin mating, often seen in nomadic tribes and common in the Middle East). Instead, nowadays, the extra digits are removed to improve the hand's function, and inbreeding is discouraged. By the way, inbreeding also leads to lower intelligence – another reason not to mate with a family member!

We could perhaps chuckle at the ridiculousness of those arguing that sex is on a spectrum if they weren't so aggressively going after those who disagreed with them, or trying to prevent research that uses male and female categories. But, we can't chuckle at them now, because they are shutting down debates and arguing for a moratorium on identifying remains by sex. Some anthropologists and archaeologists now argue that we shouldn't sex skeletal remains at all, because we don't know how these past people identified. A few years ago such statements would – rightly – have been dismissed with howls of laughter. Now, in anthropology at least, such views have become increasingly mainstream.

In late September 2023, the American Anthropological Association (AAA), along with the Canadian Anthropological Society (CASCA), decided to rescind an acceptance to a panel that I was slated to speak on – this cancellation was the first in the AAA's 122-year history. The cancellation made international headlines, appearing in everything from *The New York Times* to *Fox News*! Myself and four other anthropologists – along with moderator Carole Hooven (who wrote the book *T: The Story of Testosterone, the Hormone that Dominates and Divides Us*) – all biological females by the way – were to talk about the importance of biological sex as an analytic variable in anthropology. The panel's title, which the panel's organizer, University of Alberta anthropology professor Kathleen Lowrey, came up with was "Let's Talk About Sex Baby: Why Biological Sex Remains a Necessary Analytic Category in Anthropology." In the letter cancelling the panel, the AAA and the CASCA presidents wrote:

> This decision was based on extensive consultation and was reached in the spirit of respect for our values, the safety and dignity of our members, and the scientific integrity of the program(me). The reason the session deserved further scrutiny was that the ideas were advanced in such a way as to cause harm to members represented by the Trans and LGBTQI of the anthropological community as well as the community at large.

In their response to journalists, they doubled down on the decision to cancel our panel, writing:

> The session was rejected because it relied on assumptions that run contrary to the settled science in our discipline, framed in ways that do harm to vulnerable members of our community. It commits one of the cardinal sins of scholarship—it assumes the truth of the proposition that it sets out to prove, namely, that sex and gender are simplistically binary, and that this is a fact with meaningful implications for the discipline.
>
> The function of the "gender critical" scholarship advocated in this session, like the function of the "race science" of the late 19th and early 20th centuries, is to advance a "scientific" reason to question

the humanity of already marginalized groups of people, in this case, those who exist outside a strict and narrow sex / gender binary.

What a widely off the mark comment when one considers my talk was titled "No bones about it: Skeletons are binary; people may not be," and I wrote in the abstract that forensic anthropologists should increase efforts to determine whether a victim of homicide had undergone feminization surgery that literally changes bones. This was aimed at helping trans crime victims. But the woke warriors ignore such practical benefits, in favor of ideology.

Ironically, they use terms like "cardinal sins" and "settled science" to argue that there is no room for disagreement. Some may think that it is the cultural anthropologists who are leading the way to abandon the well-known concept of biological sex differences, but biological anthropologists are some of the worst offenders in pushing the "sex is on a spectrum" narrative. The biological anthropologists who wrote in favor of our panel's cancellation wrote: "What is typical about human sex and gender categories, is that they are not simple, not binary, are always affected by the cultural beliefs of the time, and that they shift." To support their conclusions, they use the chromosomal abnormalities discussed above and animal comparisons, including 'gender fluid' reptiles! This displays a staggering misunderstanding – or perhaps misrepresentation – of what science is, and how science works. And, science is never "settled." And, "cardinal sins" is a religious term, not a scientific one. My critics inadvertently showed their true colors.

Heterodox Academy (an organization that promotes diversity of thought and open inquiry in universities), where I'm currently a faculty fellow, rescued the panel and we gave our talks – all centered around biological sex; that sex is binary; and that it's important to look at sex differences in anthropology. My talk covered the range of male-female differences found in the skeleton, how we've gotten better at sex identification over time, and where improvement is still needed. But, importantly, I also touched upon the need to continue to look at sex and teach sex identification – something currently under attack – due to the forensic applications. If anthropologists stop identifying whether bones came from a male or female, we'll be doing a great disservice to the victims of homicide and their families. As I said in my talk, knowing sex enables more accurate age estimates, since males and females develop at different rates. In seniors, female skulls may start to take on some male features due to hormonal changes after menopause, but the pelvis and the overall post-cranial differences still reveal the individual's sex. Knowing sex and age helps the identification of the victim and, thus, may help to bring justice and closure to the victim's loved ones. As I said in my talk and later wrote in *Archives of Sexual Behavior*, if forensic anthropologists abandon their sex identification tools to appease the political agenda of erasing binary sex in anthropological research, we would be doing harm to the most vulnerable individuals – those who died at the hand of another, or who died in circumstances where they were alone and perhaps not even missed until their bodies became bones. I also highlighted the tragic irony that just as we're getting really good at sex determination (close to 100% when the whole skeletal is available), some anthropologists want to stop doing it altogether, because of trans ideology.

One may argue that this is irrelevant for research of past people, but most anthropologists who look at bones study both past and present populations. More importantly, they teach the next generation of forensic anthropologists. My area of expertise is not forensics, but I taught osteology to future forensic anthropologists. Plus, many forensic anthropologists will get their hands-on experience first in archaeological settings, such as field schools or lab classes that use teaching collections from archaeological sites. We need to protect anthropology as a research and applied field from trans activists and their allies.

Unfortunately, the American Association of Biological Anthropologists has followed the American Anthropological Association and called for a redefinition of sex as being on a spectrum, based on politics rather than science. In their "Statement in Support of Trans Lives," they wrote:

> The American Association of Biological Anthropologists, the American Association of Anthropological Genetics, the Dental Anthropology Association, the Paleopathology Association, The PaleoAnthropology Society, the Biological Anthropology Section

of the American Anthropological Association, and the Human Biology Association stand together against the escalating legislation and governance in the United States and across the globe that attacks the existence of transgender, non-binary, and gender-diverse peoples. We affirm the power of all persons to make the ultimate decisions over what happens to our/their own bodies. We oppose legislation that is rooted in and maintains rigid binary conceptions of sex and gender which impact reproductive justice and access to care for everyone. We condemn the biological essentialism driving much of this legislation. As biological anthropologists, we condemn the historical role of our discipline in producing binaries of sex, gender, and sexuality and are committed to work that enacts a more livable world. We condemn discrimination and denial of healthcare for youth and adults, including care that is gender and life affirming. We stand for the lives of transgender, non-binary, gender and sex diverse, and queer communities.

It's ridiculous that they are suggesting that the reality of the sex binary was created by anthropologists!

Had I not been used to cancel culture attacks, perhaps I would have been upset by the AAA's cancellation: rather, it was just another absurd tactic by social justice warriors who are out to destroy anthropology, due to their false perception of the field's colonial and racist roots.

It wasn't always this way. My own University at one time praised my work. They endeavored to promote the skeletal collection and the research on it. They used the skeletal collections and photos of me and students with human remains as a way to lure unsuspecting potential graduate students into our applied anthropology M.A. program, when they would be far better off in a four-field program, a program with an emphasis on biological anthropology, or even a specialized forensics program. And, at the 2017 Southwestern Anthropological Association conference – where two of my students won student prizes – I was even asked by one of my colleagues to give conference attendees a tour of our curation and lab facilities, highlighting the most interesting of the Ryan Mound individuals. Our program, built to get students in cultural resource management or the nonprofit sectors, nearly always had some physical anthropology students, and I helped them to the best of my ability. Three of them even won the University's thesis awards. Yet, they tended to have difficulty moving into PhD programs that are needed to fulfill their career goals. When the cancel culture attacks arose, they removed me from graduate student committees altogether.

Prior to 2020, my colleagues knew of my 'controversial' positions, but didn't have a problem with them; quite the opposite. When writing the recommendation for leave to write *Repatriation and Erasing the Past* my chair, Roberto Gonzalez, wrote: "her new project is likely to spark lively discussions among various stakeholders. Consequently, her book might potentially boost the department's national reputation as a center that fosters creative and unorthodox viewpoints on important public issues." And, in my post-tenure review, the committee, which consisted of my chair and two other full professors, wrote:

> Since her last review, Dr. Weiss has excelled in her scholarship, researching and writing prolifically. In addition to nine peer-reviewed articles, five non-peer-reviewed articles, and multiple conference presentations, Dr. Weiss has published three books since 2013: an edited textbook and two scholarly monographs on paleopathology and osteology. During AY 2018-19, she took a Difference-in-Pay Leave to complete another book project, tentatively entitled Repatriation and Erasing the Past (currently in press) that is co-written with an attorney...The underlying theme in this work is directly connected to Dr. Weiss's broader philosophical imperative: a steadfast commitment to advancing reason, rational thought, and the scientific method. Her future plans include further research on skeletal remains, as well as the possibility of a new book focused on objective knowledge in anthropology. The committee commends Dr. Weiss's record of productivity and looks forward to future publications.

In 2008, after my first book on repatriation came out, I was invited by the now-retired provost Gerry Selter to speak about my skeletal research and the threats to the collection, which I did! Never were there any concerns over my position – even though I knew some of my colleagues disagreed with my perspective. Furthermore, I was successful in the field beyond the University, working with co-authors from around the world, and bringing anthropology to the wider public. I was even invited to be on a PhD committee at the University of Leiden. They flew me over for the student's defense of her dissertation and had me give a talk to the anthropology students and faculty. These same folk, less than two years later, signed the open letter calling for the removal of my book from libraries.

I was also lauded for increasing the University's reputation when I helped the Milpitas Library compete for the Smithsonian's traveling exhibit on human evolution: "What does it mean to be human?" We won, and were the only library in California to get the exhibit – only 19 libraries in the whole country were chosen! During the exhibit I gave two talks, one of which focused on the study of skeletal remains.

The University's praise of my research, my promotion of the skeletal collection, and of my "controversial" perspective on repatriation all fell apart in 2020 when *Repatriation and Erasing the Past* came out. Yet, I think the fault lines were growing – at SJSU and other universities – around more than just repatriation laws and my academic book on these laws! But the fact remains: the University was happy to support me when they benefited from it; but they threw me under the bus when the tide turned. Their support evaporated. I lost my ability to study spines; my University lost its backbone!

---

[1]Ocobock, Cara, and Sarah Lacy. 2024. "Woman the hunter: The physiological evidence." *American Anthropologist* 126 (1): 7–18. https://doi.org/10.1111/aman.13915

[2]Nuñez, Xcaret. (2021, August 9). "1,000-Year-Old Remains May Be Of A Highly Respected Nonbinary Warrior, Study Finds." *NPR.* https://www.npr.org/2021/08/09/1026183914/new-dna-analysis-finds-1-000-year-old-warrior-remains-may-be-non-binary

[3]Burga, S. (2023, November 22). "U.K. museum says Roman Emperor was a trans woman." *Time.* https://time.com/6338587/u-k-museum-roman-emperor-trans-woman/

# Chapter 3:

## Fault Lines in the Bay Area

Upon returning from my first sabbatical, which I took in the Fall of 2013 to write my book *Paleopathology in Perspective: Bone Health and Disease through Time*, to work on a feasibility study on starting a donated body collection at SJSU, and to conduct research on osteoarthritis using clinical data from the National Institutes of Health, I moved into campus faculty housing. This move onto campus made it easy for me for apply to the newly-formed faculty-in-residence program that was to begin in 2016.

The faculty-in-residence program was one in which faculty lived on campus in faculty housing and spent 10 hours a week interacting with students; in exchange, faculty got to live on campus for practically nothing – just $150 a month. The program was intended to increase student involvement on campus and create an atmosphere in which students would get to know faculty. The hope was that interactions between faculty and students would make students more comfortable going to office hours when they needed help from their professors. Yet, as so often happens in academia, the program soon deviated from the plan.

Faculty-in-residence became a way for students to be treated like children with the faculty playing the role of the parent. Most faculty put together programs that would have been more suitable for elementary school students instead of even high school students. As the professors talked about "their kids," they planned friendship bracelet nights, natural hair events (for black students), and video game nights.

I tried to deviate from this norm. It's my philosophy that if you treat college students like children, they will behave like children. But, if you treat students like adults, they try to rise to the expectation and start to behave like adults. So, I decided to show documentaries like *The World Before Her* – a movie about two young women in India; one wants to become Ms. India and the other is a Hindu nationalist who is preparing to kill and die for her religious beliefs. Sometimes I showed lighter fare; on National Day of Reason, I showed Bill Maher's *Religulous*, which ridicules all religions. On Sunday mornings, I would host newspaper breakfasts, encouraging students to read newspapers and not just scroll their lives away on the latest apps. I also hosted events that were aimed at helping students attain academic success, such as a session focusing on proofreading.

My events weren't always successful, like the time I had planned for a full day in San Francisco looking at the many murals in the city – from recent ones on Haight St. to Depression-Era and Work Progress Administration ones from the 1930s to 1940s, such as the Diego Rivera mural at the now-shuttered San Francisco Art Institute. This was actually an event that the students on my floor had requested. However, after the first big hill, the students – many who were overweight and out of shape – were wiped out. Thus, they snuck down the hill towards the cookie shop and sat for the rest of the day in the park, eating sweets and playing on swings. On the bus ride home, most of them slept – exhausted by the day's adventures!

But, faculty-in-residence events aren't the only evidence of coddling. And, I am far from the first person to point out that university students nowadays are being overprotected. Jonathan Haidt, a professor of social psychology at New York University and the former president of Heterodox Academy, co-wrote (with Greg Lukianoff) a book called *The Coddling of the American Mind: How Good Intentions and Bad Ideas Are Setting Up a Generation for Failure* that came out in 2018. In this book, Haidt and Lukianoff raise concerns that safe spaces for speech and trigger warnings to forewarn students that something scary or sad may be shown (such as the recent trigger warning from the Scottish University of the Highlands and Islands for Hemmingway's *The Old Man and the Sea* that stated the book has "graphic descriptions of fishing") will result in a generation not ready to deal with adulthood. This seems to be increasingly true: people are learning to drive later, leaving home later, dating later – and less. And career aspirations nowadays seem to be increasingly dumbed down; it seems everyone wants to be a reality TV star or a social media influencer.

At SJSU, university event planners would hire bouncy castles and petting zoos to ensure students weren't too stressed before midterms and finals. And, the Health Center regularly showed Saturday morning cartoons that students could watch in their PJs while eating Froot Loops or some other sugary-sweet kids' cereal. While I was an undergraduate, movie nights included cinematic classics like the 1970 movie *The Honeymoon Killers* or the cult classic *Easy Rider*. Now, it's the latest animated G-rated film, and students discuss which is their favorite Disney princess! I'm not against enjoying childhood treats, from movies to foods, but universities needn't sponsor such things. Universities should instead challenge students – pushing then in the direction of adulthood.

When I was in high school, my friends and I were eager to enter adulthood. When I started college, I considered myself an adult – I wasn't watching cartoons; my entertainment of choice was film noir, and my favorite actor was (and still is) William Holden. If students just had childish viewing tastes that would be one thing, but this childlike behavior is pervasive in their behavior. When discussing life stages in my classes, I would often ask students if they looked forward to the next stage of life and most often they said they'd rather be younger and not older.

In other ways, the childishness manifested itself in their academic performance. For instance, the excuses made to get out of a paper or an exam were farcical; only a child would think that these excuses would pass muster. I had students, of course, who would claim their grandma died, to avoid taking tests. Mike Adams, a biology professor at Eastern Connecticut State University and a lead editor for *Nature*'s Cell Biology section, has documented this trend of false grandparent deaths, exams, and student grades for many years. He calls it the Dead Grandmother/Exam Syndrome. In a 1999 article in the *Annals of Improbable Research*, Adams started his article by noting that "the week prior to an exam is an extremely dangerous time for the relatives of college students" and wittily suggested that one possible solution is to let only orphans enroll in universities! But, sometimes students would go beyond this and provide exceptionally unbelievable excuses.

I had one student tell me his 10-year-old cousin died of type II diabetes, but there was no obituary because the cousin's parents lived in

Nigeria. Yet the funeral was to be held in Oakland, California. He provided me with a funeral notice from the church, which, oddly, was digitally watermarked with "sample" all over it. I guess the student didn't want to pay for the final version from some online memorial-creating website. Calling his bluff, I phoned the church listed on the notice he provided me, and they said that they don't hold *any* funerals! All of this to get out of a 2-page paper!

With such incidences being quite common, it's quite unbelievable that a former associate dean of SJSU's College of Social Sciences admonished professors who ask for evidence of the death. He wrote in an email that students don't lie about death. Such statements may be motivated by a desire not to be the bad guy, but they're out of touch with reality, and encourage dishonesty and cheating, as opposed to rooting it out. I did confront my student and he failed the class. However, he came to me before the following semester to ask whether he could re-take the class and whether I would hold his previous acts against him; I told him that each new semester is a new beginning, and we start with a clean slate. To be fair, the student fessed up sheepishly when I called him out. I went on to explain that had he put as much effort into writing his paper as he'd put into constructing his excuse for not writing his paper, he'd have done well. I hope it was a valuable life lesson. He did re-take the class, under what we call "grade forgiveness," he had matured, realized the joy in doing an assignment well, and did quite well the second time around.

These examples aren't meant to imply that most of the students were looking for ways to get out of work or weren't interested in learning. I had some very good students throughout the years too – students who volunteered on the weekends to gather data from the Ryan Mound Collection with me, even if it meant working from 9 AM to 5 PM without a break! I co-authored one of my papers with two such students. Then there were students who started off doing poorly in the class, but really turned things around. One student who took my general education class late in his undergraduate degree thought he'd get an easy A; after all, he was about to graduate and had been getting A's in his major courses. When he got his first writing assignment back, he was shocked to see that there was a D on it. He came to my office hours, we spoke about where he went wrong, the following papers improved, and I believe that he earned either an A or B in the class. What was astounding about this student was that he came without a chip on his shoulder and really was eager to see what he had done wrong – after all, he was sailing through his sociology or social work courses. When he graduated, we kept in touch, and he thanked me for helping him – when he applied to graduate school programs, I learned that he had been a foster child and wanted to give back and help other foster children. I am happy to say that he achieved that goal and the last time I saw him, he was doing quite well in a fulfilling career. I suspect other faculty had inflated his grades. In the current woke environment one sees this a lot, especially with black and some other ethnic minority students. But such actions help nobody – least of all the students. If somebody is underperforming, they need to be told, and need to address this. Papering over the cracks does them no favors. Taken to the extreme, such people constantly have their grades inflated, think they are A+ students, but eventually hit reality. And, often after university life, they come down to earth with a thud.

Then there are the students who are naturally talented; they immediately grasp the details of bone differences. These are the students drawn to osteology for the love of bones. They're the ones who can almost instinctively tell the difference between the left and right ulna from just a fragment no greater than an inch long! It's the hard workers and the natural talents that I will miss.

And, many students are also kind to others who struggle with the materials or to students with disabilities. It is one of the hallmarks of the American can-do attitude that we empower students who are blind, deaf, in a wheelchair, or otherwise disabled to engage in academic life. I prided myself on trying to ensure that these students got as much out of the class as other students. For instance, I had a blind and disfigured student in my general education class one semester and when passing around casts of early humans, I made sure that he felt them thoroughly so that he could get an idea of the anatomical differences between, say, a 3-million-year-old australopithecine and a 1.5-million-year-old *Homo erectus*.

Although it seemed as if students were better in my early years at SJSU, there were good, hardworking, and kind students each semester. For these students and others like them, we must try to save anthropology specifically, and academia in general.

I mentioned earlier that when students fail a class, they can retake the class, and it is called "grade forgiveness" – what a term! It used to be called "academic renewal." The University changed it for practical reasons, we were told. But other terminology was changed for political reasons; sometimes because the previous terms were considered too punitive. For example, "academic probation" has been changed to "academic notice," and the University provost Vincent Del Casino acknowledged that the reason given for this change was:

> Removing the language of incarceration from our lexicon is just one of the ways that we are working to become a student ready campus of the future. As many of you know, using the language of "probation" frames our work with students in a deficit mindset and tells them that their academic misstep is the equivalent of something criminal.

Perhaps the provost had forgotten that professors are on a probationary period until they get tenure – should we change the term for professors too?

It is my prediction that Master's degrees and programs will be named something else in the future since this may trigger students of color and cause "historical trauma" as it'll be connected to slavery.

But, it isn't just coddling of students that makes them less prepared for life after college. There are also attempts to create dependency on government programs in the student population. Students are made to believe that they are poor. SJSU is not a particularly expensive school; tuition and fees at SJSU sit at around $7,992 per year for over 90% of the students who are in-state students. And, minimum wage in California ranges from $16 to $20 per hour. So, tuition and fees can be paid for with a summer job. Rents are high, but sharing apartments or living at home is common for SJSU students. Yet, faculty and staff often lead students to believe that they are poverty-stricken, in part as a result of the high fees at the University. Food pantries are pushed, even though students are so well fed that you can't even lure them to an event with promises of free pizza. As I wrote about for the James G. Martin Center for Academic Renewal,

"SJSU used to have free grocery days, during which students lined up for their free food like Soviet peasants." And, before filling their bags full of groceries, the students were required to fill out food-stamp forms; they were being enrolled in government-welfare systems. These students weren't starving or even hungry. Often, there wasn't a single thin person in line. Yet, students believe the poverty narrative pushed onto them through university propaganda, such as food-insecurity posters that, ironically, include only fat and obese people. A poster on a colleague's door with the slogan, "when your family is hungry, nothing else matters" featured a decidedly plump family – there likely being a shortage of thin models these days.

Although this free grocery program has been shut down – perhaps one of the very few good things to have come out of the University's hysterical reaction to COVID – other free food programs are still available to students. There's an ongoing attempt to sell the poverty narrative as a way of ensuring the army of do-gooders are always 'needed.' One of the ways this has been accomplished is through the moving goalposts of definitions that define need. At one time, assistance was for those who were starving, then for those who faced hunger, and now we are concerned with "food insecurity." Throughout campuses, there are, at times, signs that announce high rates of food insecurity, but nearly everyone could be defined as food insecure. Have you ever missed a meal due to not having money on hand? Or, have you ever decided to order something less expensive due to concerns about receiving a large restaurant bill? Then you too may be food insecure – at least, according to the new definition! One wonders what genuinely starving people – Ethiopians during famine in the 1980s, or folks living in the Depression-Era dustbowl – would make of well-fed students being classified as food insecure!

Perhaps the greatest absurdities are the homeless student and faculty narratives. SJSU has claimed that slightly over 11% of our students have "experienced homelessness" (the term used because calling someone "homeless" is apparently insensitive) – this would mean that out of our 36,200 students, 4,000 would have "experienced homelessness." If this was true, of course, it would be a real reason for concern. However, it is not true because the definition of homelessness has been altered so greatly that I am surprised that the number of "students who experienced homelessness" isn't higher. In SJSU's 2021 report "being without a home for one day in the last year" qualified a student as "experiencing homelessness." The data show that the mode (which is the most often reported answer) was one day of homelessness. And, the average or mean was about three days. Most of these students reported sleeping on someone's couch and 10% said that they slept in a hotel or motel. Thus, this supposed epidemic of students "experiencing homelessness" could be attributable to people staying over at a friend's house after a party!

And, it's not just student homelessness that has been reported on. While I was in the faculty-in-residence program, which included almost completely free housing, as I mentioned earlier, the other participating faculty members were upset that the position was just for two years. They tried to argue that since rents and home prices increased during those years while we were living on campus, we'd been put at a financial disadvantage and should get another year free! One faculty member then brought up one of SJSU most famous lecturers, the homeless professor Ellen Tara James-Penney. James-Penney has been interviewed by various mainstream media and is used by the California Faculty Association Union to argue for higher wages. A cursory inspection of her story reveals that she isn't homeless because of pay; rather, she has stated that she is $143,000 in debt and has been homeless since 2007, but started teaching in 2013. In other words, SJSU gave a homeless person a teaching position, rather than vice versa. Yet, she and others who push the poverty narrative are role models for students and examples professors use to argue how hard done by we are.

As a result of the false cries of poverty, I left the union – not least because I felt this poor-mouthing was an insult to those who are *genuinely* poor. I may have been the only professor who was not a union member in my college, or even throughout the University. I joined because I was led to believe it was a requirement; when I left, I had to pay more not to be in the union than had I been a member and was paying membership dues. But, it was a matter of principle for me. Trump's election changed that and although I had already left the union, I got some of my money back in 2017. The real price I paid for leaving the union was being called a "parasite" by some of my colleagues!

Upon the election of Trump, the SJSU community had a meltdown. Professors cancelled classes, students protested – chanting "Trump's not my president," and tears were shed. In my mummy class, we were talking about Slovenian mummies on the day after the election, which sent a few of my students into tears because Melania Trump is from Slovenia. The University president also put out this statement on November 9th, 2016:

> The Residential Life Team, the Student Affairs division, and the Office of Diversity, Equity and Inclusion have collaborated to provide this opportunity to come together, help each other make sense of the election, and continue building the inclusive Spartan community to which we all aspire.

"Help each other make sense of the election" – would any such statement have been made if a Democrat were elected? No; and, then-president Papazian proved this point when she wrote about Biden's inauguration, in a message to the campus on January 27th, 2021: "Last week's Presidential Inauguration was highly uplifting, hopeful and representative of the values and traditions that Americans cherish. Still, this remains a trying period in our nation's history."

There was no neutrality. And, although things eventually settled down, COVID-19 and the Black Lives Matter movement, coupled with George Floyd's death, would once again shake things up.

At the beginning of February 2020, my husband Nick Pope, a freelance writer and media personality whose main topic revolves around UFOs, by virtue of his having investigated them for the UK's Ministry of Defence, came back from interviewing retired politician and former presidential candidate Dennis Kucinich at the former home of actress Shirley MacLaine. The field shoot producer Gabriel Rotello had told Dennis and Nick that COVID-19 was going to dramatically change all of our lives. Rotello's activism during the AIDS epidemic perhaps influenced his perception of COVID-19's impact. I brushed these warnings aside and didn't think that much would happen – after all, there was a massive viral outbreak that killed something like 240,000 in the US when Woodstock took place in 1969, and this was when the US population was much smaller (around 200 million; or about 130 million less than nowadays).

Boy, was I wrong!

As the Spring 2020 semester was underway, I was spending my weekends with the Ryan Mound Collection and two to three students. Then, we got notice that classes were going online until after spring break; shortly afterward, we were told not to come back after the break. And, before I knew it – all academic year 2020-2021 was to be remote! I hated even the thought of teaching remotely, and I had no experience in remote teaching. We were given a $1,200 stipend to take a three-week course put on by the University to improve our remote teaching techniques. Unfortunately, since this was run by "eCampus, the Center for Faculty Development, and the Office of Diversity, Equity and Inclusion," a third of the preparation was indoctrination – one of the four required modules, for instance, was titled: "Equity and Inclusion Frameworks in Design in Online Settings."

Since remote teaching was in large part unsuccessful, grades were inflated beyond anything seen before. Failing grades were turned to no credit and, thus, didn't impact students' grade point averages; academic disqualifications were put on hold; and standardized writing tests were suspended. And, although we had access to anti-cheating tools, such as "lockdown browser" – software that prevents students from Googling answers, and remote monitoring on tests, we were strongly discouraged from using them. For instance, when I had written that I was planning to use Respondus, software that uses webcams or students' phones to monitor them during tests, I was told by my chair, Roberto Gonzalez:

> There isn't really a way that you can require students to have webcams at home. (Ron Rogers has confirmed this.) As you probably know by now, not all students have reliable broadband internet access--or webcams--and there is no mechanism by which a faculty member can require everyone to have one (any more than we can require the purchase of a textbook). Additionally, some students are concerned about privacy issues (as I probably would). I suppose you could recommend it, but not require it.

I did follow up with Ron Rogers, who was the associate dean of the College of Social Sciences at the time, and he conceded that I could use the software, but did so begrudgingly.

Classes were online and the campus community – from students to faculty – were staying in their homes, only going out to protest, especially after George Floyd's death in May 2020. Our then-president Mary Papazian issued multiple statements in which support for protests was implied. In some of these statements she clearly plays judge and jury, calling the police guilty before the trial went ahead, such as when she wrote "But with recent national news reports centering on the violent killing of George Floyd by a police officer on Memorial Day," only four days after the incident. A month later she described the event as "the unconscionable killing of George Floyd by Minneapolis police officers." Yet another example where the University had abandoned neutrality.

Regardless of one's perspective on George Floyd's death, the president unfairly tainted the University police and the entire University community as a racist place. She turned the focus on "systemic racism at San José State." An investigation into University police found no evidence of racist violence or profiling. Unfortunately, these efforts were likely at the expense of a thorough investigation of Scott Shaw, the athletic faculty member who sexually molested at least a dozen female athletes over several years. The University was so fixated on looking for non-existent racists, that they missed a genuine predator in their midst.

When COVID-19 concerns subsided, the damage had been done. Even now, a large portion of our classes remain online, professors hold their office hours on Zoom, my own department hasn't held a single in-person meeting since the COVID lockdowns began, and the University halls are empty. The pandemic was (and still is) a gift to the lazy, and as we now know, of course, most students were at virtually zero risk of serious healthcare outcomes.

The damage also extends to continuous grade inflation and a focus on "systemic racism at San José State." One example of this includes the University's HonorsX program, which the provost Vincent Del Casino developed to "attract the attention of our region's BIPOC [black, indigenous, people of color] communities." Initially, there were suggestions to have an "equity application" that would award students with points, based on how much inequity they've experienced as a result of their race, gender, and sexual orientation. However, as *The College Fix* reporter Jennifer Kabbany wrote, this was "scrapped because it would run afoul of a California law that bans public universities from considering race in admissions." The program does require applicants to write a page on "What are some obstacles you have overcome and what did you learn from these obstacles?"

Illustrating the continual removal of standards in favor of social justice, Provost Vincent Del Casino questioned rigor in a campus message, sent out on September 21st, 2023:

> My concern comes to how concepts, such as academic rigor, can reinforce equity gaps, as many students need to learn not only the core concepts in their courses but the hidden curriculum and culture of higher education.
>
> …I do know that as we continue to strive to close our equity gaps and address the systemic challenges associated with student success, we have to be open to evaluating our own practices as educators. We have to avoid language that argues, for example, that we are "dumbing down" our curriculum when we talk about alternative assessment strategies or that we are "admitting students who are not prepared" when we expand access to a greater number of *qualified* CSU students.

This is the same idiotic mindset that labels virtues like punctuality and good presentation as "white supremacy." But, professors *have* been "dumbing down" their classes and university administrators *have* been "admitting students who are not prepared."

Yet, it wasn't just SJSU where such issues arose. A California law – Assembly Bill 101, which passed on October 8th 2021 – made ethnic studies a requirement. Assembly Bill 101 was sure to further dumb down the curriculum in universities. This bill revived ethnic studies, which had long been on life support – students aren't really that interested in these topics. Glynn Custred (a linguistic anthropologist who played a key role in the passing of Proposition 209 that banned affirmative action in California's public universities) and I wrote about Assembly Bill 101 for *Minding the Campus*. We wrote that this bill would indoctrinate students into critical race theory. Critical race theory, we note, is a "Marxist-inspired ideology that, if left unchecked, will form the foundation for the restructuring of America." Critical race theory claims "racism is so deeply embedded in the thought processes and the structure of American society that no white is innocent." We also raised concerns that the bill reintroduced the noble savage narrative:

> The Native American curriculum revives the old stereotypes of the environmentally conscientious Native American. They are described as those who have stewarded this land and believe that they are only "guests" on "Mother Earth." The curriculum refers to "Native American epistemology that places high reverences on land and the environment."

COVID-19, Black Lives Matter, and George Floyd's death all allowed the university to morph into a completely ideological structure; those running these institutions were no longer interested in truth, evidence, or objective knowledge. The new focus was on social justice, DEI, white guilt, virtue-signaling, anti-colonialism, and trans ideology, among other things. There isn't much time left for learning!

It was in this unfriendly environment that my book *Repatriation and Erasing the Past* came out. Due to COVID-19, many of the cancel culture attackers were shielded by computer screens – whether they were colleagues who were once down the hall from me or anthropologists from across the nation who would have been sitting in the same hotel conference room as me. Due to the growth of critical race theory, anything and anyone could be named as racist – your personal actions no longer mattered. The cancel culture attack didn't stay on the internet, as we trickled back into in-person classes; the attacks continued.

The publication date for *Repatriation and Erasing the Past* was aimed for the 30th anniversary of NAGPRA; but the publication date coincided with a worldwide pandemic, an explosion of critical race theory, a mutation of diversity and equality into diversity, equity and inclusion, and a meltdown of civility. These components led to the end of academic freedom and a cessation of open inquiry. But, I wasn't going to go down without a fight! Hell no!

# Chapter 4:

# Awakening Woke Warriors

*Repatriation and Erasing the Past* came out in September 2020; the publisher, University of Florida Press, which is an imprint of University Press of Florida, is considered a top peer-reviewed academic press for archaeology and, more specifically, bioarchaeology (i.e., the study of skeletal remains from the archaeological record). They even publish the prestigious journal *Bioarchaeology International*. My co-author Jim Springer and I were thrilled to have our book come out, and in time for NAGPRA's 30th anniversary, as planned.

The book was thoroughly reviewed by independent reviewers after delivery of the manuscript, in accordance with standard practice for such academic books, and there were quite a few changes made along the way, especially to make our two writing styles and the sections of the book come together more cohesively. In the end, we had a book to be proud of – we accomplished our goal: to have a book that takes a critical view – yet explains both sides – of repatriation laws and ideology.

*Repatriation and Erasing the Past* is split into an introduction, three sections ("The Science of Human Remains;" "Human Remains and the Law;" "A Critique of the Repatriation Movement"), and a conclusion. We lay out our position in the introduction where we explain that repatriation ideology means "any ideology, political movement, or law that attempts to control anthropological research by giving control over that research to contemporary American Indian communities." We didn't limit it to the laws or the practice of repatriation.

In our introduction we also explain the origins of repatriation ideology, which we tie back to the postmodern movement. The postmodern movement, which began in the late 20th century, attacks the concept of objective knowledge as fraudulent. As we noted, "To the postmodernists, what was supposed to be objective science and scholarship was, in fact, an expression of the ideology of the dominant classes or subcultures." Thus, in postmodernism, "the perspectives of the oppressed groups should be given special credence and deference to make up for suppression in the past." It is our opinion that repatriation ideology, due to its postmodern origins, puts victims' narratives over objective knowledge and scientific discovery. And, legitimate anthropological research is maligned as "racist." Repatriation ideology is rife with Native American "spokespeople" who compare anthropologists to "graverobbers" and even "satanists." The outcome of this ideology is that "indigenous knowledge" is better than objective knowledge obtained through data, and Native Americans should be the only ones telling the story of America's past. Furthermore, Native Americans, especially elders, are credited with powers of memory that extend beyond anything credible; their "oral histories," which are most often religious tales, cannot be challenged. In short, in repatriation ideology – as in all postmodern ideologies – who tells the story is more important than whether or not it's true. Postmodernists reject the concept of truth.

One of our main criticisms of repatriation is that the laws, such as NAGPRA, violate the Establishment Clause of the First Amendment of the US Constitution. This means that the federal government should be neutral towards all religions and must avoid favoring any specific denominations. The US Government generally avoids supporting or discriminating against specific religions, as Jim documents in *Repatriation and Erasing the Past,* yet Native American traditional Indian religions are the exception to the strict adherence to the First Amendment's Establishment Clause. Native American traditional Indian religion is given preferences that no other religion is provided in the US.

The second main issue revolves around race preference; as we explain in *Repatriation and Erasing the Past,* "racial discrimination is at the heart of NAGPRA." Some argue that it's not about race, but rather about politics, and point out the sovereignty of tribes. However, NAGPRA's rights and privileges are dependent upon a tribe's descent from a biological population that occupied America before Europeans arrived.

Thus, with our perspective laid out in the introduction, we delved into the first section: "The Science of Human Remains." In this section, there's a chapter on Paleoindians, who are individuals whose remains date to over 7,500-years-old. We covered the Paleoindians discoveries, such as the 1963 discovery of the 9,700-year-old Gordon Creek Woman who was found during a watershed improvement project in the Roosevelt National Forest. Archaeologists from the University of Colorado excavated these remains, associated stone tools, and animal bone artifacts that would otherwise have been destroyed. Much of US archaeology revolves around salvage sites; the remains and artifacts would have been destroyed by progress had it not been for archaeologists.

We also looked at some of the research on these remains and what has been learned about the earliest Americans. Many of these remains had excessively worn teeth, which could lead to an early death. For example, the 10,600-year-old Nevada skeleton Wizard Beach Man's teeth were worn down to the roots (a result of his high-grit diet) and pulp chambers were open as a result, which likely led to dental abscesses. Wizard Beach Man also had evidence of severe bone infection called osteomyelitis – probably indicative of blood poisoning from bacteria that entered through the open pulp chambers, streamed through the blood, and infected his entire system. [1] This likely killed Wizard Beach Man.

Other research has revealed trauma that belies the narrative that violence occurred only upon increased population density in the Americas, or after the arrival of Europeans. It appears that Kennewick Man, the nearly 8,000-year-old Minnesota teenager Pelican Rapids Woman, and the 10,000-plus-year-old Texas Horn Shelter Burial One all have evidence of trauma that was likely a result of violent encounters. Kennewick Man, the Paleoindian from Washington state that I mention in Chapter 1, was injured in multiple ways: he had an arrowhead lodged in his hip, his chest had evidence of multiple healed rib fractures, he had broken his funny bone – which he probably didn't think was funny at all – and at one point in time he had been hit on his head. [2]

There are about two dozen Paleoindians who have been discovered through time that could help us understand America's first peoples. However, about half of these individuals have been repatriated, reburied, or are unavailable for study as a result of repatriation ideology. In some cases, no study of the remains has ever been conducted; for instance, Wet Gravel male and female from Nebraska were reburied even before their true antiquity could be confirmed. And, in other cases, tribes that are nearly 500 generations removed from the remains have been allowed to repatriate and rebury the remains with only decidedly suspect oral history to support a connection, such was the case in Spirit Cave Mummy from Nevada, possibly the world's oldest human mummy with a date of 10,600-years-old. It's a bit like me demanding to be given the remains of Ötzi the 5,600-year-old iceman found in the Alps, simply because I too have European ancestors. Laughable, of course. But not if you're Native American.

In the next chapter, we reviewed North American mummies that have helped us understand the horrendous hardships faced by prehistoric peoples. My favorite example involves the Frozen Family of Utqiagvik and the story of a middle-aged female whose spirit must have been truly remarkable. In the Frozen Family of Utqiagvik a collapsed igloo preserved a family of five; the family was found in 1982 and using radiocarbon dating it was determined that the site dated back to about 1510 AD, give or take 70 years. Three of the individuals were skeletons, but a female in her forties and another female in her mid-twenties were mummified. Both females had anthracotic lungs (which is now most often associated with extreme heavy smoking), likely a result of the many hours stoking fires in the enclosed igloo to keep the family warm. Osteoporosis, which is bone loss usually found in post-menopausal females, was also discovered in both females. The early-onset bone loss was likely the result of a low calcium diet. The older female, who may have recently been lactating, although a baby was not found, had hardened arteries, evidence of heart inflammation that had healed (likely from a near-death experience with an infection), and kidney failure. Anthropologists have suggested that this older female may have caught pneumonia, a common illness in Alaska, followed by pleuritis (or inflammation of the lung tissues), which may have been complicated by bacteria in the blood that would have resulted in infection of the inner lining of the heart tissues, and then the health problems resulted in partial kidney failure; but even with these severe health issues, the female made a full recovery! A parasitic trichinosis infection was also discovered in the older female, which is assumed to have arisen from consumption of undercooked polar bear meat, since the *Trichinella* larveae live in the muscle tissue of bears; extant populations living in the region have been infected by the same parasite through undercooked polar bear meat.[3] Nearly all mummified remains from North America have been repatriated and will no longer be used to reconstruct the lives of these remarkable people – giving them a true voice in a way that oral myths cannot. Anthropologists honor these people by telling their stories. After repatriation – often to people with no genuine close connection to the remains – these stories end.

In the middle chapter of this section, we examine the peopling of the Americas and the biological connections between past and present Native Americans. In this section, we explain why remains cannot be easily tied to modern tribes. Modern tribes do not use genetics to determine who is a member, instead they use "blood quantum," which amounts to evidence of family ties through genealogies. Most of the remains predate contact and, thus, lack historical accounts (bear in mind that pre-contact Native Americans had not developed a written language), or have generic artifacts that cannot be linked to a specific tribe. Nearly all the affiliated remains have been repatriated long ago. This likely represented about 10% of the remains in university and museum holdings. Anthropologists who work with DNA understand that "genetic information and other analyses to pinpoint the exact origin of hundreds of individuals is expensive and time consuming."[4] But, they also know that the DNA will not provide affiliation to a specific tribe. There are no genetic markers for specific tribes, tribes have merged and changed over time, and gene flow has revealed that many who consider themselves Native American are more similar genetically to Mexican-Americans and Europeans than to Native Americans from hundreds of years ago.

In the last chapter on the study of human remains, we highlighted the controversial topics that have been misreported as a result of repatriation ideology. These myths continue the "noble savage" narrative, falsely constructing a past in which Native Americans are portrayed as the first environmentalists, peaceful, exceedingly healthy and that this utopia was destroyed by the arrival of Europeans. For instance, in an education packet by the Natural Resources Conservation Service, a part of the US Department of Agriculture, Native Americans are described as having "thousands of years of peace pre-1492" and that they created "no complete annihilation weapons (Hydrogen Bomb)." Although it's true that Native Americans did not create the H-bomb, it's intellectually dishonest to give them credit for something that there was no way they could have created or conceived – remember, pre-1492 Native Americans were basically a stone age people – no writing, no metals, not even the wheel! But, they didn't live in peace, as illustrated by the Paleoindians; and, later, evidence of violence is also abundant. For instance, we wrote about research from Mississippi State University anthropologist Anna Osterholtz and University of California, Berkeley anthropologist Tim White, both of whom examined 1,400-year-old Southwestern Anasazi Native Americans. Osterholtz, looking at the Anasazi site from Sacred Ridge, Colorado, found that in the 33 individuals at the site, every body part of each individual had been cut at around the time of their deaths. These people had also been scalped, defleshed, mutilated and burned. There is good evidence that some of this was due to cannibalism. And, no one was spared, all ages were represented among victims, and both sexes were affected.

Other claims that we take on are that Native Americans were healthy before contact. Although some diseases were brought to the Americas by Europeans, tuberculosis, syphilis, staphylococcus, tapeworms, hookworms, and many more bacteria, viruses and parasites have been found in pre-contact sites in mummies, coprolites (fossilized feces), DNA, and bones! There's a false narrative that has been widespread, in part because of Howard Zinn's immensely popular history book, *A People's History of the United States: 1492–Present*, that has been used in classrooms across the nation; it posits that North America likely had 10 million Native Americans before contact and that this was quickly reduced to a million as a result of Europeans' spread – sometimes intentional – of disease, and their violent attacks on the peaceful Native Americans. Yet, as we reviewed the literature on demographics, we found that research on the population of North America suggests that the population before contact was likely between 1.2 million and 2.7 million. Fewer Indians than people in the city of Phoenix, Arizona now! Furthermore, the population decreased prior to contact, with the onset of agriculture, which did decrease health among Native Americans. There had been no devastating "genocide." Even the spread of diseases was likely far lower than previously assumed; the low population density made epidemic spread, that was seen in European cities, exceedingly unlikely.

In the next section of the book, Jim and I reviewed repatriation laws and find fault with NAGPRA, especially in its violation of the First Amendment Establishment Clause, which states: "Congress shall make no law respecting an establishment of religion." It has been widely explained that this means the federal government should be neutral towards all religions, avoiding favoritism or preference to any denomination. NAGPRA violates this establishment clause by allowing Native American oral history and creation myths to be used as evidence in repatriation – similar 'evidence' of Christian creation myths would not be treated as evidence in the courts. It also prefers a specific religion when it requires that the NAGPRA committees have at least two "traditional Indian religious leaders." It's not good enough to have Indian religious leaders; they must be "traditional Indian religious leaders." Further issues arise with the definition of "sacred objects." Jim and I have been writing about the violation of the First Amendment and NAGPRA for decades and I will continue to fight against this deviation from the US Constitution!

Also in this section, the legal aspects of cases such as Kennewick Man are reviewed. One such case involved the around 9,000-year-old remains from the San Diego area; these remains, found on the University of California, San Diego campus in La Jolla, were repatriated and reburied before research on the remains was conducted. Like the Kennewick Man case, anthropologists, led by Tim D. White of University of California (UC) Berkeley, fought for access to the remains. Unfortunately, the judge decided that the case would be dismissed since the tribe was an essential party to the case, but couldn't be sued due to their sovereignty – ensnaring the plaintiffs in a Catch-22. My own case against SJSU would face the same challenge, as we'll see in a later chapter.

My favorite chapter in the book is in the third section – it is the one in which Jim takes a deep look at treatment of remains. He did an excellent job of describing the many ways in which Native Americans in the past treated human remains: cremation, scaffolding, and trophy-taking to name a few. For instance, "among some groups, the body of the deceased, after being allowed to partially decay, was defleshed by particular individuals whose job it was to perform that service. The defleshed bones were then collected in a box or hamper and kept by the relatives of the deceased." And in the Arctic and the western subarctic, treatment of enemies would sometimes involve beheadings and the cutting off of genitals![5] This chapter brings home the point made in our introduction that "the current Native American view that remains should be reburied is a modern, political construct and not a genuine reflection of historical Native American cultural beliefs." Prior to the modern repatriation movement, even as late as the 1960s, Native Americans regularly assisted archaeologists in excavations, and the Native Americans weren't concerned with reburial of these human remains.

The third section is also where Jim and I worked most closely together. In this section, titled "A Critique of the Repatriation Movement," we examined the effects of repatriation ideology on the scientific study of human remains from the archaeological record. Of course, the loss of research collections results in the loss of data, and we predicted that in fifty years' time all research collections will be lost forever! Since *Repatriation and Erasing the Past* was written, repatriation ideology has grown and spread, collections are being lost at an alarming rate, teaching collections are being targeted, and museums are hiding artifacts from display that Native American repatriationists deem too sensitive or "powerful" to be shown, as I found out in protocols for the American Museum of Natural History, where a whistle was removed from display because it may be used to conjure up evil spirits! More about this insanity in a later chapter!

We also found that censorship blossoms when repatriation ideology takes over. For instance, Native Americans have been able to stop the publication of research; repatriation activists, such as Devon Mihesuah, who is a historian of Choctaw descent and the former editor of *American*

*Indian Quarterly*, argue that "researchers need to allow Native Americans the right of determining whether research should be published, what should be published, and where the research should be published." And, self-censorship is also abundant. Terms, such as "cranium" and "burial" that were once considered normal are now apologized for.

Beyond censorship, repatriation ideology spreads to allow for the acceptance of discrimination – a topic I will return to in a later chapter. In short, collaboration – even in politically-correct havens such as California – may mean accepting practices, such as barring "menstruating women" (or "menstruating personnel," as my own University calls them!) from field sites, keeping them from activities, and making them eat apart from the group because they're considered unclean! Such ignorant and offensive discrimination has no place in the 21$^{st}$ century, but is often not challenged if it comes from indigenous people. However, *true* equality means calling out such discrimination, *whoever* it comes from.

Our solution, which we cover in our concluding chapter, is to return to objective knowledge, which we explain through the views of Karl Popper – one of the 20th century's most influential philosophers of science. Objective knowledge doesn't depend on the person providing the knowledge; it transcends any single individual; and, it can be expressed in written language and other forms of physical data, such as maps, images, and numbers. Objective knowledge is always being tested, revised, and reviewed. And, knowledge grows with each new data point that has been proven through time, tests, and re-tests. This objective knowledge is what science is composed of, and it is the search for the truth; perhaps never obtaining it.

*Repatriation and Erasing the Past* received some good reviews. For instance, Dwight Read, a retired professor of anthropology from University of California, Los Angeles, wrote in *Choice Reviews*:

> [T]he authors address a long-standing issue regarding who owns the past: the indigenous groups to whom human remains discovered as part of archaeological research are repatriated or the broader public to fulfill the human desire for an objective account of the past. According to the authors, there is no common ground permitting a simple resolution to this issue. As they conclude, "the

free search for objective knowledge through scientific research ... should never be considered a luxury" because "objective knowledge is universal, not 'European' as repatriationists try to argue, thus it benefits all humans" (p. 218)... Referencing is extensive, and exhaustive information on all human remains dating back at least 7,500 years is presented in tabular form. However, one question remains unanswered: with the passage of time, at what point does the connection to the dead become subject to the objectivity of science in lieu of the subjectivity of the living wanting to be tied to their ancestors?

And, Geoffrey Clark, a retired professor of anthropology at Arizona State University, wrote:

In short, and inarguably, *Repatriation & Erasing the Past* is good science. I read it, and consider it to be a well-balanced, empirically supported defense of the opposing position taken on repatriation by evolutionary anthropologists and bioarchaeologists world-wide, and by a substantial part of the archaeological community.

J. Kenneth Smail, a retired anthropology professor from Kenyon College wrote:

Weiss and Springer provide a useful and necessary counterbalance to this regrettable trend, given their emphasis on: (1) well-established scientific methodology and research in both physical anthropology and prehistoric archaeology; and (2) a detailed legal review and analysis of current Indian law (including NAGPRA) and its historical precedents.

Furthermore, *Repatriation and Erasing the Past* was listed in the "Top 75" highly recommended titles for community colleges by the Association of College and Research Libraries, a division of the American Library Association.

Yet, just days before Christmas, on December 16th, 2020, our publisher's marketing manager Rachel Doll emailed me, and copied it to Romi Gutierrez, the University Press of Florida director, to let me know that there was a "discussion currently underway across Twitter and

Facebook surrounding your book" and that I and SJSU were mentioned in several posts. She included a link to some of the Tweets, which included statements, such as "it's time to stop reproducing our racist discipline, starting first with our (white settler) selves & our workplaces." They also called our perspective "outdated, racist ideas." Doll then ended her email with a request to speak to me, hopefully that very day. In the telephone call, Romi Gutierrez and Rachel Doll let Jim and I know that they were in "crisis mode"! As it turned out, a group of woke anthropologists had decided that they'd try to get our publishers to pull the book! At the beginning of this campaign to get our book banned, I was not on any social media and, thus, I wasn't aware of the trouble brewing. Shortly after the cancel culture mob started, I joined Twitter, using the handle @eweissunburied!

It's worth noting that on December 16th, I also received my first positive email as a result of the "discussion" on Twitter. A state archaeologist, who did not want to be named, in an email titled "congrats on the book" wrote:

Based on my Twitter feed, I would imagine you might get some hateful feedback on your book in the coming weeks, so I felt compelled to reach out and let you know you're not alone. I haven't read the book yet (just ordered it) and might not agree with it all, but that's not really the point. Regardless of the specifics, the orthodox trend in anthropology (especially pernicious on Twitter) really bothers me and your willingness to engage this issue in a public way is heroic.

And, the archaeologist also noted that:

...the Twitter comments are one-sided because a small, vocal group of young archaeologists totally monopolizes archaeological discourse on Twitter and piles on anyone who breaks from their narrative to make their lives miserable for a few day...It's the same group that has been trying to bring down the SAA. Hopefully your publisher understands that. That group of folks strategically orchestrates their attacks to maximize impact and they've been really successful at controlling the narrative on that website.

I passed this on to Rachel Doll and Romi Gutierrez, hoping that they'd ride out any storm, and stand behind their authors and their title. But they decided to apologize for the publication anyway. And, in response to the Twitter storm, on December 18th, Gutierrez sent an email out to stakeholders in which she wrote:

> University presses are methodical, and our processes can seem slow...Because the gears of the publication process do move gradually, a flawed editorial decision made in the past has consequences today.
>
> Those consequences, in this case, include harm to voices we sincerely value, the potential to undo important progress, and injury to relationships we have long worked to foster. I apologize for the pain this publication has caused. It was not our intent to publish a book that uses arguments and terminology associated with scientific racism. I assure you that, months ago, changes to our editorial program had already started to take place, including greater focus to inclusivity and sensitivity, and we will continue and redouble these efforts.

In other words, although the book had been accepted and published in accordance with their standard practices, in order to virtue-signal to a woke cancel culture mob, a former employee was blamed and thrown under the bus with the comment about a "flawed editorial decision." More evidence of a lack of backbone in academia.

Gutierrez, however, made the decision not to pull the book from publication. I wonder if Jim's legal reminder that they had signed a contract to publish and promote the book played a role in their decision. Afterall, Jim, as a retired attorney, would have known enough about contract law and possibly have enough connections to enable us to sue if they had pulled the book. Jim hinted at this in the "crisis mode" call we had with Gutierrez and Doll! Gutierrez struck back, bizarrely suggesting that we had hoodwinked the publisher – making them believe that the book would be a balanced view because we mentioned that we'd discuss both sides of the debate. We do indeed explain both sides of the debate, but as we always made clear, we were writing a book critical of repatriation – even the title should have given it away. Our proposal included that we would write a "critique of repatriation and reburial laws and their effects on scientific endeavors" and the table of contents includes chapter subtitles, such as "Critiques Specific to NAGPRA" and "Biases in Interpretation Promoted by Repatriation Ideology/Pressure." Yet, Gutierrez was using a common tactic of the spineless to try to explain why they accepted a now-undesirable manuscript, paper, or conference panel. This type of false claim was made by the American Anthropological Association to cancel the panel that I was slated to be on that was about the binary nature of sex. And, as I will discuss in the next chapter, such bogus allegations were made against Jim and I in regard to our presentation at the 2021 Society for American Archaeology conference.

Yet, Romi Gutierrez gave as the reason to keep the book published:

I worry, too, that such a withdrawal might risk future editorial decisions that forget these lessons learned. To retract a work already published also preempts continued dialogue surrounding its publication and stifles the scholarly challenges that normally follow in post-publication reviews.

Gutierrez, however, was not done groveling. She listed a series of actions the publisher was taking to atone for this grievous publication error. These steps included: "redoubling our commitment to amplifying Black, Indigenous, and other marginalized voices in archaeology, as well as every other field we publish in," "accelerating the time frame for our long-planned graduate diversity fellowship," and "friends of the press will make a donation to the Association on American Indian Affairs as a show of support of their work."

They'd gone full-on woke!

A nearly identical message would be provided to the wannabe book-banning anthropologists after an open letter against the book came out.

On December 19th, 2020 an open letter addressed to the publisher, Jim and I made its appearance on social media websites. The letter was calling for the publisher to cease open access (which basically means access through libraries or other means in which people do not have to pay for the book). It quickly got nearly 900 signatures – and, I'm sure that many of those came from "scholars" who had not read the book. Otherwise, it would have been the most read academic anthropology book of the year, if not the decade!

The open letter was written by two New Zealand anthropologists, Siân Halcrow at the University of Otago and Amber Aranui at the Museum of New Zealand; one Canadian anthropologist, Stephanie Halmhofer at the University of Alberta; and three American anthropologists, Annalisa Heppner at Brown University, Kristina Killgrove at University of North Carolina at Chapel Hill, and Gwen Robbins Schug at University of North Carolina at Greensboro and Appalachian State University. In the letter, they wrote: "…this work is reminiscent of colonial scholarship from more than a century ago," that they are "deeply concerned with the explicitly racist ideology espoused by the authors," and "this volume promotes racist ideologies." They argue that the book should not be made open access, "as that may cause further harm to Indigenous communities and scholars."

The authors also mentioned a book, *Reburying the Past: The Effects of Repatriation and Reburial on Scientific Inquiry,* I wrote that came out in 2008. This book, unfortunately, didn't turn out as I had hoped – I had posted several messages on community websites asking if anthropologists would talk to me about their experiences and the book was planned as a narrative from multiple perspectives. But, no one reached out to me with their experiences and, thus, I did a rush job on the book with materials that I had on hand. It was also my first book. There are good sections in there, and others that could have been far better.

An interesting aspect of the open letter was that the authors mentioned that there had been an earlier version of the letter that called for the book to be completely de-published.

The earlier letter calling for our book to be banned was marked December 17th, 2020 and addressed only to University Press of Florida. It appears that this letter was sent to the publisher and the publisher's response was identical to the stakeholder email. It could be that the second open letter was more moderate because the publishers didn't retract the book. It's likely that if Gutierrez had answered differently, the whole repatriation activist mob would have been for banning the book. Thus, it's hard for me to believe the statement in the open letter that "while some of us favor retraction of the volume, we recognize that not everyone shares that view." In this December 17th letter, written by the same authors as the later open letter, they write: "UPF should cease selling this book or providing electronic access to this book immediately."

As the Twitter storm was still rumbling along, Jim and I decided to issue a short statement in response that could be shared with my University media director. We wrote:

> We recognize that repatriation and reburial is an emotive issue and if publication of *Repatriation and Erasing the Past* leads to a constructive debate about this, and about the intersection of science, religious beliefs, law, and politics, then we welcome this discussion.

On December 19th I contacted my chair Roberto Gonzalez and my dean Walt Jacobs to let them know of the cancellation campaign. Both expressed support for academic freedom. For instance, Walt wrote: "As you know, SJSU strongly supports academic freedom." But, they'd sing a different tune in the upcoming weeks and months.

It was in these early days that I also started to communicate with journalists regarding the attack on *Repatriation and Erasing the Past.* The first journalist to break the story was Christian Schneider of *The College Fix.* He reached out to me after his initial article on the issue on December 18th. In this article, he quotes anthropologists' tweets, such as Sara Parcak at University of Alabama-Birmingham, who said the book "is racist garbage and needs to be pulled immediately." And, Kristina Killgrove – one of the authors of the open letter – who acknowledged that she didn't read the whole book and yet stated: "Hoo boy, I did not expect it to be *this bad*." Considering that this tweet occurred only one day before the open letter calling for the book to be banned and she was one of the authors of that letter, it makes me wonder if she wanted it banned before she even read the book!

In a follow-up article, on December 23rd, Christian Schneider quotes Jim and I for the first time and the Twitter mob began to realize that we weren't backing down. Our quote was: "Falsely playing the race card — as has been done here — to try to ban a book simply because one doesn't agree with the contents is unhelpful to the fight against genuine racism."

Even after University Press of Florida decided to continue to publish and sell *Repatriation and Erasing the Past* (by issuing a groveling, virtue-signaling apology while continuing to sell the book, they were arguably wanting to have their cake and eat it too), Jim and I were still responding to cancellation attempts and the number of signatures on the open letter was continuing to grow. Thus, we issued a statement on the 28th of December in response to the open letter. In our letter, we wrote: "We encourage anyone who has signed the letter or is thinking about signing the letter to read *Repatriation and Erasing the Past* in its entirety and with an open-mind." And, we also noted that:

> [R]eaders will find that the legal issues surrounding repatriation are complex and, thus, required an author with both extensive legal expertise and deep knowledge on case history to explain the problematic legal ramifications and entanglements associated with repatriation laws, especially with regards to the US Constitution's First Amendment, which separates Church and State.

And, we hit back at the accusations of racism with: "readers will discover that the allegations of racism are absolutely false and, in fact, our case against repatriation ideology is built on the concept of treating everyone equally. We focus on data rather than the identity of who provides the narrative."

Perhaps most importantly, we challenged repatriationists to provide "evidence that proves the validity of oral traditions, showing that these narratives should be used in repatriation cases" and pointed out that we had provided evidence to the contrary, with my favorite example:

> Columbia River tribes' use of tales about the trickster coyote whose steamboat was left in a dry channel, which would later become a running river, to claim their connection to the region where Kennewick Man was found, even though Native Americans did not have steamboats prior to contact with Europeans.

We argued that impossible events, such as miracles and polygenesis creations, that are enveloped in oral traditions, "should make oral traditions inadmissible in claims for repatriations." No evidence to the contrary was provided – and I'm still waiting!

When I posted our response to the open letter on my department's listserv, my chair Roberto Gonzalez – all of a sudden no longer concerned about academic freedom – emailed me that:

> I don't think that it's appropriate to use the departmental listserv for this purpose, and in fact I think these kinds of messages may unintentionally undermine the hard work that has gone into building a viable online communication and networking infrastructure.

Then he suggested that I publish my materials elsewhere. But it *was* an appropriate use of the listserv. Previously, announcements of works had been posted there, political statements were also made there, and calls to consider using "anti-racist" databases, such as Cite Black Authors, were put up on the listserv. More on that later! Most importantly, I made the decision to post it on the listserv because I knew that many of those who were on the listserv had also signed the open letter against the book. By then, half of the department and all of the current graduate students had signed the open letter. Roberto's commitment to open debate and academic freedom suddenly and mysteriously evaporated, and he started monitoring posts, policing what went up, and even non-controversial posts of mine are often barred to this day!

The small band of vociferous Twitterers turned into letters from esteemed organizations: the Society for American Archaeology (SAA), that notes on its website that since 1934 the society "has been dedicated to research about and interpretation and protection of the archaeological heritage of the Americas" and the British Association for Biological Anthropology and Osteoarchaeology. The SAA issued a statement that stated that the book is "unduly divisive and promulgates scientific racism to our students and the public." But, it was the British Association for Biological Anthropology and Osteoarchaeology's December 22nd statement that Jim and I felt the need to respond to – in their statement, they wrote that they "encourage the University of Florida Press to withdraw from sale and digital access *Repatriation and Erasing the Past*." Our response, which was sent to the association and which we asked be shared with people they sent their letter to, stated:

> In regards to the letter put out by British Association for Biological Anthropology and Osteoarchaeology: we find it ironic that they call to ban *Repatriation and Erasing the Past* when censorship is a key issue discussed at length in the book. Those who call for a ban on *Repatriation and Erasing the Past* are strengthening our case against repatriation ideology and playing to type. Our suggestion is for everyone interested in this debate to read the book in its entirety and come to your own conclusions.

Perhaps because of these association statements, *Repatriation and Erasing the Past* seemed to have mysteriously disappeared from the University Press of Florida catalog. We immediately contacted Gutierrez and let her know of this slight. The book was relisted! In a similar incident, *Repatriation and Erasing the Past* was removed from my department's webpage – along with Roberto Gonzalez's latest book, which was likely accidentally taken off when they attempted to remove *Repatriation and Erasing the Past*. I pointed out this 'error' and both books were put back up!

As the holidays ended, the attacks on *Repatriation and Erasing the Past* continued and especially came home to my college community. On January 4th, 2021, Roberto emailed me that he was writing a statement to the anthropology community because he had "received numerous emails and calls from colleagues who are quite concerned and even upset about" my book. His statement, he noted, would support academic freedom, but would also include an ending critiquing *Repatriation and Erasing the Past*. Although he may have thought that he was being fair – on the one side standing up for academic freedom and on the other side providing his perspective – he grossly misrepresented the book:

> On a personal note, I want to let you know that after having carefully read the book, I disagree with both the substance and style of *Repatriation and Erasing the Past*, including its dismissal

of Native American epistemologies and indigenous scholarship, its Victorian-era approach to anthropological inquiry, and its linear, pre-Kuhnian view of scientific progress. Our discipline has long played a signal role in recognizing the insight and benefits that can come from understanding different lifeways and cultural perspectives, and I'm confident that we will continue doing so in the future.

These misrepresentations required a response and one sent out to the same people as Roberto had sent his letter to. So, I drafted a response; to be fair, Roberto did send it out. In it I corrected his false claims, noting that Thomas Kuhn and Karl Popper were contemporaries and that thus "to portray *Repatriation and Erasing the Past* as antiquated because we don't use Kuhn, but rather cite Popper, is an unfair representation." I also wrote that we – Jim and I – and Popper do not support a linear view of scientific progress and that in our book, we wrote of the "unpredictability and uncontrollability of knowledge while noting that knowledge is not an unfolding sequence, but rather a messy endeavor that is in constant flux."

Roberto's letter really made me question his honesty – had he really read the book? Perhaps he did, but didn't comprehend our argument – which brings into question his reading comprehension skills.

I ended my letter discussing the *ad hominem* nature of the attacks of *Repatriation and Erasing the Past* and indicated that I would not be fighting against these attacks in such a poor manner; I quoted Michelle Obama: "When they go low, we go high." The majority of the comments regarding *Repatriation and Erasing the Past* did not focus on any substance – it was mainly focused on calling Jim and I "racists," "colonialists," and referring to us and our ideas as "garbage," "trash," and "shit." Some social justice warriors were offended that Jim had been a lawyer: "seems fitting for trash like this to be pub. Dr. Weiss of San Jose along w/a lawyer (enough said)." Isn't it ironic that someone concerned about social justice would be against legal help? Yet, this anti-law sentiment is published in some of the "noble savage" propaganda that we discussed in *Repatriation and Erasing the Past*. For instance, from the US Department of Agriculture website, "Native American Contributions," a list of pre-Columbian Native American characteristics states, as evidence of their genuine goodness, that pre-contact Native Americans had "no lawyers" – the assumption is that they wouldn't have needed any!

Other tweets included statements like: "Eww…no what the fuck," "gross white Eurocentric trash," "trash archaeologists" and "this piece of shit."

In upcoming attempts to cancel me, the social media posts would become even nastier and more personal.

The day after my email response went out, I received possibly the saddest email, from a former student who wrote:

> It took me all day to decide if I should email you using my SJSU email or my personal one.
>
> I want to let you know that although I have not read your book and its content, my experience with you as your former undergraduate and graduate student was positive…You always treated me as equal to those born here and are light skin. It saddened me to read that you are being accused of such a horrible thing. I just want you to know that you have a student who had a positive experience with you as my professor.

Her support for me was sad because it demonstrated her concern about showing support, perhaps worrying it might cost her her job, since she was employed at SJSU. And, she was clearly worried that the SJSU thought police might be monitoring her email and might retaliate against someone expressing support for me. This fear-ridden environment is the result of cancel culture and spineless administrators, like Roberto, who feel that they cannot just say "I support academic freedom," and allow a free debate; but rather, they need to virtue-signal that they too are condemning the work and scold me for use of a departmental listserv.

At the end of his letter, Roberto promised to "coordinate a series of virtual events that address topics having to do with inequity and bias in the social sciences, so that we can all be well informed about these crucially important issues." Roberto invited four speakers, but only two spoke – the others cancelled and were never rescheduled. The first speaker was Agustín Fuentes, a professor of anthropology at Princeton University and a classic race-baiter who sees white supremacy everywhere he looks.

Fuentes came across as angry, argumentative, and bitter. Everything – to Fuentes – was evidence of "racism" and "white supremacy." When I questioned him about black on Asian crime, which had spiked in the Bay Area at the time, Fuentes blamed it on whites. If whites didn't treat blacks so poorly, blacks wouldn't be lashing out against Asians. These people have no shame.

I asked Roberto if I could have a series on academic freedom and diversity of thought as a counterbalance to his series. Roberto quickly said there was no money or time to hold such a webinar series. I offered that we hold it the following semester. He pawned me off to Walt Jacobs and the Center for Faculty Development. The Center for Faculty Development staff wouldn't even talk to me. And, Walt pushed me back to the department. The outcome was that Roberto – likely with the help of Walt – came out with an old set of guidelines from the college on how to invite a speaker to campus (even though this was all online due to COVID restrictions). Roberto, then, held retroactive votes for his speakers! And, stated that I would have to follow the guidelines – guidelines that we had never used before! Upon complaining of this unfairness, Roberto held a meeting to discuss this issue. It was the one time that I lost my cool – tears of anger welled up when Roberto lied and acted like he just found these guidelines floating around, rather than the truth that he was using them to try to prevent me from inviting speakers. In the end, the department drew up, with my input, new guidelines that were supposed to prevent vetoing speakers based on one's personal ideologies. Yet, each time I submitted an application for speakers, I never got the votes to sponsor them, regardless of the speaker or topic. I could have resurrected their hero, Thomas Kuhn, and asked the department to sponsor my efforts to bring him to campus and they'd have voted against it! Fortunately, when I was suing my University – more on that later – Roberto decided to play nice and sponsored speakers from the chair's office, even when the department voted against the speakers! But even here, this was likely a tactical ploy. I doubted that he'd genuinely rediscovered his supposed commitment to academic freedom.

By the end of January 2021, most of the *Repatriation and Erasing the Past* cancellation attempt had died down. Although there were over 940 signatures on the open letter, the book was still being sold and is available in nearly 900 libraries, which was likely useful, since a flurry of book reviews were published on *Repatriation and Erasing the Past*. The *European Journal of Archaeology* had three reviews in one issue! Some reviews were written by multiple authors – the highest number was seven, in the *International Journal of Cultural Property*. One reviewer just focused on a single page! And, perhaps forgetting that you shouldn't judge a book by its cover, a review in the *Southeastern Archaeology* journal complained that the cover was "glib" because it uses an image from a noncontroversial and European site. If the author of the review had contacted us, he would have learned that the choice was made because of the image-Nazis in anthropology conference bookrooms, who won't allow books displayed with realistic images of bones or photos of skeletons – creating a noncontroversial cover can be difficult! Ironically, the *Southeastern Archaeology* journal, which is the official journal of the Southeastern Archaeological Conference, has been in the news over such issues. Their editor even got in trouble for using an image of 'sacred' pots for the journal's cover and thus offended indigenous members. Of course, they had already banned all images of human remains – both in the journal and on covers!

Before leaving the cancellation attack on *Repatriation and Erasing the Past*, I'd like to note that even when such cancellation campaigns aren't successful, they can have devastating consequences, especially for untenured faculty. There is, of course, the culture of fear that they generate. But also, my ability to publish was affected. This was most evident with my article about a bump on the head on a prehistoric skull from the Ryan Mound, which turned out to be a ballooned osteoma, likely from being struck on the head in a violent blow. In September 2020, just days after my book came out, I sent the article, that I co-wrote with Gary Heathcote, for review to the journal *Bioarchaeology International*. At the end of November, we received reviewers' feedback and made every requested change. We resubmitted the article on January 6th, 2021. When I initially sent in the article, the cancel culture campaign against *Repatriation and Erasing the Past* had not yet begun. Yet, in January, I saw that the editors of *Bioarchaeology International* were two of the authors of the open letter against *Repatriation and Erasing the Past*. I thought they may still publish this exceedingly uncontroversial article. I received an odd letter from the associate editor at the end of January, which seemed to imply the article would be accepted. Yet another round of revisions was requested, this time by the editors – rather than by reviewers who had already indicated that the article was acceptable for publication – at the end of March. We made these additional changes and resubmitted the article two days later. After nearly a month, on April 27th, we received a rejection! And, the rejection letter was identical to the previous letter we received in March. I was confused; had I sent in the wrong version? Yet, their reply – which had a nasty tone about it – made it clear that this decision was based on their contempt for my perspective on repatriation. Never before had I received a rejection after reviewers had recommended that a paper be accepted. I do wonder if they were trying for months to figure out how to reject the article. Another possibility is that my Society for American Archaeology talk in early April enraged them so much that they decided to reject my paper – more on the SAA in the next chapter!

---

[1]Edgar, Heather, and Joy Hecht. 1997. "Paleopathology of the Wizards Beach Man (AHUR 2023) and the Spirit Cave Mummy (AHUR 2064)." *Nevada Historical Society Quarterly* 40: 57–61.
[2]Owsley, Douglas W., and Richard L. Jantz, eds. 2014. *Kennewick Man: The Scientific Investigation of an Ancient American Skeleton.* College Station: Texas A&M University Press.
[3]Zimmerman, Michael R., and Arthur C. Aufderheide. 1984. "The Frozen Family of Utqiagvik: The Autopsy Findings." *Arctic Anthropology* 21 (1): 53–64.
[4]Ridler, Keith. (2018, February 7). "500-Year-Old Skeletons Sought by 3 Native American Tribes." *Idaho State Journal.* https://idahostatejournal.com/news/local/year-oldskeletons-sought-by-native-american-tribes/article_cef4ca31-7ca2-529e-bde9-6be72618d7ac.html
[5]Chacon, Richard J., and David H. Dye, eds. 2007. *The Taking and Displaying of Human Body Parts as Trophies by Amerindians.* Boston: Springer.

# Chapter 5:

# Academic Debate
# is Buried by Support for Creationists

As the winter months passed and spring was upon us, Jim and I were preparing to present at the April 2021 Society for American Archaeology (SAA) annual meeting. The SAA is the largest of the anthropology societies that focusses on archaeology; it consists of around 7,000 members and has been around since 1934. According to its website, the SAA is "dedicated to research about and interpretation and protection of the archaeological heritage of the Americas."

We submitted our abstract back in September 2020 at around the time *Repatriation and Erasing the Past* came out. In early November, thus, before the open letter against *Repatriation and Erasing the Past,* our abstract was accepted and I was asked to chair a session. At this time, the assumption was that the conference would be in-person and in San Francisco, which is one of the reasons that I made the decision to submit my abstract – San José is just an hour and a bit train ride from San Francisco. Yet, as a result of COVID restrictions, the SAA board made the decision in early February 2021 to hold the conference online.

Jim and I had written an abstract that was about the issue of whether indigenous creation myths should be used as evidence for repatriation. We had written on this topic in *Repatriation and Erasing the Past* and thought that presenting this sliver of the book at an academic archaeology conference would be a good way to further share our perspective, get feedback from those in the field, and perhaps spark a civil conversation over such issues. After all, many of the conference attendees deal with repatriation issues, and repatriation issues have been debated at this conference before. It was the ideal venue to get the conversation going!

Since the conference was to be held online, the talks were prerecorded. During the actual conference days, which were held from April 15<sup>th</sup> to 17<sup>th</sup>, the talks were aired. Comments and questions could be posted during the initial airing of the talks in a side box; speakers then could answer questions during this time. At least one of the authors of each talk was required to attend the session in which their talk was aired. For Jim and I, this meant that I would attend the session; I was also the one who gave the talk.

Our talk, which was titled "Has Creationism Crept Back into Archaeology?," aired on April 15th, 2021. The talk was 15 minutes long and started by highlighting the times when the SAA and similar organizations took a stand against Christian Creationism. We defined creationism as "belief in the origin of the universe through a series of miraculous events which cannot be accounted for by natural processes such as we can observe today." For instance, we noted that on the SAA website there are teaching guidelines that include statements like "Fully modern humans (*Homo sapiens sapiens*) have existed for about 100,000 years, and they have occupied the Americas for approximately 12,000 years." And, that "archaeology follows the scientific process." The American Association of Physical Anthropologists (now known as the American Association of Biological Anthropologists) has an anti-creationist statement too and it "condemns any effort by the state to dictate specific religious instruction to the people." And, the American Anthropological Association (AAA), which is an organization that covers archaeology, physical anthropology, and cultural anthropology, states that "evolution is a basic component of many aspects of anthropology." In the AAA's statement on evolution and creationism, they write that "anthropologists are encouraged to use their knowledge both of evolution and of human social and cultural systems to assist communities in which evolution and creationism have become contentious." Thus, the three biggest and most prestigious anthropology organizations in the world all take a strong stand against creationism – at least when it comes from Christians! Yet, creationism is embraced by anthropologists when it's indigenous creationism, and coupled with repatriation ideology. The double standards are sickening. But, they're indicative of a wider suspension of critical thinking whereby anthropologists – and academia more generally – go all misty-eyed over anything "indigenous," which is automatically seen as a good thing – even when it isn't.

We also highlighted how NAGPRA – a federal law – props up and promotes indigenous creationism. Thereby, NAGPRA helps to "establish" the Native American traditional religion. We reminded our listeners that both Thomas Jefferson and James Madison took strong disestablishment positions on religion. We noted that the Lemon test, named after a legal case and not the fruit, has been widely used as a way to determine if a law violates the Establishment Clause of the First Amendment. The Lemon test, it seems now, has gone out of favor recently, but when this talk was given there was still much support for it. The Lemon test basically states that a law must have a secular purpose, its primary effect cannot advantage or inhibit religious practice, and it must not foster entanglement between the government and religions. NAGPRA does not pass this test – there is advancement of Native American traditional religion in the form of the requirement that at least two members of a NAGPRA review committee must be traditional Native American religious leaders. This requirement can also cause entanglement, because the Secretary of the Interior appoints the committee members and, thus, needs to decide who is a traditional Indian religious leader and perhaps even what traditional Indian religion is, since they have no texts that can be looked to for guidance – as pre-contact Native Americans never developed a written language.

But, most pertinent for our talk was that oral tradition can be used as evidence for repatriation claims. NAGPRA doesn't say religious doctrine or beliefs can be used, but oral tradition nearly always includes religious tales – many of them creation myths. We gave the example of the case when the Zuni origin myth, which includes "tales of a watery underworld creation and guidance by gods coupled with migration through the region that included transformations from webbed-feet, horned creatures to humans," enabled them to claim Southwest lands that were far outside their current reservation. We noted that the "judge acknowledged that their tale was one of "religious history," but accepted the story without realizing that to do so meant that he should have to determine what aspects were true and what were not." Another example we gave related to the 2017 case of *Navajo v. United States Department of the Interior*. The Navajo Nation sued to repatriate 303 sets of human remains from Canyon de Chelly National Monument, located within the Navajo reservation. The human remains, which included mummies, were curated at the National Park Service Center in Tucson, Arizona. The Navajo argued that the National Park Service didn't have lawful possession of the remains under NAGPRA since the remains belonged to the Navajo. The appeals court accepted the Navajo creation myths, which included supernatural events in the canyon, even though the defendants pointed out that historical and archaeological evidence proves that the Navajo were relative latecomers to Canyon de Chelly and that the early inhabitants were more likely related to the modern Hopi or Zuni! This type of thinking is rampant with repatriation activists. They start from a mythological assertion that a tribe has been in a certain location "since the dawn of time," and confound this with a false narrative that implies that tribes have been static over time. In reality, of course, Native Americans are like any other peoples in human history, and have been constantly on the move.

We also pointed out that repatriationists also promote some very unscientific ways of understanding the origins of all peoples. For instance, some promote polygenesis, which is a common concept found in Native American oral traditions that means distinct origins for different people. Polygenesis was scientifically disproved by Charles Darwin over a hundred years ago. Polygenesis was once used by racists to argue against the notion of a common ancestor to the different races. We also note that "some Native American repatriationists have even adopted the Christian creationist catchphrase about evolution — "it's just a theory" — to dismiss research published on migrations into the Americas."

We ended our talk by suggesting that as scientists, we should strive to conduct research with an emphasis on seeking the objective truth, and we should work to prevent the promotion of creationism ideology. And, that repatriation decisions should be made on evidence obtained through research, rather than through beliefs. Our final sentence was:

> Let us encourage an anthropology that looks at the world through the lens of reason and keep ourselves free from the entanglements

of religion as the First Amendment of the US Constitution intended.

All this shouldn't have been controversial. In no place did we say that all repatriation should stop, but rather that NAGPRA shouldn't use creation myths to determine links between past peoples and modern tribes. We didn't say that Native Americans shouldn't practice their beliefs, but rather that these beliefs shouldn't be treated as factual. And, others collaborating with Native Americans should not be made to follow protocols that are anathema to the Western ideology of equality – protocols like barring female students and professors from handling warrior remains! And, barring "menstruating personnel" (alternatively known as women) from conducting research.

I've written about my perspective on religion for the Libertarian site Libertyunbound.com. My views are quite simple – the US Constitution supports freedom *of* religion, and this includes freedom *from* religion, since the government is not supposed to establish a religion or promote one religion over another. I respect people's right to their beliefs and religious practices, but these should not interfere with others' academic freedom, scientific research, and human rights. It would never cross my mind to go to someone's church, temple, or home, and try to get them away from their religion, interrupt their sermons or prayers, or destroy their religious texts. Importantly, I also think religions need equal treatment by the law and in universities – too many anthropologists embrace religion and support people's right to practice only if it's non-Western religion. Universities, for instance, celebrate World Hijab (i.e., the Muslim head covering women wear) Day, which is held on the first day of February (a day that coincides with the return of Ayatollah Ruhollah Khomeini to Iran from his exile, and this led to mandatory wearing of hijabs in Iran), by hosting events like wear-a-hijab day. And, posters proclaiming "Everyone Is Welcome Here" display a female in a hijab.

Interestingly, upon the 2016 election of Donald Trump, a slew of "Islamophobic attacks" seemed to have occurred on campuses across the country; even at SJSU a Muslim student claimed that she was strangled or choked by a white male with her hijab the day after Trump won. Initially the attack on the SJSU student was said to have occurred on election day, but then the Muslim student changed her story and said it happened after Trump was elected. These attacks didn't result in any arrests; no other witnesses came forward; and in one case one of the 'victims' was discovered to have made up the attack and was subsequently arrested![1]

There's another aspect here that exposes the hypocrisy of today's academia. All this "loving hijabs" seems to largely ignore protests by women who regard the hijab as being a repressive tool used by patriarchal societies to subjugate women and to erase their individual identities. Woke white westerners may embrace the hijab, but when women in countries like Iran protest against it, academia is mysteriously silent. And, the feminist movement is largely silent too – as they are on the issue of biological males in women's sports. The tragic murder of Mahsa Amini, who was beaten by the Iranian morality police because she was accused of wearing her hijab "improperly," may have slightly tempered academia's love of the hijab. But, the Israel-Gaza war that started as a result of the October 7th, 2023, Hamas attacks, which included an attack on a music festival in Israel, have caused academics to reembrace Islam. More on that later.

On a related issue of double standards, academics accept Christianity if it comes from liberal minorities, like the black professor who proclaimed on her faculty-in-residence profile "I sing, pray and have an inextinguishable addiction to God." Yet, when conservatives – even black conservatives – express religious views, they're mocked. Ben Carson's beliefs have been mocked at academic conferences that I've attended, but Biden's Catholicism has been celebrated. Much of this, it seems, boils down to the Left's views being embraced, but the Right's vilified.

Now, this doesn't mean that I believe all religions are the same. I'm not a religious scholar, and I'm a lifelong atheist (3rd generation on my mom's side, which makes me wonder about the genetics of skepticism, on the one hand; and the genetics of religiosity, on the other). But, it seems to me – from having lived in the Bible Belt as a young teenager and having spent a year in Egypt during my last year as an undergraduate college student – that mainstream Christianity treats women far better than mainstream Islam. And, certain religions have embraced science and progress more than others – mainstream Judaism and Catholicism have supported science in ways that we don't see in fundamentalists, like the Amish.

Going back to the SAA conference, even though our points may sound like simple common sense, that shouldn't have been controversial, all hell broke loose! The first actions taken were that some conference attendees started to contact the ombudsmen to demand that the talk be pulled before it was even aired. In a post-meeting write-up, the ombudsmen noted that over 80% of the complaints were about our talk. For instance, one attendee wrote on social media:

> Emailed the president, annual meeting email address, and the ombuds of the @SAAorg to tell them to remove this talk. Let's see how long it takes to get a reply and some action.

Another wrote: "The session is scheduled to start in ten minutes, so quick action would need to be taken." The conference organizers and the ombudsmen acted too slowly or had decided not to pull the talk. The talk was played.

Quickly, social media pages and the comment box during the playing of our talk were filled with nasty attacks of no substance. And, as of now, we haven't seen any criticism that takes on our claims – i.e. why is it that indigenous creation myths can be used for repatriation and why haven't the anthropology organizations called for an abandonment of this practice, in favor of a return to the evidence? For instance, there were comments that the content of our talk was: "thinly veiled racism" and "racist, anti-indigenous bullshit with talking points from white supremacy." Other comments were more personal, such as calling me a "dumb bitch" and a "fucking clown." Some even wrote vague threats to me via email, such as the one that ended with "So politely, choke on a bag of shit, Elizabeth." Perhaps most disturbingly, a Twitter thread pointed out that our talk was in session 88, a white-supremacist signal; as if we had planned this!

Still more comments revolved around being "triggered" and "traumatized." For instance, one of the other presenters in my session wrote:

I watched her record this and it's just as scary as the abstract seems. I had to ask the guy recording to give me like 10 mins to recover bc I was so shocked at what I had just watched and was shaking.

And, another attendee wrote: "This is harmful, triggering, and beyond unacceptable. What an absolute joke of a society to welcome shit like this again and again."

At one point, someone implied that I wasn't in attendance, as required, since I hadn't responded to these attacks. Yet I "spoke up" and made it clear that I was there, and said if there were any legitimate questions, I would be more than happy to try to answer them. And, I did attempt to answer the two or three real questions – out of the over 100 comments!

In addition to these goings-on, there were also posts that questioned whether I was actually a member of the SAA – implying that I somehow snuck in. I had been an SAA member since about 2015. Others questioned whether I had sent in a misleading abstract, which is a common accusation, as I mentioned in regards to the American Anthropological Association panel on sex that had been cancelled. I hadn't. This is what Jim and I sent in:

Archaeologists and anthropologists have been at the forefront of supporting the spread of science over creationism religion. For instance, the Society for American Archaeology posts teaching guidelines that includes statements that dinosaurs went extinct 65 million years ago, the Americas were inhabited about 12,000 years ago, and that archaeology follows the scientific process. The American Anthropological Association, on their policy page, states that "Evolution is a basic component of many aspects of anthropology (including physical anthropology, archaeology…)." And, the American Association of Physical Anthropologists has an anti-creationist statement in which it "condemns any effort by the state to dictate specific religious instruction to the people." However, archaeologists and anthropologists have nearly unanimously supported the Native American Graves Protection and Repatriation Act (NAGPRA). NAGPRA violates the First

Amendment in multiple ways; for instance, "traditional" religious leaders are required for the review committee, "traditional" prayers open and close NAGPRA meetings, and decisions to repatriate remains are made on the basis of creation stories. With NAGPRA, archaeology has become entangled with religion in a way that would never be accepted if the religion was Western-based. We propose a different perspective on human remains and artifacts based on objective knowledge rather than creationism.

They cried about how this abstract could have escaped review. It hadn't, of course. One person, Michael E. Smith, noted that the abstract wasn't really problematic. He would later lead the committee to ensure someone with our views doesn't get on again! And, in *Science* magazine, the incoming president, Deborah Nichols, mentioned that during the review process "no one flagged Weiss's and Springer's abstract" although our argument was "dated."

Twitter feeds were filled with #IAmNotTheSAA and calls to start a new organization due to the SAA's initial response by the outgoing president Joe Watkins that supported the inclusion of my talk:

Discussions involving NAGPRA and related issues are highly sensitive. SAA unequivocally supports NAGPRA and advocates for its increased funding. We are also redrafting our Statement on the Treatment of Human Remains.

As a professional organization, SAA hosts the annual meeting to provide a space to offer diverse viewpoints. Providing a place to exchange differing ideas does not equate to an endorsement.

SAA recognizes some will find some certain positions in presentations objectionable or even offensive, and we do not want to minimize those feelings. The conversation reflects the broader discussions happening in our field. Scholarship requires the opportunity for rigorous interrogation of diverse views. We invite all participants to explore the broad range of research and information shared throughout this meeting.

This support for free speech (or as one person put it "freeze peach" so as not to validate the concept of free speech) and diverse perspectives was not as robust as Jim and I wanted, but at least our right to present was just about supported.

Yet, this statement of support soon evaporated! The SAA leadership caved into the Twitter cancel culture mob, which seemed to be made of every social justice warrior tribe imaginable: Native American indigenous scholars, queer and trans archaeologists, Marxists, and Branch Covidians, (with Twitter handles and titles like Vaccinista, Social Agitator, and Queer Archaeology).

Most of the comments were coming from single individuals, but three groups posted responses: the Black Trowel Collective, the Indigenous Archaeology Collective, and the Queer Archaeology Interest Group. The Black Trowel Collective, which is focused on getting micro-grants to students based on race, class, and gender, stated that "These events are just one act in a long history, and ongoing present, of racist, misogynistic, and colonial discourse and action."

The Indigenous Archaeology Collective wrote that our the talk "impedes efforts, like ours, to decolonize the field."

The Queer Archaeology Interest Group wrote that Jim and I "(re)traumatize Indigenous attendees/viewers" and called for "[m]andatory training" to deal with "problematic papers." But, they also called for an end to tolerance:

> Develop an environment not of tolerance, but of genuine inclusion, in which no member feels marginalized for their identity or ideas (provided they are in keeping with the Society's stated ethics and goals).

In other words, if you agree with us, then you are welcome here – otherwise, we will not tolerate your presence!

Although the talks were supposed to be up for two months, ours was removed from the platform immediately and the SAA wrote to me:

> After careful review of the recording, the SAA board finds that the presentation "Has Creationism Crept Back into Archaeology?" does not align with SAA's values, and so has chosen to not re-post it at this time.

And, they issued a second statement about our talk, in which they wrote that the "Board of Directors collectively apologizes to those who were harmed by the inclusion" of our presentation. Furthermore, they noted that they'd be making changes to the submission and abstract acceptance policy.

The SAA lost its way; they decided that hurt feelings of woke warriors were more important than science and reconstructing the past as accurately as possible. They've embraced indigenous religion to the extent that the conference is now more powwow than archaeology.

Was our talk racist? Actually, Jim and I have a perspective that is the opposite of racism. We were surprised to be attacked as racists as a result of this talk, because as we told Christian Schneider, who was a journalist for *The College Fix* at that time, "in our talk, there was no mention of race." Plus, we told *Science* writer Lizzie Wade that: "[T]o us there are no indigenous archaeologists and no non-indigenous archaeologists – there are only archaeologists…We think that the validity of any argument does not depend on one's race." And, in our response, which was published on the National Association of Scholars website, we wrote:

> Our talk made no mention of race and we were specific in criticizing the use of creationist arguments in archaeology. Instead, we were making a case for science and objective knowledge over the religious literalism of creationism. Yet, the constant cry of racism is practically a requirement in the social sciences today. And, objective knowledge is now viewed with suspicion because facts may support a version of history that does not align with the social justice activists who see racism in every corner.

In addition to cries of racism, it is also interesting how many of the statements focus on concepts of harm, trauma, and violence. What harm could they be talking about? In the coddled academic environment, "words are violence" and, thus, censorship is embraced. Interestingly, "silence is [also] violence" and, thus, anyone not willing to jump on the cancel culture bandwagon will also be accused of causing harm. This may explain why Michael E. Smith (who initially stated that my abstract was not problematic when asked about how it could have been accepted) changed his tune. When confronted with his initial response, he started to approach the subject from a different angle – saying that the abstract should have been rejected because of my book *Repatriation and Erasing the Past*. But, even more absurdly, he called up my marriage to Phil and to my current husband Nick Pope to criticize me.

As I mentioned earlier, Nick is a freelance journalist and TV personality who covers topics on the paranormal, most often on UFOs. He worked for the Ministry of Defence in the UK for 21 years; and, during that time, he spent a few years at the desk that researched the unknown – from crop circles to UFO sightings. Nick's been on shows like *Ancient Aliens*, *The Unexplained*, and *NASA's Unexplained Files*; he's also written both fiction and nonfiction books on the topic of UFOs. Nick and I agree on a lot of topics – from the uselessness of the COVID restrictions to the importance of being free speech absolutists. However, we do not agree on the likelihood of extraterrestrial explanations to the UFO phenomenon. I'm an extreme skeptic on the issue and I'd describe Nick as hopeful that aliens do exist and that some of these sightings are from ETs. Nearly all couples don't see eye-to-eye on everything – would I doubt Charles Darwin's commitment to his theory of evolution by Natural Selection because his wife was very religious? This type of attack on my credentials is uncalled for and sexist.

Smith ended up leading the committee on submission guidelines; a committee that was created in response to my talk, as noted by the SAA: "It was formed in the aftermath of widespread concern about a paper presented at the 2021 annual meeting by Elizabeth Weiss and James Springer." These guidelines are meant to prevent any debate on repatriation or on the validity of indigenous knowledge. Ironically, the new guidelines include a requirement that you accept all the principles of the SAA. These principles focus on preserving the archaeological record. For instance, their first principle is stewardship, and at that time it included the statement that archaeologists should:

> [W]ork for the long-term conservation and protection of the archaeological record by practicing and promoting stewardship of the archaeological record. Stewards are both caretakers of and

advocates for the archaeological record for the benefit of all people.

The 7$^{th}$ principle put forth that "Archaeologists should work actively for the preservation of, and long term access to, archaeological collections, records, and reports."

When I last submitted an abstract to their annual conference in 2022, I was given a rejection because, supposedly, I wasn't adhering to their second principle, accountability, which stated:

> Responsible archaeological research, including all levels of professional activity, requires an acknowledgment of public accountability and a commitment to make every reasonable effort, in good faith, to consult actively with affected group(s), with the goal of establishing a working relationship that can be beneficial to all parties involved.

However, it is clear that they decided to reject the abstract based on who I was rather than the submitted materials, since the abstract was about working with university administrators and tribes to try to come to an agreement about the continued care and accessibility of x-rays that were taken with the tribe's approval. I'd been blacklisted!

Although our talk centered around repatriation and the use of creation myths as evidence, there are other topics which have now been removed from academic debate. Bruce Gilley, a professor at Portland State University, has been the subject of a vicious cancel culture attack that involved a journal even withdrawing a previously peer-reviewed and published article. Bruce's 'sin' was to write an article reviewing the effects of colonialism, and he found that not all of the effects were negative. Looking into any benefits of colonialism is taboo. He republished his article, "The Case for Colonialism," in *Academic Questions*, which is the in-house journal of the National Association of Scholars (NAS). The NAS is a nonprofit organization that "upholds the standards of a liberal arts education that fosters intellectual freedom, searches for the truth, and promotes virtuous citizenship." I too have published in their journal and on their website. In 2023, I was elected to be a board member, which is a role that I'm honored to hold.

Questions regarding the validity of claims about clandestine graves at Indian Residential Schools in Canada and the US are also grounds for cancellation. Frances Widdowson has been compared to a Holocaust denier for looking into the allegations of clandestine graves – and even possible murders – at the Kamloops and other Indian Residential Schools. The biggest case involving Indian Residential Schools revolves around a May 27th, 2021, announcement by the Tk'emlúps te Secwépemc (formerly the Kamloops Indian Band) in British Columbia, Canada, which supposedly revealed "the confirmation of the remains of 215 children who were students of the Kamloops Indian Residential School [KIRS]" that had been buried in an apple orchard near the school. As a result of this announcement, there were headlines around the world, such as the one from *The New York Times* whose headline was "Horrible History: Mass Grave of Indigenous Children Reported in Canada." For five months, Canadian flags were flown at half-mast in government buildings. And, Canadian university presidents sent out statements on the remains of indigenous children found, encouraging their employees to help indigenous students through the grieving process. Following the Kamloops 'discovery,' which was based on ground penetrating radar (GPR) and not excavations, other searches in the US and Canada followed. More GPR data was said to support the existence of buried children. Headlines about 53 burial grounds in the US also spread after a government report on Indian Residential Schools in the US. It seemed that there would be a whole slew of bodies to excavate and rebury in their indigenous homelands. And, sure, there were cemeteries of known graves – sometimes unmarked because wooden crosses rotted away – that even included teachers who had been buried at schools. These may be sad, but they're not evidence of "genocide," "murder," or an indigenous "Holocaust." After all, child deaths were quite common in prehistory, and even relatively recent historic periods. Frances has never argued that deaths didn't occur, but, rather, that deaths aren't evidence of murder; the graves aren't clandestine; and that there isn't any documentation or reliable oral tradition to back up claims about missing children. To say otherwise is just not true. In our joint article for *Minding the Campus*, we question why there haven't been any excavations at Kamloops; and, we suggest it's because other sites that had been excavated – like at Holy Rosary Mission in South Dakota – revealed no remains of murdered children.[2]

> At Holy Rosary Mission (now known as the Red Cloud Indian School) in South Dakota, it was also reported that multiple GPR anomalies were discovered. An excavation found the anomalies related to building products and animal activity. Some animal bones were also discovered, but no murdered children.

For her skepticism, which is supported by the fact that all excavations have turned up zero bodies, Frances lost her job as a tenured professor at Mount Royal University.

Another topic that is rarely discussed is pre-contact slavery among the indigenous peoples of the Americas. In most of the literature that does touch upon this issue, indigenous slavery is downplayed and made to seem not so bad. For instance, in Camilla Townsend's 2021 chapter in *The Cambridge World History of Slavery*, she writes in the abstract that "[s]cholars have long avoided the subject due to their concern that indigenous Americans are already too much associated with savagery," but she notes that "the information only helps us to humanize and comprehend ancient Americans." And, continues with the line:

> In Mesoamerica and South America, agricultural states did demand contributions from communities of laboring people; but though these people were diempowered [sic] dependents, they were not slaves. The vast majority of those who really were enslaved were prisoners of war who were maintained as domestics, most of them women.

In my June 2021 article posted on Libertyunbound.com, which I titled "Slavery: It's All Bad," and my subsequent talk about slavery for History Reclaimed, an independent group of scholars who think that history is too important to use as a propaganda machine, I noted that "slavery is all bad" rather than trying to minimize the impact it had on indigenous peoples. Slaves from the Americas were tortured; they had their Achilles tendons sliced to prevent them from running away; they would have the finger that is required for drawing a bow cut off, and in the Northwest Coast, slaves were slain at potlatches (i.e., tribal ceremonial feasts) just to show off wealth! Could this be the reason why colonial Europeans banned potlatches?

Recently, another tactic to discuss indigenous slavery is being batted around – blame European scholars! For instance, at the 2023 SAA meeting, there was a two-part session titled "Misinformation and misrepresentation: Reconsidering "human sacrifice," religion, slavery, modernity, and other European-derived concepts." The abstract explains that:

This session examines how European-derived analytical concepts that have gained academic legitimacy and given rise to particular methods of understanding have fostered misleading claims, ideas, images, and narratives about ancient Mesoamerica. The presentations reconsider and reevaluate concepts that have gained ground as valid sources of insight into conditions, motivations, and representations in civilizations and societies of the past. Although Mesoamerica figures importantly in this session, the discussion of the prevalent use of European-derived analytical concepts and how usage impacts our understanding of ancient cultures is pertinent to all archaeologists working in non-European contexts.

Although I wasn't able to be there to hear this session, it appears that they are reconsidering "human sacrifice" – when someone was sacrificed in ancient Mesoamerica, it wasn't really sacrifice – like Europeans have claimed! When indigenous peoples regularly murdered children in this way, the approved woke term, apparently, is "ceremonial deaths"!

No bad words will be spoken or written of indigenous people. The woke myth is that indigenous knowledge is science; Native Americans were wise, peaceful, and environmentally-conscientious "from time immemorial," and that they still retain these qualities! We'll see that these are indeed myths in later chapters!

---

[1]Greenfield, Daniel. (2016, December 22). "The fake hijab witch hunt." *Israel National News.*

https://www.israelnationalnews.com/news/348529

[2]Widdowson, Frances and Elizabeth Weiss. (2023, November 9). "Empty Graves: the Genocide that Wasn't." *Minding the Campus.* https://www.mindingthecampus.org/2023/11/07/empty-graves-the-genocide-that-wasnt/

# Chapter 6:

## Diggin' Up Grandma:
## Ghoul and Graverobber

Throughout the multiple cancellation attempts on me and the ramifications of those attempts – from the open letter against *Repatriation and Erasing the Past*, to the deplatforming of my SAA talk, to my chair's talk titled "What to do when a tenured professor is branded a racist," to my court appearance – the social justice warriors always fought dirty. The use of *ad hominem* attacks on my character and appearance was non-stop. Mentions of my marriages were used to try to discredit my work and my anti-repatriation, anti-superstition, pro-science, and pro-research positions.

Some people – on both sides of the cancel culture spectrum; those doing the cancellations and those being targeted – use crude language to get their points across. And, parody profiles on social media platforms and satire are common tools for those fighting against politically-correct censorship driven by the woke; the tweets from parody accounts may mimic *ad hominem* attacks to make the point that the social justice warriors and cancel culture mobs have no evidence or legitimate arguments to back their claims. Yet, this use of humor is distinct from *ad hominem*, since it's attacking a technique and not an individual. Three excellent satirists on Twitter are Gad Saad, Frances Widdowson, and Titania McGrath. Gad Saad, wearing a blue wig, a nose ring, and a pronoun pin, becomes his alter ego "Fierce Sally." Gad humorously writes that they are "related through my mother's side (who is my father because my dad self-identifies as a woman I think)." It's obviously satire and quite effective at pointing out the absurdity that social justice warriors promote. Frances Widdowson's satire character is "francXs mcgrath (NOT frances widdowson)" and she will retweet stories from those who've been cancelled (including herself) with messages, such as "FAKE NEWS!," and in relation to questions about the Indian Residential Schools "YAASSSS!!!! violent hate facts and epistemic terrorism have no place in a genocidal settler colony." Titania McGrath, who I believe is a male, describes herself as "Activist. Healer. Radical intersectionalist poet. Nonwhite. Ecosexual. Pronouns: variable. Selfless and brave."

Frances Widdowson has gotten into trouble at Mount Royal University, where she was a professor before they fired her, for her social media posts, including a tweet in which she spoofed the ever-expanding LGBTQ acronym and the trauma caused by "misgendering fatigue." When the University asked her to stop naming specific Mount Royal University professors, she did. But, that was not good enough – it seems that woke academics and administrators have no sense of humor!

These efforts to bring humor into the very real issue of censorship should be lauded; it's not a technique that I would excel at, but I have cried tears of laughter from the efforts of those mentioned above. There are many others – usually their username, like "Ann Lesby, PhD (she/her)," makes it obvious that they're parody sites. However, there have been times when the lines of reality and satire blur! And, it's increasingly becoming more difficult to tell what is satire and what is real outrage from social justice warriors. I've always tried to ensure that I haven't confused the two!

In my situation, the attacks from social justice warriors weren't humorous; rather, they were mean and free of any substance criticizing my positions. There were tweets that just called me "ugly," such as one from a religious studies graduate student who called me an "ugly cow" after she saw my op-ed that was published in *The Mercury News*, which criticized California's reburial law.

Then, there are those who got personal about my hair or my weight. Those who make fun of the way I speak or the clothes I wear. There is something fundamentally different when one is criticizing a model's appearance or a magazine's use of unattractive models, such as when Jordan Peterson (a world famous psychologist) stated that the obese models were not beautiful – since that person's job and the publication is about appearance, whereas my appearance plays no role in my work and, thus, shouldn't be used to criticize my work.

There are others who call me a "bitch," such as the mask-wearing mother who wrote:

"Science over Religion" my ass, you grave-robbing bitch. I'll be calling the administration today. You should be removed from teaching if this is what you believe.

It saddens me to think that such a censoring and vulgar individual would be someone's mother. Ironically, she stated that she was a SJSU alumna with a minor in anthropology – obviously, universities are partly to blame for these unreasoned attacks, since our job is to teach critical thinking and encourage civil debate.

The most common name calling revolves around two words and one phrase: "ghoul," "graverobber," and "digging up grandma." For instance, an author of Native American themed children's books wrote: "WTF is wrong with you? Ghoul!!! Shame on you!" after I tweeted about the publication of my *Mercury News* op-ed. And, "They should be reburied you ghoul, they don't belong to you" was written by an art history professor. Also, "You sound like an actual ghoul: complaining about the unfairness of having to return a hoard of stolen remains of the ancestors of genocide survivors," by an archaeologist with a PhD.

"Graverobber," along with accusations of eugenics and racism, was posted on Twitter with an image of marching Nazis by a professor of indigenous literature. And, a recent Penn State PhD wrote: "Every one of those humans would've hated your colonizer-graverobber guts, Beth."

Digging up grandma type comments include state teachers of the year, to the judge who was assigned to my case against SJSU, such as one internet user who wrote: "Go dig up your own grandmother, you fucking ghoul."

I point all these out to illustrate that although some of the internet posts come from young people without the educational ability or maturity to argue against my position with facts and reasoned criticisms, many come from well-educated individuals in my field or adjacent fields. Some come from those claiming to be Native American, but many are from non-Native Americans. And, although it is difficult to assess, there seem to be more female bullies than males.

In trying to understand the phenomenon of internet bullying and name calling, I recalled something that Jordan Peterson said at the Stanford Academic Freedom Conference: these internet trolls often had female personality traits, but negative ones such as narcissism, and they tended to be Machiavellian (i.e., a trait that's characterized by interpersonal manipulation). The Stanford Academic Freedom Conference was held in November 2022 and I had the great privilege of speaking at the event in a panel with Frances Widdowson, Joshua Katz (who was fired from Princeton), Amy Wax (whose honest discussion on the topics of race and achievement gaps resulted in administrators at University of Pennsylvania attempting to fire her), and an empty chair for Mike Adams. Adams was a professor at University of North Carolina Wilmington who was nearly fired for satirical posts and holding conservative positions, but he settled out of court with the help of FIRE (the Foundation for Individual Rights and Expression); after his settlement, he committed suicide.[1]

The Stanford Academic Freedom Conference's goals were to tackle the censorship of academics, looking for ways to fight the problem, and bringing about changes. There were many different topics and tactics discussed. For instance, some, such as Gad Saad and Frances Widdowson, made good arguments for the use of satire, while others, such as Peter Arcidiacono at Duke University, suggested embracing and befriending our detractors. Peter Thiel, the tech billionaire who made much of his wealth as a result of founding PayPal and investing in Facebook, gave an impassioned plea for us to steelman our arguments and, thus, win by reason. Steelmanning is the opposite of strawmanning, and involves highlighting and then addressing an opponent's strongest argument, as opposed to a weak argument that they haven't actually made.

It was during those two days in November that I really began to realize the seriousness of the problem, but also discovered how those who've been subjected to cancellations are strong, smart, and dedicated to not backing down. It was there that I had the opportunity to hear Jordan Peterson talk about cancel culture attacks and, thus, after the conference I reached out to him via email to see whether I could understand the phenomenon better – not least because I was being asked to write about the conference for the online magazine *Quillette*.

Jordan Peterson, even though he has millions of online followers, took the time to answer my questions; and, thus, he gave me further insight into online bullying. Psychology research, using personality surveys, has found that those who troll – which is basically described as a chronic bully, or someone who posts to deliberately offend – tend to have sadistic tendencies, in that they like to see people hurt. They also are Machiavellian and display subclinical psychopathy.[2] It appears that narcissism is found in those who want to debate others online, whereas there is a slightly negative correlation with narcissism in trolls. In other words, trolls don't like themselves very much. These are part of what psychologists call the Dark Tetrad, and in the case of the internet bullies, it takes the form of a negative feminine personality. Now, I may have some of this wrong (after all, I am not a psychologist), but I do find it interesting that so many of those who are throwing out vile comments to me are female, especially since more males tend to troll. Yet, I also wonder if many of these bullies would define themselves as trolls, or rather that they would see themselves as debating the issue; in which case, they may be narcissists! In short, they're not mentally healthy!

Nearly all of those commenting have declared their pronouns, many are nonbinary or trans, they often are still wearing masks, and many claim to be vegan, into yoga, and care about the environment. Claims of being kind, coupled with statements about "Black Lives Matter" and "Indigenous Lives Matter," pollute these people's profiles too. Such profiles illustrate how interlaced identity politics is with the Native American repatriation issue. All of these tribes – the queer archaeologists, the trans anthropologists, and nonbinary teachers, the public health pushers – recognize the importance of tribalism, which may be why attacking an individual's appearance, speech pattern, or dress is considered an appropriate way to respond to an argument. Yet, watch out if someone else speaks up against fat models, such as when Jordan Peterson did; then you're coming after the "body positive" tribe, and that must be protected. None of them recognize the importance of the individual. And, they cannot understand how someone from their generation who went through the same education can think differently from them. Thinking differently used to be an important component of liberal education and was celebrated in popular culture as part of the progressive movement. A good example of this was the Apple computers Think Different ad, which featured individuals like Albert Einstein, or their iconic 1984 Superbowl ad.

Many great thinkers didn't want to be defined by their group or the tribe in which others thought that they belonged. For instance, Ralph Ellison, the American novelist and scholar best known for his novel *Invisible Man* which won the 1952 National Book Award, was frustrated by being referred to as a great black writer; he wanted to be known just as a great writer. Yet, social justice warriors want everyone not only to think the same; they want everyone to fit into a tribe. Tolerance for the individual is nonexistent.

Tribalism is anathema to America, which was built on the importance of protecting individual freedoms. It is freedom for each individual to worship (or not worship!) and speak as they wish; individual merit is what makes one great. We have the tales of great individuals – Benjamin Franklin, Walt Disney, Bette Davis, Babe Ruth, to name just a few. We know the names of those who made great strides in civil liberties, like Rosa Parks. And, the stories we tell are framed not around groups, but around people, such as documentaries on Ruth Bader Ginsburg or Muhammed Ali. Others too have written about the issue of tribalism and how it goes against the American and Western way; one of my favorite takes on this issue can be found in Gad Saad's *The Parasitic Mind: How Infectious Ideas are Killing Common Sense*, which came out in 2020.

I place a large part of the blame on universities; where, as I mentioned before, affiliation group dorms, like the Black Scholars Hall, are encouraged. Classes on identity politics, such "Trans Studies: Identities, Embodiment & Politics" are little more than indoctrination sessions. And, new professors are leading the way in cancel culture attacks, as I saw with the open letter calling for the banning of *Repatriation and Erasing the Past.* The newest hires at SJSU were also the most adamant in their attempts to derail my ability to conduct research. Yet, older professors too have been caught up in the tribal warfare – after all, they don't want to be considered old, and they really don't want others to go after them!

The accusations against me also fit in with the movement to "decolonize anthropology" – in other words, remove Western concepts, like progress, civilization, objective knowledge from the field and fill it with indigenous fairy tales to perpetuate the noble savage narrative. Thus, in order to destroy anthropology, accusations of being a ghoul (which is an evil spirit that robs graves and feeds on the dead) or just a non-supernatural graverobber play on the misconception that anthropologists and archaeologists illegally dig up graves. There definitely has been graverobbing in the past by anthropologists, medical doctors, and just plain robbers. Looting of graves goes back millennia – even in Pharaonic Egypt there was looting, which prompted the clergy class to hide royal mummies and even disguise them as ordinary individuals, to prevent looting. These early movements of bodies and deceptive practices to preserve the bodies are two reasons why it is sometimes difficult to identify a royal mummy as actual royalty! I'm obviously not for the continuation of this practice of graverobbing, but I don't see what good can come of burying bones that have been successfully curated for decades and used in research, sometimes in ways that help the living – especially when all living relatives are long-since deceased.

Putting that aside, many cemeteries have been excavated for legitimate reasons – building roads, dam construction, and urban development are all factors that would destroy the remains and artifacts if excavation hadn't occurred. Archaeologists and anthropologists are not graverobbers, but rather salvagers. Salvage archaeology protects what would otherwise have been destroyed and, thereby, allows for us to research the remains and learn about the past. We can also use the remains to help present day people, especially through forensic training. Most collections in the US that have been excavated since the 1930s have been salvage archaeology. And, as I discuss in *Repatriation and Erasing the Past,* as America became a car nation, the building and improving of roads, especially highways during the Eisenhower administration, led to the Federal-Aid Highway Act of 1956, which included key provisions that authorized state highway departments to spend money on archaeology. This helped to create a new type of archaeology—highway archaeology. The 10,000- to 12,000-year-old Buhl Burial, a female Paleoindian discovered in Idaho, was found as a result of highway improvement. Unfortunately, this oldest Paleoindian has now been reburied. Yet, even large sites, with many burials, can be salvage sites. In the building of the second Aswan dam in Egypt, archaeologists feverishly worked to save as many mummies as possible. And, even the Ryan Mound, from which the collection at SJSU was recovered, was a salvage site.

Another form of excavation occurs mainly in Europe; cemeteries are sometimes excavated due to space limitations. The remains are then curated and made available for research. We see this in the Museum of London's archaeology section, where there are cemetery collections dating from the Pre-Roman period (which ran from about 800 BC to 43 AD) to the post-medieval period, which include remains from 1547 to 1852 AD.

Furthermore, when accusations arise that "white folks" wouldn't want the remains of *their* loved ones and relatives studied or utilized, I point out that this is actually not true. The vast majority of bodies on exhibit, such as in the world-famous Gunter von Hagen's Body Worlds exhibits found in museums around the world, come from white people. Research and display of white people can be found across Europe, without issues from their descendants. These include donated bodies, but also ancient remains, such as the bog bodies of Northwestern Europe that date from about 500 BC to 100 AD, and the 5,300-year-old alpine iceman called Ötzi. It also includes the catacombs in Paris and Italy, which contain thousands of individuals that are on display. In the Mütter Museum, in Philadelphia, there are examples of white people who wanted their bodies displayed to educate others about the pathologies they experienced.

Forensic collections – such as University of Tennessee's Bass Collection and the newer collection in San Marcos, Texas, that is associated with Texas State University – are made up mostly of white people who donated their or their relatives' bodies. For some forensic collections, they have so many white, adult males, that they aren't even taking any more of them! White people also donate more organs and more bodies for medical schools. The body used to understand Egyptian mummification in the *National Geographic* special was also from a white person who donated his body for the experiment and display. Even the "visible man" and "visible woman" – early attempts to slice the body into 10 centimeter pieces that were then digitized and put on display – are from white people, including one who was executed, but wanted to do something good with his life to atone for his actual crimes!

Thus, to act as if only Native American remains are excavated or studied is a falsehood. And, when I'm asked about whether I would like for *my* grandmother to be dug up and studied, I honestly say that not only would it not bother me, but I'd be genuinely happy for it. The funny thing is that when I give this answer, then all of the sudden the person who asked the question gets defensive and says something along the lines of "well, they're not your grandmother" or "well, that's you and not everyone else." I never claim to speak for everyone else, but the social justice warriors do!

My parents have assured me that they're donating their bodies to science upon their deaths. I plan to do the same. I hope that readers will consider the same. Let's remember to make ourselves useful after death through organ or body donation. These are honorable acts. Research on human remains and celebrating the study of the dead through photos, books, and museum exhibits are not matters of disrespect, but rather the opposite. They are ways to respect those who have come before us. I will return to this issue again, especially in regards to photography!

I want to add that we don't know what these people who we study would have wanted. As I stated in an article that I wrote for Libertyunbound.com:

In my field of biological anthropology, which involves studying past populations, especially Amerindians from prehistoric cultures, we sometimes assume that those who lived in prehistoric times would have liked to be treated or buried in a single way, but I am sure that there were individuals who thought independently and differently — maybe there were some who didn't even believe in an afterlife. Thus, I ask you, who are we to say that the current tribes know what past individuals would have wanted to happen after their remains are discovered?

And, as Christine Quigley noted in her book on mummies called *Modern Mummies: The Preservation of the Human Body in the Twentieth Century*, sometimes you don't get what you want – Joseph Stalin wanted to be preserved and displayed forever and he has been buried. Vladimir

Ilyich Lenin didn't want to be preserved, displayed, or idolized, as he saw it unfitting with communism, and yet, he is still preserved and displayed in the Kremlin!

My maternal grandfather Gustav never wanted to be buried. He had a lifelong fear of being buried alive; a common fear during his time. Jan Bondeson's book *Buried Alive: The Terrifying History of our Most Primal Fear*, which came out in 2001, is an excellent account of the history of burials and the fear of being buried alive. Nevertheless, Gustav was buried, dressed in a white suit (which he also would have hated) as a result of his wife's decision. His grave was considered a protected grave as a result of the family's prominence in art and philosophy, but because one of his sons forgot to keep up the required paperwork in relation to this historical protection, Gustav's body was exhumed and cremated to make room for others. This upset some of my relatives, but not my mother. And, in fact, as soon as Gustav was dead, what happened to his body really was irrelevant to him!

---

[1]French, David. (2020, July 6). "A eulogy for a friend, a lament for the nation." *The Dispatch*.    https://thedispatch.com/newsletter/frenchpress/a-eulogy-for-a-friend-a-lament-for/

[2]Buckels, Erin E., Paul D. Trapnell, and Delroy L. Paulhus. 2014. "Trolls Just Want to Have Fun." *Personality and Individual Differences* 97–102. https://doi.org/10.1016/j.paid.2014.01.016

# Chapter 7:

# Ten Little Indians

The Native American Studies minor at SJSU had been housed in the anthropology department for decades. It included archaeology, cultural anthropology, and physical anthropology courses along with a bevy of courses from art history, sociology, and history. Students could also use courses, such as Women of Color in the US, and courses from Chicano/Chicana Studies. The paucity of courses directly on Native Americans, rather than Mexicans and other Hispanics, is likely a result of our student body, which is in large part Hispanic – about 28%. Nevertheless, anthropology courses, such as Native California Past and Present, and Anthropology of Native America, helped to maintain the overall Native American theme in the minor. My course, Bioarchaeology, covered research on Native American collections, especially research using the University's Ryan Mound Collection. In this way, I was also able to recruit student volunteers to collect data on the skeletal remains from the Ryan Mound Collection. Given the recent incendiary problems over studying and handling Native American skeletal remains, one might think that I would have had difficulty recruiting student volunteers, but this was never a problem – until it was! An interesting clue that these recent taboos are activist-created, and don't reflect any genuine reluctance to work on Native American skeletal remains.

From February 2017 to February 2020, our department chair was actively fighting to keep the Native American Studies minor in anthropology. He even enlisted my help in putting the work of past and present anthropologists in a perspective that included the positive influences anthropologists had on Native American communities, the collaborative efforts of archaeologists and Native American tribes, and the research conducted that helped to reconstruct the past lives of Native

Americans who left without leaving behind any written records. He and others in the department strongly believed the minor should stay in anthropology. Furthermore, with 2020's ethnic studies requirement, known as AB1460, all California State University students would be required to take an ethnic studies course, and this may include Native American Studies courses – perhaps, this could be a windfall for anthropology. That was the thinking.

The ethnic studies requirement, which was signed into law by California's governor Gavin Newsom, was considered legislative overreach by some – some academics wanted more flexibility for campuses, suggesting that there could be a requirement for ethnic studies or social justice studies, such as those which may focus on the women's rights movement or global human rights. Furthermore, ethnic studies is a narrowly-defined field that specifically focusses on "Native Americans, African Americans, Asian Americans, and Latina and Latino Americans." Thus, other minority groups, such as Jews, are excluded from ethnic studies. The requirement of ethnic studies – first in the California State University, then in the University of California, and finally in high schools – breathed new life into ethnic studies departments that weren't attracting enough students to keep afloat.

On the other hand, it was no windfall for anthropology – as politically correct as anthropology is, it cannot keep up with the wokeness of ethnic studies departments! The general education page on ethnic studies at SJSU states that:

> Ethnic Studies courses give students the knowledge and skills necessary for comprehending continued sovereignty movements, the racial and ethnic dynamics, and settler colonial histories and social justice movements in the United States, and the socio-historical origins, processes, and consequences of racial construction, racialization, and racial oppression in the society in which they live.

The guidelines for the ethnic studies general education requirement make it clear that the purpose of these classes is to indoctrinate students into critical race theory. For instance, in a veritable buzzword bingo of wokeism, student learning outcomes include to:

> Analyze and articulate concepts such as race and racism, racialization, ethnicity, equity, ethnocentrism, eurocentrism, white supremacy, self-determination, liberation, decolonization, sovereignty, imperialism, settler colonialism, and anti-racism.

And, also, students should:

> Apply ethnic studies theory and knowledge to describe and actively engage with anti-racist and anti-colonial issues and the practices and movements that have and continue to facilitate the building of a more just and equitable society.

These courses are intended to create activists, not scholars or critical thinkers. The new ethnic studies general education requirement forces students to take these brainwashing classes – it's practically a welfare program for ethnic studies professors!

Anthropologists may have felt doubly slighted, because the requirements to teach these classes state explicitly that an instructor must have:

> [A]n appropriate terminal degree, or master's degree with demonstrated knowledge and expertise in ethnic studies or related fields such as: Native American Studies (NAS/AIS), African American Studies (AFAM), Asian American Studies (AAS), and Chicanx/Latinx Studies (CCS).

Anthropologists were out of luck (or, more accurately, the deck was rigged) and our department lost the Native American Studies minor – it has been discontinued as of 2023, but stopped accepting students in 2022. There is an assumption that Native American Studies will be resurrected in the University's new Ethnic Studies Collaborate, which aims to create an undergraduate minor in "Comparative US Race and Ethnic Relations" and bring the ethnic studies departments together. And, of course, the new classes will be taught by new hires with PhDs in Native American Studies.

In early December 2020, SJSU placed a job advertisement for a new faculty position to lead the way for a new "independent" – of anthropology and other 'settler colonial fields' which rely on 'evil' Western concepts like data and objective knowledge – Native American program "that is grounded in Ethnic Studies perspectives and practices." The ad further stated that there would be support from the University and college for developing Native American Studies. Thus, the new hire would work on creating classes that "address issues of settler colonialism, racial capitalism, immigration, and racialization." These classes will also focus on "experiential knowledges [sic]." In other words, they wanted someone who has looked at people's "lived experiences" or perhaps, even better, the professor would use his own "lived experiences" rather than scholarship to teach the courses. This would fit well with the committee's desire to hire an actual Native American.

The search committee, which was made up of about four or five faculty members (including one of my departmental colleagues), winsomely hoped that the hire would be Native American and would likely give any applicant of Native American ethnicity a more favorable vote than a better candidate who was white. Of course, this is illegal, as stated on the bottom of each job advertisement. For this particular advertisement, the legal statement read as follows:

> San José State University is an Affirmative Action/Equal Opportunity Employer. We consider qualified applicants for employment without regard to race, color, religion, national origin, age, gender, gender identity/expression, sexual orientation, genetic information, medical condition, marital status, veteran status, or disability. This policy applies to all San José State University students, faculty, and staff as well as University programs and activities.

How can an institute be both an affirmative action employer and an equal opportunity employer? Affirmative action is not equal because it revolves around activities that are designed to increase minorities (and, in some cases, women – although there are more women than men in university jobs) hires. It makes no sense that equality and affirmative action can be present at the same time!

The more recent statement is even more inclusive, opening with the line that SJSU "prohibits discrimination on the basis of Age, Ancestry, Caste, Color, Disability, Ethnicity, Gender, Gender Expression, Gender Identity, Genetic Information, Marital Status, Medical Condition, Military Status, Nationality, Race, Religion, Religious Creed, Sex, Sexual Orientation, Sex Stereotype, and Veteran Status"!

Why is the phrase "We are an equal opportunity employer" not enough? And, perhaps, a statement that "we do not tolerate discrimination of any kind?" Because otherwise one ends up with some new category (or perceived category) feeling aggrieved at being left off the list, and then getting themselves added. The same thing, of course, happened with LGB, which expanded step-by-step and now stands at LGBTQIA2S+ (though some versions are even longer!) – this may have expanded further by the time this book goes to press! The point, of course, is that this 'just one more' expansion never ends, becomes farcical, and the whole thing loses its meaning and any power it may once have had.

Or, perhaps, wouldn't it just be easier to say we hire people on merit? Unfortunately, these statements are sometimes contradictory, oftentimes meaningless, and usually promptly ignored. But, it's worse than that. Statements like "we are an equal opportunity employer" are probably seen by some as "hate speech," like saying something 'subversive' such as "All Lives Matter." Imagine the short shrift someone would get at a faculty job interview if they responded to the inevitable DEI question with "I treat everyone equally," without name-checking a veritable laundry list of victims (or perceived victims). I've seen this happen when an interviewee for an office staff position responded to a question on diversity by saying that she treats all people equally and respectfully; afterwards the rest of the committee mentioned that they were aghast at her answer and didn't even see her out.

Hiring is often based on race and gender. Diversity hires are abundant in academia. And, these don't usually end well, as with the recent resignation of Harvard University president Claudine Gay, a black woman. Gay flubbed her response to the US Senate in regards to campus antisemitism during the Israeli-Gaza war that started after the Hamas terrorist attack in October 2023; asked whether calling for the genocide of Jews was counter to Harvard's policies on bullying and harassment, she replied "it can be, depending on the context." She was also caught having plagiarized more than half of her academic scholarship. Her publications, nearly all of which contained plagiarism, were so few that any white male wouldn't have been hired even as an assistant professor at Harvard, much less rise to their highest position.[1]

The hiring committees sometimes get around the legal prohibitions by asking for "experiential knowledge." And, the required diversity, equity, and inclusion statement at SJSU for all faculty applicants comes with guidelines in which the first suggestion in regarding how one may understand "diversity, equity, inclusion, and belonging" is that "understanding could be shaped by personal experience."

Yet, what caught my eye in the SJSU job ad was the line: "We currently enroll approximately 700 students who identify as Native American." 700 Native American students! As I wrote in an article to *The College Fix*, which I titled "San José State U. massively inflates Native American student population to justify ethnic studies expansions":

> A number that high would put SJSU in the top 10 of universities with the highest number of Native American students – nestled between University of Alaska at Anchorage and Northern Arizona University.

Throughout my time at SJSU, I never got the sense that there were many Native American students on campus – they weren't in my large general education class, Introduction to Human Evolution, and they weren't in my other classes either, even the class that was listed as a course which could fulfill a requirement for the Native American Studies minor. So what was going on?

I needed to get to the bottom of this number – after all, a lot of resources were being thrown at this student population: new faculty hires, a resource center, and a new major – possibly even a new department along the way. Unlike most faculty positions, this one was even listed as starting as an associate or full professor. In other words, this person wouldn't be required to do the six-year probationary period before getting tenured and, basically, having a job for life!

Upon seeing this number, I reached out to one of my departmental colleagues who was on the search committee. I thought that she may be able to provide me with the reason behind the number. I wrote to her that:

In the Office of Institutional Research, the number is listed as 25. If you count Native Hawaiians or Other Pacific Islanders, that brings the total up to 192. Perhaps this is an erroneous assumption, but do the rest of the 500 come from those who list two or more races? If so, then that would be remarkable because it means that a third of those are listing themselves as Native Americans and some other race.

My colleague got back to me with: "Good question, but I have no idea about that specific number! I think that was written by the diversity officer or other administrative offices...."

She also noted that the University "now allows students to respond to the demographic info with more detail (like, listing multiple ancestries), in an attempt to capture a better picture of the student body."

In order to get a better understanding of the number, I next decided to reach out to the committee chair, who also didn't know where the number came from. She noted that "[t]he committee did not write that part of the ad, so unfortunately I cannot answer your question, though I will do my best to find out where the query should be directed."

She did follow up with a second email, and found that the number was provided by the Office of Diversity, Equity and Inclusion – quelle surprise! She also acknowledged that the figure of 700 included students who identify with multiple groups (e.g., Native American & Latino).

After several email exchanges with the director of the Office of Diversity, Equity and Inclusion, I received this confirmation:

The number reflects students who have indicated that they identify as Native American plus one or two other racial/ethnic identities. A significant number of Native and Indigenous identified students also identify as Latinx. The count from the CSU system of 25 or so are those students who only identify as Native American.

Yet, this answer left me with more questions than before. Obviously, most of those who were identifying as Native American were actually Hispanic. This is problematic, because the national standard for data collection provides the guidelines that Hispanic students should not be listed as "two or more races." Afterall, Hispanics are *already* a combined race category: Spanish European and Indigenous Central and South Americans. Moreover, if Hispanic students don't have any indigenous genes or ancestry, then they're just Spanish – thus, Europeans and white!

Plus, indigenous populations that are not in North America are not usually considered Native American; there is an ongoing debate about this issue, but the ad stated "Native American" and not "indigenous." Archaeologically and culturally, the indigenous of Central and South America, such as the Aztec, Mayans, and Inca, are distinct from Native Americans. (There are a few exceptions to this, such as border tribes like the Apache.) They had developed civilizations that far outpaced Native Americans in regards to writings, societal organization, and even architectural structures. They are fundamentally different peoples, and this is the key point, surely?

I mentioned the issue of demographic standards to the director of the Office of Diversity, Equity, and Inclusion; along with the link to how SJSU's own Office of Institutional Research collects data:

> [P]ersons who are Hispanic should be reported only on the Hispanic line, not under any race, and persons who are non-Hispanic multi-racial should be reported only under "Two or more races."

Furthermore, to be Native American, one must maintain "cultural identification through tribal affiliation or community attachment;" just claiming to be part Native American, like Senator Elizabeth Warren did, should not be counted, according to the University's own standards. People who falsely claim Indian ancestry are sometimes called Fauxcahontas, or Pretendians, and I will discuss this issue in a later chapter.

Even indigenous people from Hawaii are separated out in the count of Native Americans; they are considered Native Hawaiians or Pacific Islanders.

Although I was never able to get the raw data that added up to 700 Native American students, I was able to look further into whether there was evidence for a large Native American population at SJSU. In my examination of the data from the Institutional Research Office, I found that since 2009 the highest number of Native American students was 120, which likely was still a vast overcount. Some years the number was as low as 20 students. From 2013 to 2023, the number of Native American students never reached above 50, and the student population hovers around 30,000!

As for the anthropology department clinging to the Native American Studies minor, it really wasn't worth it. Since the Fall semester of 2013, we've never had more than three students enrolled in the minor and never more than one Native American student at any one time. Considering that students take about four years to graduate and, thus, each count is not necessarily a different student, the numbers are ridiculously low. In other words, there were less than two dozen students enrolled in the minor over a period of 10 years, and no more than seven of them were Native American. In some years, we had no Native American Studies minors at all!

Of course, not all Native American students would be drawn to a Native American minor, but we'd expect to see more than this with 700 Native American students! In actuality, most ethnic studies classes are filled with students of that ethnicity, which is one of the reasons that these classes were struggling. Black students at SJSU, according to the Institutional Research Office data, are always the majority of students in African American studies, for instance. The same is true for Chicano/Chicana Studies. And, at SJSU, the number of Native American students in the Chicano/Chicana Studies courses was even lower than that of the Native American Studies minor. For multiple years there were no students in these courses that identified as Native American.

But, the low number of Native American students is evidenced also in more subtle ways. The Native American Student Organization has defunct

Instagram and Facebook pages. On their website, their last post was over six years ago in 2018! And, the photos of University events celebrating Native Americans show only a handful of the same individuals – some of whom are the administrators happily grinning at the new expenditures!

In the Spring semester of 2021, the SJSU senate passed a "Sense of Senate Resolution, Requesting the Appointment of a Presidential Task Force on the Needs of Native Students, Staff, and Faculty." In this resolution, they recommended that "the task force should include Native faculty, staff, and students." Furthermore, they called for SJSU to use "aggregated Native and American Indian student data that account for the fact that many Native and American Indian students are identified in other racial and ethnic categories," as this will big up the numbers and increase the likelihood of getting resources.

They also asked that:

> The Native Task Force members be compensated with release time and/or a stipend to complete the work of gathering data, formulating a survey, conducting interviews, and writing a report with recommendations.

This is a perfect example of a self-licking lollipop!

Seven months later, in October 2021, questions were asked about why there hadn't been progress made on the task force. The answer shouldn't be surprising if you realize there are few Native Americans at SJSU at every level – from undergraduate students to university administrators and full professors. It "has been slow in getting off the ground because decisions were being made about how to parse out the work among the few identified Native and Indigenous faculty and staff on campus." Much of SJSU's staff is made up of current and former students and, thus, with 700 Native American students it should've been easy to get the lower-level tasks, such as putting together events, accomplished. And, thus, they branched out to more explicitly include other indigenous groups. They called the new group GAIN, which stands for Gathering of Academic Indigenous and Native Americans. Yet, even with this expansion, the numbers stay low and progress for change has been slow.

Although there were rumors that SJSU couldn't attract anyone to the position due to my presence, a new Native American Studies assistant professor was hired. Shortly after being hired, he published a study on Native American students at SJSU. This 8-page report, written by Kerri J. Malloy (who states that he's enrolled in the Yurok tribe and of Karuk descent – both Northern California tribes) and four colleagues, came out in September 2023. As resolved by the senate, the authors were likely well compensated for this little undertaking. It's called "Native American and Indigenous Student Experience at San José State University." In this short report, the authors discuss their findings from interviewing students in three focus groups, with each group containing between two and five students. In other words, between 9 and 12 Native American students were interviewed for this report!

What Malloy and his colleagues discovered was that the students felt isolated; not surprising when there are so few other Native Americans around! For instance, a student said "we're not very large numbers and pretty scattered, so it's hard to kind of just meet students or other faculty . . . It's hard to connect with other Indigenous folks."

And, "I'm fairly certain, I'm the only native student in my department of about three hundred people. So I think it's been very isolating."

They also complained of being mistaken for Mexicans, such as when one said that: "They're like, 'Oh, yeah, well, you're nothing,' or else 'You're Mexican,' and that's all they will ever refer to me as."

Yet, these few students have many demands (again, quelle surprise!): dedicated personnel in the financial aid office and in the Student Outreach and Recruitment office; dedicated guidance and academic counsellors; a physical space for the Native American and Indigenous Student Success Center with a program coordinator; a monument to tribes of the region; and, a Powwow! Some of these demands have been provided for the handful of students! This situation reminds me of Winston Churchill's quote: "Never was so much owed by so many to so few" – yet the "few" in Churchill's quote were those Royal Air Force pilots who fought in the Battle of Britain, fighting for the liberty of all during World War II.

The reason that these few students can be catered to is because of the funny numbers that I mention in this chapter. Numbers which are intended to exaggerate the population in order to get resources. The provost – discussing the number of Native American students on a webinar panel about building a Native American Studies Program that I discuss in the next chapter – admitted that the official number was about 20 students, but that when you dig deeper and allow students to identify as multiple races then the number increases to about 800! One of the panelists then suggested looking for even more Indians by looking at students who marked "decline to state ethnicity" – perhaps, they listed their tribe.

The Office of Diversity, Equity and Inclusion Director further revealed the identity politics shuffle – the bureaucrats' way of squeezing every last drop of money out of taxpayers – when she wrote, in regards to demographic standards:

> The protocols, national guidance and governance for counting racial and ethnic groups are devised for different reporting purposes. The national guidance, I would imagine is being used for reporting HSI [Hispanic-Serving Institutions] status for federal funding and programming (as well there may be other reasons). There can be other uses of data that are not official reporting but programmatic based on grant requirements, research protocols, programming initiatives, etc. which are not necessarily for the purposes of reporting.

Different standards for defining ethnicity are used for different pots of money. Make no mistake, the 700 number is an intentional massive inflation to get resources. And, then, the diversity bureaucrats will place these same students in other identity cubbyholes to enable them to grab even more taxpayer money.

As I mentioned in *The College Fix*, hiring decisions, course offerings, and money distributions are all made in large part as a result of demographics and, thus, the claim of 700 Native American students enables the University to justify a Native American Studies hire – one that is even being hired as a tenured professor, as opposed to the usual hiring of a faculty member as tenure-track, where the hired person must prove their worth through six years of service, teaching, research, and publications.

This is only possible with the exaggerated number of Native American students, even when all the other data disprove this number of 700, such as the less than five students a year who are interested in a Native American Studies minor.

Three general points emerge from all this. Firstly, it's difficult to escape the conclusion that someone cooked the books, massively inflating the number of Native American students for political and resourcing purposes. Secondly, the bureaucratic runaround that I got from the Office of Diversity, Equity and Inclusion shows that despite DEI being a growth area in academia, their actual output is poor. Thirdly, if an apparently simple question like "how many Native American students do we have at SJSU?" can be so badly messed up (the claim of 700 Native American students is 28 times higher than the likely actual figure of 25!), then what else has been messed up – either by accident or by design?

Yet, ironically, as the University is double-dipping – combining Mexicans and Native Americans to get their numbers up – Native American scholars and students, such as the one mentioned above, insist on keeping the groups distinct. We will see more of this intertribal bickering and racism in the next chapter!

---

[1]National Association of Scholars. (2024, January 2). "Going, Going, Gone: Claudine Gay resigns as President of Harvard University. *National Association of Scholars.* https://www.nas.org/blogs/press_release/press-release-going-going-gone

# Chapter 8:

# See Something, Say Something

On December 3$^{rd}$, 2020, SJSU's provost Vincent Del Casino hosted a webinar on how to create a successful Native and American Indian Studies program. The webinar ran for 90 minutes and had over 100 attendees. The three invited speakers were Joely Proudfit, Cutcha Risling Baldy, and Craig Stone.

Joely Proudfit spoke first. Proudfit, who the provost mistakenly referred to as Proudfoot a few times, is a Native American and a professor at California State University, San Marcos. She was appointed by President Obama to the National Advisement Council on Indian Education. And, she has played key roles in developing Native American Studies programs in the California State University system. Her mentor, who she holds in high esteem, is the late Vine Deloria Jr., who held vehemently anti-Western and anti-science views. In *Repatriation and Erasing the Past,* Jim and I explain that according to Deloria miraculous events and supernatural phenomena have greater validity than data from physical anthropology and archaeology. His work is the epitome of the postmodern perspective – the victim narrative is all that matters and there is no such thing as objective truth. Repatriation ideology, which I mentioned earlier in this book, is a specific postmodern ideology, dealing with Native American issues from repatriation to understanding past lives, that places who tells the story above scientific evidence; in this case Native American repatriation activists are defined as the victims who get to tell the story. Deloria was one of the most extreme repatriationists. His 1997 book *Red Earth, White Lies: Native Americans and the Myth of Scientific Fact* (1997) is an attack against natural sciences and any non-Indian understanding of the world. For Deloria, biology, evolution, migrations into the Americas, evidence of the extinction of New World megafauna by early Native Americans, and many more such topics were fictional tales that biased, racist researchers, who claim to be objective, tell. Instead, Deloria used American Indian religion to reconstruct the past and suggested that we must accept, as literal truths, creation myths that include magical transformations and supernatural beings.

Cutcha Risling Baldy, also a Native American, is a professor at Humboldt State University. She's a feminist who believes that Native American menstrual taboos (which require women to sequester themselves away from others, including eating separately and staying away from elders) are about the power women hold during menstruation, rather than a regressive way to keep the 'unclean' away! Baldy repeatedly stated that Native American Studies was about decolonization and deconstruction of Western ways of thinking. Yet, towards the end, she claimed that it was about the Native Americans themselves, and not just oppositional.

The third speaker, Craig Stone, wasn't Native American. He's a retired professor from California State University Long Beach (CSULB) who has been key in contaminating high schools with ethnic studies. He helped CSULB become the first college to bury remains of Native Americans, even before the enactment of NAGPRA. Stone also led the way to the removal of CSULB's mascot Prospector Pete and the taking down of the Prospector Pete statue. Prospector Pete was removed because indigenous groups claimed that the gold rush harmed Native Americans. Ironically, the mascot was created in the image of CSULB's founding president Pete Peterson, in the 1940s, not the gold rush of the 1840s. Peterson famously said that he had "struck the gold of education" with the creation of CSULB![1] But Stone wasn't going to let the facts get in the way of a good story – especially when the story is a narrative with Native Americans as the victims.

These three scholars of Native American Studies were asked how to build a successful Native American Studies program. The answers they gave were shockingly discriminatory and revolved around nepotism and activism rather than scholarship. Throughout the hour-and-a-half, they repeated that the main recipe for success was the hiring of Native Americans from the region; to avoid hiring Hispanics; and to allow non-

Native American professors to be only allies (and not to be involved in the actual creation of the curriculum). Furthermore, they noted that the programs needed to be autonomous – independent from other university input – although all other programs go through curriculum committees at the college level (as in the college of social sciences) and the university level!

Joely Proudfit started with a call to treat indigenous knowledge as valid. Indigenous knowledge, according to Proudfit, is distinct in being place-based (i.e., each tribe has knowledge about their region) and sovereign. I am not sure how knowledge is sovereign; shouldn't it be shared and fit along with the bigger picture? And, isn't it either correct or incorrect? I suspect what Proudfit was referring to is that Native Americans should be able to retain the knowledge or control who gets the knowledge. After all, Native Americans often refer to "knowledge keepers" or "knowledge holders" (phrases that make proponents of the noble savage myth go all misty-eyed, but which don't, in fact, mean very much). She further noted that Native American Studies was not about teaching culture, but to enhance tribal culture and sovereignty. Thus, courses invite tribal engagement and focus on experiential knowledge – the lived experience. The core of Native American Studies is not scholarship, but activism. The intent is to decolonize and deconstruct what came beforehand to empower students and communities. Whether something is true or not, doesn't matter. And as for Proudfit's distinct, place-based knowledge, Native Americans have been just as mobile as most other peoples in world history, so have no better and no worse insights into their homelands as anyone else.

Unlike classic disciplines, the field of Native American Studies, Proudfit announced repeatedly, should not be centered around interesting research areas or scholarship. Native American Studies, according to the speakers, needs to be centered on community activism. You're not going to be studying anything about the Native Americans. The intent is to hire Native Americans, bring them onto campus, and give jobs to the community – the jobs may not be needed, and the students may learn little, but that isn't important in an activist field. So, non-Natives can be hired, but only if they are helping the Native Americans at the university and in the community. Any non-Natives who want to "colonize" the discipline are to be challenged. This is why Proudfit sees a linguist's argument that teaching about Native American language belongs in linguistics (a logical, commonsense point of view) as threatening, and a form of colonization. Proudfit stated no other academics are facing such issues, which is just a blatant lie, especially coming from someone who has been in academia for 27 years at the time of the webinar! Throughout my years at SJSU, whenever new classes are brought up, other fields will try to make the argument that the new class encroaches on their discipline. When anthropologists try to bring economics-focused classes, such as Money, Gifts, and Exchange, into the department's course list, economics professors complain. When environmental science professors suggest "culture of waste" courses, anthropologists complain. This territorial bickering is the norm, not the exception!

All three speakers tried to argue that Native American Studies should be autonomous, as I mentioned before. They shouldn't have to ask the university community about their hires, courses, program, or scholarship. Yet, academia is a community, and we get judged and aided by our peers. From hiring, to promotion, to course development, and research, decisions are made at the department, school, and university levels! A typical faculty hiring, for instance, involves input from students after the job candidate gives a classroom lecture; input from the department after a research talk; input from the dean after discussion of service duties and curriculum; and even after all this, the final decision may lie in the president's office – from the provost, or the president himself! Instead, Native American Studies programs want the tribal communities to make the decisions and only Native Americans to be decision-makers. Stone, for instance, stated that his courses in Native American Studies were vetted by the tribal community of 80 individuals; these individuals likely got paid handsomely for their input. Yet, more importantly, they're not scholars and cannot make educated decisions about course content that may include the reading load, assignment timings, and the balance of topics!

Cutcha Risling Baldy was perhaps the most outrageous of the speakers. She railed against "settler colonialism," argued that Native American Studies was about learning from Native Americans and not learning about them, and wanted to blow up the Western disciplines. Ironically, she also said that all these Western fields come originally from Native Americans. To her, climate change, politics, and health are all things that Native Americans know more about than other communities. For instance, she said "Let me tell you how it was Native people who built these historic Western disciplines." And, the discoveries of Western science – well, according to Baldy – those were made by Native Americans too! In her view (where "our" refers to Native American): "our community has the most knowledge; and our peoples have the most knowledge; and, our land has the most knowledge." How land can have knowledge, I fail to understand. Of course, Baldy isn't correct; the disciplines, such as anthropology and history, could only be developed within cultures that had written languages – something missing in Native Americans until European contact.

In order to push back against the West, Baldy reiterated that Native Americans must be hired. Proudfit and Stone agreed. Hiring Native Americans is the key to Native American Studies programs success, and it's even better to hire those in your region. Stone told the story of office staff hires that went awry. He said:

> If you're going to hire a secretary or an administrative support coordinator, hire someone the community [in this case, he's speaking about the tribal community] trust. Don't share that staff person with another department. It's gotta be autonomous and for years we had Latinas as our secretaries or our administrative support coordinators. And, our Native people would show up and they'd speak Spanish to them and if you're a California Indian or a Native person the last thing you want to do is show up to a Native Studies Program and have somebody assume that you're not from here. So, one of the first things we did when we restructured ourselves was hire a person when people show up and they're like 'oh my gosh, I know you.' That connection is so vital.

In other words, they fired people based on their race and hired people based on their race! This is illegal! He went on to add that universities "mess up all the time" when they think that they can train somebody to work with "Injuns" (as he repeatedly called them). Stone insisted that one must hire the "families that are already there"! There is no other way to have a successful program.

But, also, the University has decided that Hispanics are Native Americans; and, the vast number of those who list themselves as Native American in California are actually originally from Mexico! Thus, this exclusionary practice against Hispanics is doubly troublesome. Once again, this illustrates the fudging of statistics to support high-cost and low-demand programs.

Upon hearing these statements and those from Baldy regarding the superiority of Native Americans, I decided to ask a few questions. Afterall, we've been taught at SJSU to speak out when you hear racism or discrimination; our culture is one of "see or hear something, say something." My questions were as follows:

Isn't it quite racist to say that "our" group has the most knowledge? All people have knowledge – are you saying that Native Americans have more knowledge than Blacks, Whites, Asians, Hispanics?

and

Are you saying that only Whites should teach Western Civilization? Or that only British should teach Shakespeare?

With these two questions the provost's face sunk into a deep furrowed frown; Joely Proudfit was visibly angry and looked like she was chewing a wasp. Proudfit, Baldy, and Stone weren't able to ignore these questions and their remarks showed an unwillingness to see my point – not that Native Americans shouldn't teach these courses, but that teaching courses should be based on scholarly merit and not race.

Proudfit's response was:

I'm reading some of the questions here, and there are several that I find disturbing written by the same person. I don't know if this is an ignorance of American Indian Studies, but to ask the question in 2020 do you think only Native people can teach Native American Studies, isn't that racist? That in of itself is really racist...If I'm an American Indian content expert and I also happen to be from a local tribal community of which my campus resides, doesn't that bring opportunity and attributes to the students and the campus community. The fact that my students can see me as one of the relative descendants who share the same language – if they can see it, they can be it. Don't our students and community deserve the role modeling opportunity to be in the classroom as well?

So, I go back to this person who's asked this question and say "sit with your thoughts for a minute before you feel like you need to lay claim to our discipline, our stories, our courses, our language, our history, and our future."

If we have American Indian scholars capable with the knowledge – right? – both cultural and academic knowledge of being able to do that, why wouldn't you invite us to do that and to lead because to not do that is a form of academic genocide and that should stop now?

I don't know you, and I don't know your discipline, but I can take a guess. And, it's the same discipline that has been attacking and trying to encroach upon and colonize American Indian Studies for all these years. So again, appreciate our knowledge, our academic degrees, our publications, our expertise, and our cultural knowledge that we bring to these campuses, these communities, to our students.

Let us mentor our students, speak our language on our tribal land within these institutions. Many of these institutions house the ancestral bones of our people and many of these can't even be returned because these tribal communities don't fall under federal recognition status or don't have land where to bury them.

So please sit with that for a minute before you ask a question like isn't that racist that American Indians should be the ones to teach American Indian Studies and to make the same kind of analogy that only Europeans should teach Shakespeare. Come on, you're an academic that is beneath you.

And, Cutcha Risling Baldy also chimed in:

...together we're going to tell a very different story about this land, about this history, about this culture, and about what it could be and when you start to learn that way, you learn a couple of things. One, none of this makes any sense: patriarchy, capitalism, colonialism, doesn't make any sense. Two, you start to figure out that you are responsible to [sic] that colonialism because you, in certain instances, have benefited from that. So, this is what I say when people ask me can anybody teach Native American Studies. Yeah! Can anyone major in it? Of course. Can other departments teach classes about Native Americans? Sure. But for over 500 years, your departments benefited from being the ones with the privilege to be included as part of higher education.

What is your responsibility now? We have the PhDs, we have people doing the research, we have the people doing the interventions. Don't you want to take a step back because you're done benefiting off our genocide, the theft of our land, the taking of our peoples, the kidnapping of our women and children? You're done. And, if you're ready to be done, you're going to build a program that's far more powerful. You're going to step into a situation where you're empowering the voices to teach you to view this world in a way where we can build futures without dams, where we can all breathe. I don't think that's too much to think in terms of what we think this future could look like and I know it's possible because I've seen it happen in multiple generations.

And, Stone noted that Native Americans should teach the courses, because they are teaching something that impacts them and their families. And, this is the "beauty" of ethnic studies. However, it is also why ethnic studies, including Native American Studies, is not scholarly!

None of the speakers truly answered my question, of course. I wasn't saying that Native Americans shouldn't teach such courses, but that what you teach shouldn't depend on your race.

One may wonder why I attended the webinar. Did I just want to troll the session? I truly didn't understand the very regional focus on Native American Studies; that the most important point was to hire Native Americans from the region was news to me! I, further, was unaware of how off-the-rails Native American Studies had become – no longer is it the study of Native American culture, history, and politics. It has abandoned all scholarly pursuits for activism. Now, it's about destroying Western knowledge and replacing it with whatever Native Americans say – the important feature is who the speaker is, not what is being said. That's why it doesn't matter that in one instance Baldy claims to want to "blow up Western knowledge," while in the next instance she claims that this knowledge is actually from Native Americans. They don't need to make sense – they need only to belong to the right race!

But, more importantly, what these speakers were saying was true racism. At SJSU, we have a mandate that racism should be reported, racists should be confronted, and, thus, I did my job. I was hearing racism and I pointed it out. Their anger validated my concerns. Never once did I say or imply that Native Americans shouldn't teach the classes, but, rather, hiring people and assigning courses based on race is racist. If one were to exclude non-Britons from teaching Shakespeare, that would be racist! At many universities, German language and culture courses are not taught by Germans or Austrians, which is perfectly fine. If a non-German's skills are better than that of a German's skills, why wouldn't we want to hire the best candidate? If this is okay, then why must Native American language classes be taught by Native Americans? The 'unique ways of knowing' argument may be a nice soundbite, but it is just a soundbite!

One may question whether a non-Native American could teach these courses better or engage in tribal activities better than a Native American. We don't have to look hard for an example; in July 2022, a story broke in the media about the British Columbian Kamloopa Powwow. The organizers had decided to require those who take part in the Powwow's dance competition to be "at least (1/4) Native Blood," and proof of "tribal identification/status may be required."[2] They immediately received backlash, with some claiming that this resurrected "colonial blood quantum" rules. They also noted that the dancers must be of the "correct gender for that category," which also received backlash because of the exclusion of the two-spirit people – the sex binary is also "colonial" to postmodernists! As I mentioned in Chapter 2, the term "two-spirit" was just recently coined – in 1990 – by Myra Laramy at the Third Annual Intertribal Native American, First Nations, Gay and Lesbian American Conference in Winnipeg. But, going back to the requirement that the dancer have "Native Blood" – this came about because in the previous year, a German (Shock! Horror!) won the dance competition! According to the news article, "the now-controversial rules stemmed from a German participant in the powwow who won an event one year, upsetting some participants...." There's a word – that my German mother taught me – for enjoying this backlash: *schadenfreude*. The unique satisfaction derived from someone suffering a consequence of their own misdeeds, especially when they've engaged in hypocritical actions.

Furthermore, arguing that one's people are better and hold more knowledge, especially when untrue, is racist. It is Native American supremacy. Native Americans didn't build the Western disciplines. Modern anthropology, for instance, came from England, can be traced back to Charles Darwin, and includes some of the research on the earliest discoveries of Neanderthals in the 1870s. Perhaps the first anthropology textbook was written by Sir Edward Burnett Tylor, who published *Anthropology, an Introduction to the Study of Man and Civilization*, in 1881. This book included information about cultures that Native Americans had never even heard of. I am not aware of any early work by Native Americans that discuss early humans, from australopithecines to Neanderthals! And, history as a discipline could only be developed by those with written language! These are just flagrant falsehoods similar to the African Athena argument found in the 1970s through to now, which puts forth the lies that Socrates was black and that Aristotle stole his ideas from Africans. Mary Lefkowitz (whose book *Not Out Of Africa: How "Afrocentrism" Became An Excuse To Teach Myth As History* came out in 1997) was an early proponent of teaching true history and not allowing the Afrocentric movement to take over real history by teaching postmodern myths to students in universities. For her brave stand, she became an early victim of cancel culture.

The webinar ended, but the drama wasn't over! Shortly after the webinar, I received an email from another professor at SJSU who wrote:

> I don't know you but as your colleague at SJSU, I did not appreciate the attacking tone of your messages to our Native

Scholars. It was extremely disrespectful and I was embarrassed that they experienced that level of hostility from a faculty member on our campus.

My response was:

I am just sorry that there was no true discussion. If there had been, then people may not have been so upset. I find it offensive when I hear any people say that "our" culture is the best and knows the most (on every topic), regardless of the people who are saying it. Knowledge is best pursued by all people. I think that if we all keep an open-mind, then we can learn from one another rather than a top-down approach regardless of who is at top.

The professor replied to my response, even more upset:

Your attack didn't signal discussion – it was clear you were not there to learn anything. Your casual mention of "people" being upset magnifies what I and other colleagues saw in the q&a – you were clearly the most upset by this.

You and I are scholars in fields that have committed cultural and physical genocide on Native communities in the name of "research." I ask that you sit down and listen to Native scholars and allow them to teach us how to do better by them. And yes, entertain the notion that they may be smarter than you and me on many many subjects.

I'm exhausted and disgusted by Karen antics that silence BIPOC voices in the academy.

I decided it was time to end the email squabble and stated: "You are entitled to your opinion as I am to mine. I hope you have a good weekend and a good rest of the semester."

With the end of the email thread, I thought that the issue was put to rest, but more was to come! A few days later, I received an email from my chair, Roberto Gonzalez. He wanted to chat on the phone; something that is rarely done! In his call, he said that he was sympathetic to my perspective and that these events are echo-chambers. But, then, he warned that my questions and appearances at such events could harm junior professors' chances at getting tenured. He then asked how I would feel if I was a junior faculty member, and a full professor hindered my ability to gain tenure. Of course, Roberto was trying to imply that professors would retaliate against others in my department for my views, but this isn't necessarily true – especially since most of those in the department are achingly woke and politically correct! Even if it were to occur, the correct course of action would be to file a grievance or complaint against the Retention, Tenure, and Promotion committees for making decisions not based on scholarly output (such as publications), teaching, and service to the university. My response to Roberto was that I would support my colleague's freedom of speech and academic freedom. And, I would hope that they too would do so if the shoe was on the other foot. He ended with reiterating that he'd like me not to attend such events in the future. Little did I know that my dean and Roberto would use this incident and the publication of *Repatriation and Erasing the Past* as examples in a joint presentation, outrageously titled "What to do when a tenured professor is branded a racist."

---

[1]Mikelionis, Lukas. (2019, April 27). Cal State campus ditching 'Prospector Pete' mascot after complaints that Gold Rush hurt indigenous people. *Fox News.* https://www.foxnews.com/us/cal-state-campus-ditches-half-century-old-mascot-to-replace-it-with-either-basic-moniker-or-non-mascot

[2]McSheffrey, Elizabeth. (2022, July 13). B.C. powwow organizers apologize after identity-based event rules spark outrage. *Global News.* https://globalnews.ca/news/8988494/powwow-organizers-apologize-outrage-kamloops-bc/

# Chapter 9:

# What to do When a Tenured Professor is Branded a Racist

On June 3rd, 2021, using my personal email address, I attended a Zoom webinar titled "What to do when a tenured professor is branded a racist." This presentation was being given by my chair Roberto Gonzalez, who was hosted by my dean Walt Jacobs. They decided to present this informative session to the Council of Colleges of Arts and Science (CCAS). The CCAS was founded in 1965; it's a national association that has around 2000 members from over 500 universities. About 100 people attended Roberto and Walt's session. I am not a member of the CCAS, but the Zoom link was open, and no password or registration was needed to attend. I was made aware of the session by my sister, who was a chair in an English department in Tennessee at the time. She received the email notification of the webinar because her training for being a chair included attendance at a CCAS leadership conference.

The title of the talk could be taken to mean that perhaps the colleague in question had been falsely accused of being a racist; or maybe it was an entirely hypothetical exercise; but knowing what had come before from Roberto and Walt led me to conclude that this wasn't the case, and that this would be a direct attack on me, and certainly not an even-handed and fair representation of the accusations against me. Sadly, my prediction was correct.

By this time, I had already weathered Roberto's unfair interpretation of *Repatriation and Erasing the Past*, including the statement that Jim and I had used a "Victorian-era approach to anthropological inquiry" and that we viewed scientific progress as "linear." Both accusations that I had corrected him on, but I shouldn't have had to if he had read the book with an open-mind. After all, we clearly stated that scientific progress was both unpredictable and uncontrollable and noted that scientific "knowledge is not an unfolding sequence, but rather a messy endeavor that is in constant flux."

Further reason to doubt an even-handed account of the accusations about me included Roberto's insistence that I do not attend events that involve Native American Studies topics, as I mentioned in the previous chapter.

But, perhaps, most insidiously, Roberto and Walt were in cahoots to prevent me from holding a webinar on academic freedom as I mention in Chapter 4. Roberto's virtue-signaling anti-racist series of Zoom talks were put on without any debate and with no required vote. When I wanted to hold a similar series of talks, but on the importance of academic freedom, or even one talk, obstacles were put in my way, including digging up obscure guidelines that had never been used. After all, speakers in Roberto's anti-racism series argued that views like my own should be silenced. Roberto acted as if he had just come across these guidelines of departmental support for invited speakers that he was insisting should apply to my request. And, we held a department meeting to discuss these guidelines. This is the only time I really lost my composure – and Roberto mistakes this as hurt feelings in his CCAS talk – but really I was just completely incensed that he'd blatantly lie about how he came across the guidelines and why we would now be using them. I even wrote to Walt about it stating:

> After having received the email from Roberto regarding the retroactive vote for Dr. Fuentes and the late vote for the next speakers, I was incensed that he would try to spin this as a false narrative. I had initially typed the following email to send to my colleagues, but decided not to since I don't like reacting in anger. I do think that Roberto is being unsupportive; I was wondering if you and I could schedule a meeting to discuss this situation.
>
> *Dear Colleagues: Roberto didn't just remember the guidelines, which are not attached; he remembered them because I had proposed a counter symposium and he now wants me to follow the guidelines that he failed to follow. Plus,*

*the guidelines also note that there should be a discussion about the speakers – not just a vote. Had such a discussion occurred, I would have suggested a balanced speaker series with multiple perspectives presented. I will not vote retroactively. I hope that we are not heading in a direction where some event topics are okayed through a different set of guidelines than other event topics.*

Finally, the fact that neither Roberto nor Walt decided to inform me of this CCAS session enabled me to correctly assess their angle – to further brand me as a racist!

The session was an hour long. About half of the time Roberto painted himself as a victim and maligned my views and my character. For instance, he repeatedly implied that he had no awareness of my work on repatriation issues before he became chair. After talking about my osteology research, he said:

When you're in a department, you're focused on your own research and you're not necessarily focused on all the different dimensions of your colleague's research. And so what wound up happening once I became chair is that I discovered that there was a different side of her research. And I found that she had published a couple of articles in fairly obscure journals in which she was somewhat critical of NAGPRA -- federal NAGPRA, as well as California State NAGPRA legislation.

He also alleged that before *Repatriation and Erasing the Past* that none of my books had "anything to do with NAGPRA."

These statements are not only inaccurate, but I don't believe that Roberto hadn't known about my repatriation work prior to being chair. My first book, which came out in 2008, was called *Reburying the Past* and it was about NAGPRA. Furthermore, the "obscure journals" included the Cambridge University Press's *Politics and the Life Sciences* – it was in this journal that I published *Kennewick Man's Funeral*, an article that I submitted to the hiring committee before I was even hired at SJSU. Roberto sat on that committee.

Furthermore, in 2006, only two years after being hired, I published in *The SAA Archaeological Record*, which is the newsletter for the largest academic and arguably most prestigious archaeology association in the US! In 2006, I presented my views on repatriation and reburial at the American Association for the Advancement of Sciences, which has around 120,000 members and is the publisher of the journal *Science*. And, in 2008, I presented my views on NAGPRA at the American Anthropological Association.

In 2010, I gave a talk in the "San José State University Scholar Series," which is hosted by the provost. It's one of the most prestigious scholarly honors one can receive at SJSU. My talk was about the importance of preserving skeletal collections and the negative effects NAGPRA has had on research. I was also featured in *Science* in their 2010 issue on repatriation and 20 years of NAGPRA.

All of this happened before Roberto was made chair in 2016. During those times, he would have seen flyers about some of these events, the publication of my book in the display case, and heard of my work – just as I had heard about his work in regards to his concern of anthropologists working for the US military or CIA. We are a small department with less than 10 tenured or tenure-track professors; thus, we're well aware of one another's work through program review periods, curricular discussions, peer-observations, and even Retention, Tenure, and Promotion committees at the departmental, college and university levels! Roberto was most definitely on at least one of these Retention, Tenure, and Promotion committees while I was going up for tenure and promotion before he became chair. Thus, he would have seen my publications before becoming chair. It is possible that he erased all this from his mind, but I have a difficult time believing this. And, even if he had, there would be no reason to dismiss my work as appearing in "obscure" publications. Simply put, either *all* this had been mysteriously erased from his memory, or he was telling lies.

Even if he hadn't been aware of any of this before being chair, upon becoming chair in 2016, he supported my efforts to write and talk about my controversial perspective before the cancel culture attacks. As I mentioned earlier, Roberto wrote (actually in his recommendation for my leave of absence to write *Repatriation and Erasing the Past*!) that my controversial position is "likely to spark lively discussions among various stakeholders" and suggested that my book "might potentially boost the department's national reputation as a center that fosters creative and unorthodox viewpoints on important public issues."

Cast-iron proof that not only was Roberto aware of my views, but also, he was happy to reap the perceived benefits of these views.

While in front of the cancel culture firing squad however, he took a very different perspective; at the CCAS talk he said:

> And her argument is – was and is essentially this. Returning remains to Native American communities stands in the way of the kind of progress of objective Science with, you know, capital S. And in my mind, that's a very kind of antiquated position. I disagree with that entirely as do all of my colleagues, and as I said before, the overwhelming majority of anthropologists in the United States. But this was the focus of her most recent book which was published last summer by a major university press, who – I'll get to that part of the story in just a moment. So she co-published this book with a constitutional lawyer. And this – the central argument of the book is this, that NAGPRA is a bad idea. That it is also – that it violates the separation of church and state to the extent that universities – public universities, for example, that receive federal funding – are basically buckling to the religious demands or religious beliefs of Native American communities, and so on. In my mind, personally, it's a really flawed argument. I think it borders on incompetence – professional incompetence. But one of the – one of the issues with a full-tenured professor is that you have very few mechanisms, I think, to sanction that person unless the person is in clear violation of the law.

Roberto has no law degree and, thus, he's overreaching by judging the legal argument that Jim, who is a retired lawyer, and I make in regards to NAGPRA's constitutionality. This is a complex issue, which Jim and I dissect in *Repatriation and Erasing the Past* in a manner that – to my knowledge – no one else has done. The real problematic issue here is that Roberto is alleging that I am "incompetent" – this is language used to try to fire professors, even tenured ones! This was a real red flag.

Roberto noted later in his talk, in relation to post-tenure reviews, "If I was on the committee, I might make the argument that this is academic incompetence because I think the arguments are so scientifically shaky." There was that accusation of *incompetency* again. Yet, my arguments against repatriation are mainly legal and philosophical!

In addition to attacking my scholarship, Roberto also decided to bring up the issue of the department's email listserv in relation to one of my colleague's suggestion that we should use a database called CiteBlackAuthors.com. My colleague wrote:

> I would like to share an important resource that just went live a few weeks ago. Cite Black Authors, a searchable database of Black scholarly journal articles, books, and expert listings, will launch to the public on November 16, 2020, at CiteBlackAuthors.com. The website is an interdisciplinary effort to enhance and recognize Black academic voices for better representation in scholarship. Sparked by the death of George Floyd and ongoing racial conflicts in the United States, a team of nine people, including researchers, developers, and graduate students, curated citations and designed a searchable website for researchers, educators, and the general public.
>
> We are overwhelmingly grateful for the support of contributors and the team behind the initiative.
>
> Please share the attached release with your friends and groups - and help us to spread the word and the WORK of Black, academic professionals.

In response to this email, I wrote:

> Although the intent of Cite Black Authors may be well-meaning, as a scholar in search of objective knowledge, I encourage researchers to look for the best source material and realize that an author's ethnicity, race, or color of their skin has no actual bearing on the validity of their contribution.

This comment from me started a slew of reactions from the graduate students on the listserv disagreeing with me. None of the comments went beyond what I would call civil disagreement. Although one student did say that my comment "saddened" her. Yet, Roberto painted a different picture of this thread and incident; he claimed that I responded in an "extremely insensitive way." And, he went on to say:

> Now you can imagine the reaction of graduate students reading this kind of thing from a full tenured professor, one of the senior faculty in the department. It was devastating.

It was this accusation of being racist because I didn't think that race matters when citing one's work that caught the media's attention, even as far away as Australia! It is ridiculous to think someone is racist for not taking race into account – being colorblind is now being racist! We're back to this crazy, woke situation where phrases like "I treat everyone equally" are smeared as being right-wing dog whistles. In the new DEI world we not only have to discriminate in favor of various groups of people, but signal our virtue with misty-eyed eulogies of Saint George Floyd, and so forth.

Even though Roberto said in his CCAS talk "I'm not going to call her a racist;" he immediately followed with "I've read her book and her [sic] – the talk that she gave at the conference closely enough to know that she's making some classic scientific racist arguments in her work." Later, he also said about *Repatriation and Erasing the Past:* "it's scientific racism, so it's a sort of racism that's subtle and couched in the language of research."

However, beyond calling me a racist, he also maligns me personally by stating "I would hardly describe her as a warm and fuzzy person" and suggested his tactics prevented me from "making obsessive demands all the time." He also claims that I set traps "trying to prod and provoke people into irate responses."

I am not sure what Roberto would call "warm and fuzzy," but I would say that I had been an outstanding and collegial colleague. When a lecturer got sick and couldn't teach her class anymore, I took over her teaching on overload without asking for extra pay. When one of our colleagues quit in the middle of the semester, I stepped in, didn't ask for extra compensation – and I didn't receive any. I signed every card for farewells, get wells, congratulations, and so forth. And, when office staff had babies, I crocheted baby blankets! I was friendly, reliable, and never spoke badly about any of my colleagues throughout my years at SJSU. Never did I get into an argument or row with colleagues. If this isn't "warm and fuzzy," I don't know what is!

Even after many of my colleagues stopped being civil to me, I retained my civility. I've never spoken bad about colleagues to students, and I consistently took the high road. But, the farcical lies Roberto told didn't end there!

"Obsessive demands?" Up to that point, I had only asked for an academic freedom webinar, nothing more! I've never demanded a particular schedule or raises. I sat on any committee that I was assigned – and without complaint! It just isn't in my nature to make demands – upon leaving SJSU, I even was still working on my 12 year-old laptop.

Roberto laid out his five takeaways, which included to be prepared for the worst, such as in the case where he imagined that I would lock myself in a curational facility and prevent the repatriation of remains. Although he acknowledged that he didn't think it would happen, he did put it in his mind that if this did happen, he'd have a plan! Of course, this wouldn't happen – I have always made it clear that I obey repatriation laws, even while disagreeing with them. I had even assisted the NAGPRA coordinator in assessing human remains of a few boxes in order to repatriate the remains to a tribe.

He also stated that he'd keep resources away from me by requiring everything to be voted on; this is how he'd managed to squash a webinar on academic freedom. Finally, he also said that messaging was important and so, the department voted on two messages – one about racism and one about NAGPRA. I voted against both of these statements.

The "Anti-Racism Statement" states:

The San José State University Anthropology Department stands in opposition to all forms of racism and prejudice. We also reject persistent patterns of anti-Blackness in America and endemic discrimination against Native American, Asian/Asian-American, and Latino/a communities. Such racism has continued manifesting itself in acts of repression, violence, and murder.

Our department is committed to supporting anti-racism and efforts to dismantle structures of inequality in our discipline, in our University, and in American society as a whole.

I made the argument that the first line is sufficient, because otherwise there will always be a group that you leave out! Ironically, while Roberto is so concerned about racism and prejudice, he had no problem erasing my Jewish surname of Weiss and replacing it with a very white surname "Jones" throughout the talk as my pseudonym. This is of importance, because one of the attendees noted that a professor had used the N-word when reading a historic document, but she knew the professor wasn't racist because she was Jewish. Would the audience have been more sympathetic or granted me the benefit of doubt had I been called "Weiss" or another Jewish sounding name? At the time, this might have been the case, though the wave of on-campus antisemitism that followed the Hamas terror atrocities of October 7th, 2023 means that if this happened now, using Weiss (or any Jewish name) might harden attitudes against me.

The attendees lapped up this tale of the hidden racist professor that Roberto spun! An attendee, however, did challenge Roberto's depiction that I was isolated; instead, according to this speaker, I was "reinforcing, like, a 500-year-old militarized system that's committed to genocide."

And, then, the question of the ethics of me being in the classroom arose! One of the attendees asked:

> [I]f this person has shown themselves publicly to hold these belief systems, is it ethical to expose students to them, right? It's an ethical question for me as well. Like if this person holds deeply, like, held white supremacist values, right?, which is what scientific racism is, it's an expression of white supremacy. Does exposing students to that in the classroom cause an ethical barrier? Like what does that mean?

Roberto stated incorrectly that I don't teach my perspective to students. He said:

I think it certainly would but in this case, it's an interesting situation because she's never brought this into the classroom. She's never talked about her writings in the classroom. She's never had any of her writings in this subject area on her syllabi. So it's kind of a strange situation. I have done a lot of that in my own work. You know, I love talking about my all aspects of my research. But she's kind of strange that way. She's not -- she's decided not to do that. And I think she understands that that very possibly could have damaging consequences for her career at San José State if she were to take that path.

This was all nonsense, of course. For over 15 years I'd been open with my students about my pro-science and anti-NAGPRA views. Though I'd always taught both sides of the argument and never once gave someone a lower grade for disagreeing with me – because that's what any honest professor should do.

Walt then responded to Roberto's point with an "uh-huh." Roberto went on to say that he had "gotten zero complaints about students hearing these things in class" and also claimed to "always review the syllabi before to make sure that I understand what's being taught in the classroom so then I can do the mentoring or advising to the faculty if I see a problem." He ends with another career-threatening statement:

If it was in the classroom, I would – I think I would – have a very different approach to this.

It was this statement, in conjunction with the references to incompetence, that made me realize that my job was on the line and that I would need legal aid!

After this June 3rd talk, I looked for legal help to protect my job. After all, Roberto and the dean had agreed that if I taught my perspective, I should be removed from the classroom. Roberto called me incompetent and suggested that he would state so in my five-year post-tenure review! Thus, I submitted the case to Pacific Legal Foundation, who are a national public interest law firm. As they state on their website, they "sue the government when it violates Americans' constitutional rights." And, they "believe in individual liberty." They represented me free of charge and I will be forever grateful for their help.

Glynn Custred, a retired professor of linguistical anthropology from California State University, East Bay, had worked with Pacific Legal Foundation lawyers on California's Proposition 209, which opposed affirmative action in the state. Proposition 209 passed in 1996 with 55% of the vote in favor of the proposition. Glynn had also given *amicus briefs* for both Kennewick Man and Spirit Cave Mummy – two Paleoindians who are now long lost to science following repatriation and reburial, despite there being no meaningful connection to the modern-day tribes to whom they were ultimately given. Glynn explained to the courts that oral tales cannot survive for thousands of years and, thus, should not constitute evidence! And, thus, it was Glynn who suggested that I reach out to Pacific Legal Foundation; this was perhaps one of the best pieces of advice I had ever received. And, throughout the years, Glynn has been a supportive colleague and friend.

Pacific Legal Foundation took up my case, first helping me write emails to ask for assurance that I was not in peril of losing my job. So, I emailed Roberto:

> I wanted to let you know that I listened to your June 3rd presentation, hosted by Walt, to the Council of Colleges of Arts & Sciences. You incorrectly stated that I have previously not taught from my writings on the topic of repatriation of remains; if you review my Bioarchaeology syllabi (ANTH156) you will see that I have assigned my books and covered repatriation (sometimes described as ethics). The last time I taught the course Fall 2020, I even used *Repatriation and Erasing the Past* (see attached syllabus). For the upcoming semester, Fall 2021, I plan to use a portion of *Repatriation and Erasing the Past* and to cover the importance of collection preservation in my Mummies (ANTH159) course. I believe teaching both sides of the repatriation issue, including using my own scholarly writings, serves an important pedagogical function: basically, I give students a balanced perspective and allow them to come to their own conclusions. I would like assurances that neither you nor the

university will take action to prevent me from teaching these issues and assigning texts in the manner that I see fit, or retaliate against me for doing so.

Roberto's response started with "Glad that you got a chance to hear the CCAS talk I gave earlier this month"! I sincerely doubt that this was the case! I suspect that while he was happy to virtue-signal to the CCAS audience, he'd never expected it would get back to me (let alone expect that I'd been in the audience!), and that he was horrified that he'd been busted!

He further added: "I didn't realize that you'd been teaching from your NAGPRA writings...I see now that your Fall 2020 syllabus does explicitly include your readings, and I obviously overlooked that." He ended by referencing the SJSU policy on academic freedom – a concept that's central to academia, but which he'd mysteriously forgotten during his CCAS talk, and during his previous (and future) moves to block any speakers I proposed.

This wasn't good enough! I wanted a reassurance that he wouldn't take actions against me and a retraction of his planned actions. Both of my attorneys, Ethan Blevins and Daniel Ortner, agreed that this wasn't good enough too! And, thus, I emailed Roberto again:

Thank you for your response. I appreciate your reference to academic freedom, but I remain concerned by comments you made during the CCAS meeting which indicate that I may face retaliation if I express my viewpoints on repatriation in the classroom, particularly during the last ten minutes or so. For instance, someone during the event declared that allowing me to teach about repatriation or express my view on the subject in the classroom would be unethical. You agreed that "it certainly would." You also stated that there would be "damaging consequences" for my career at SJSU if I were to express my views or teach from my materials on this subject in class. While you noted somewhat ruefully that I'm tenured and had just had my five-year review, you then stated that if I taught about repatriation in class, you "would have a very different approach to this." You also refer to me as your "racist colleague" and suggest twice that my work rises to the level of academic or professional incompetence.

I hope you can see why these statements cause me some concern, given that I do plan to teach on this subject and assign readings from my book, as I've done before. What "damaging consequences" will I face if I do so? Although I enjoy tenured status, I worry about efforts to withhold resources, block me from teaching certain classes, or otherwise impair my ability to teach my viewpoint on an issue of academic importance.

Roberto's next response was less than friendly. He denied that chairs are in a position to retaliate against faculty or "even take disciplinary action." And, he ended his email with a threat:

PS: I never gave my consent to have the CCAS talk recorded or distributed. You might inform the person who recorded the meeting about our state's privacy laws, particularly California Penal Code 632.

He'd been busted, he knew it, and he was probably squirming – wondering what other false and defamatory remarks he made.

Informing my lawyers of Roberto's response, I also clarified that although Roberto plays the helpless chair – he can't do anything against me – this just isn't true. A chair can retaliate and Roberto did! Chairs make the schedules (including assigning classes and the times for those classes), determine the distribution of resources (and even if there is a department vote, he determines if there will be a vote, which meeting to have the vote on, and then makes the final decision – regardless of the vote), and write evaluations (such as for post-tenure review). And, thus, although the chair doesn't have the final say on aspects of firing and promotions, he would have a great deal of input into it and can strongly influence the dean. Chairs can also refer professors to deans or higher ups for disciplinary actions.

I also reached out to Walt. He didn't want to write emails and preferred phone calls. In the first phone call, Walt started off with an apology and stated that he didn't think that I was a racist. Walt is black; he sat on the committee that chose faculty for the faculty-in-residence program. He may have remembered that coincidentally my student references were black too. I'd never been accused of being a racist by any student in my class, and even Roberto had to admit this. Walt decided that he'd try to get a letter written to assure me that my job was secure that there would be no retaliation against me. I thought that it may have ended there. My two Pacific Legal Foundation lawyers, Ethan Blevins and Daniel Ortner, and I worked on my requests for the letter. So, hopeful, I wrote to Walt that I would like the official letter to address:

1) My freedom to assign whatever books, articles, or other materials in my classes, provided that they are on-topic.

2) My freedom to hold controversial debates, talks, and lectures both inside and outside of class, thus, exposing students to a diverse range of views. As I mentioned in the conversation, I have never penalized students who hold views counter to my opinion and I never will.

3) My freedom to speak publicly in the media about my views on repatriation (such as in op-eds, interviews or articles) without threats or punitive actions even if I present views that run counter to the university, college, or department positions.

4) My right to fair and equitable treatment with regard to scheduling, class assignments, service assignments, access to resources, platforming of materials, departmental support, and any other conditions of my job.

5) My right to have continued access to and use of skeletal collections for research and teaching, subject to any federal or state laws, which I will comply with -- as I always have.

6) A commitment to refrain from false accusations against my character or performance and to respect the University's Guiding Principles of Shared Governance including the principles of collegiality and civility.

7) Finally, I believe that this letter should be shared publicly with those who participated in the June 3rd CCAS event or at the very least that I should be able to share this letter freely without any constraints and requirements of confidentiality.

I ended the letter with: "I look forward to your response and the official university letter, which I hope that I can whole-heartedly accept." If I had received such a letter or even a modified version of it, I would have likely ended the legal action. However, I was soon informed by Walt that the University would not allow him to provide me with an official letter of assurance. And, thus, the case moved forward.

With the threat of taking me out of classes looming, Pacific Legal Foundation's Ethan Blevins and Daniel Ortner, who now works at the Foundation for Individual Rights and Expression (FIRE), wrote to the University administration in August 2021. This was the first time SJSU knew I had legal representation, though they may have suspected this. The gloves were off.

Pacific Legal Foundation's 7-page letter included citations to several Supreme Court cases on free speech and academic freedom, such as this one:

> As the United States Supreme Court has explained: "Scholarship cannot flourish in an atmosphere of suspicion and distrust. Teachers and students must always remain free to inquire, to study and to evaluate, to gain new maturity and understanding; otherwise our civilization will stagnate and die." Sweezy v. State of N.H. by Wyman, 354 U.S. 234, 250 (1957).

And:

> The Supreme Court has long held that freedom of expression "is nowhere more vital than in the community of American schools," Shelton v. Tucker, 364 U.S. 479, 487 (1960), and that the First Amendment "does not tolerate laws that cast a pall of orthodoxy over the classroom." Keyishian v. Bd. of Regents of Univ. of State of N.Y., 385 U.S. 589, 603 (1967).

They also noted that:

> Professor Weiss's speech is unquestionably about a matter of public concern within her profession. Publishing a book and assigning her students to read from her book does little to "impede[] the teacher's proper performance of [her] daily duties

in the classroom" or "interfere[] with the regular operation of the schools generally." To the contrary, the discussion and debate of potentially controversial viewpoints is the essence of the university experience and merits rigorous First Amendment protection.

They ended the letter with:

Professor Weiss's scholarly publications and speech are directly germane to the subject of the classes she teaches. She encourages her students to engage with, debate, and discuss her work and the arguments to the contrary. And there is not even a shred of evidence that Weiss's views are harassing or discriminatory. Accordingly, any attempt to "mandate[] orthodoxy" and silence Professor Weiss would not be justifiable.

The Pacific Legal Foundation will be watching closely to ensure that Professor Weiss's rights are protected. If the University takes any further action against her, then we will not hesitate to take further steps to vindicate her rights.

We'd need to wait further! But, no one could ever have guessed what lay ahead – an op-ed and a photo led to new series of cancel culture attacks, retaliatory actions at the highest level of the University, front page headlines, and global media coverage of my case!

# Chapter 10:

## Back with Old Friends
## and Finding New Enemies

On August 31st, 2021, I got an op-ed published in *The Mercury News*, the Bay Area's main daily newspaper, on the recent changes to California's repatriation laws. The changes to CalNAGPRA, as these laws are called, under the newly-passed AB275 included allowing traditional knowledge as evidence and preventing transparency of the evidence. I wrote:

> NAGPRA's allowance of folklore and oral traditions as evidence is problematic. However, at least NAGPRA does not say that oral tradition and folklore are superior to other evidence. CalNAGPRA defines cultural affiliation in the same way and allows the same type of evidence as NAGPRA. However, CalNAGPRA adds "traditional knowledge" as allowable evidence, defined by AB275 as "knowledge systems embedded and often safeguarded in the traditional culture of California Indian tribes and lineal descendants."

Furthermore, I pointed out that CalNAGPRA states "[i]f there is conflicting evidence, traditional knowledge shall be provided deference." Then, I explained that oral tradition doesn't hold any factual information after less than 1,000 years (it's like a game of telephone, where the original message is slowly, but surely, lost over time, becoming increasingly degraded with each repetition); that tribes create symbolic links between themselves and past peoples even when no such links exist (which has been dubbed "neo-traditions" by Alex von Gernet); and, of course, that traditional knowledge is "awash with tales of creation, mythical creatures and supernatural events."

My argument was – and still is – that CalNAGPRA is destroying research and chooses religion over science; and, perhaps, in a stroke of creativity I concluded that: "With AB275, CalNAGPRA is like NAGPRA on steroids."

I tweeted:

The skeletal collection I curate @SJSU is in danger of being reburied -- as are all California Native American collections! Here's my @mercnews & @eastbaytimes op-ed on this issue, championing science over religion. #NAGPRA #anthrotwitter @SJSUNewsroom

And, things were quiet and calm. I hadn't seen any responses that would lead me to think another wave of cancel culture attacks were coming. Little did I know that a tsunami of a cancel culture attack was just over the horizon.

After a long hiatus brought about by COVID restrictions, I re-entered the SJSU curation facility, which held the skeletal collections that the University curated, to do my duties that included ensuring that human remains were not accidentally placed in faunal (i.e., nonhuman animal remains) boxes and vice versa. I had just reunited some human hand bones to the skeleton that they belonged with. And, during this time in the curation facility, I was truly happy. Happy to be back in the room with all these fascinating remains. Human remains that I had cared for, researched, and helped others gain access to for their own research – these tasks I undertook gladly for 17 years! Thus, upon opening a box and seeing a beautiful skull from a young child, I took it out – I had to, in order to put some bones in the box – and snapped a photo. Thinking of all the wonderful images that drew students to the field of anthropology, and having been actively encouraged by my department to promote the University, the department, and our collections through the use of social media. And, we – the University, the college, the department, and I – had a history of doing so with no previous problems. Furthermore, the consultations with Muwekma Ohlone tribal members never mentioned any prohibitions on photos before this image was posted. It was a complete non-issue. Until it wasn't!

Hence, when I posted the tweet "So happy to be back with some old friends @SJSU #anthrotwitter #archaeotwitter" with the now infamous photo (that graces the front cover of this book) on September 18th, 2021, I had no way of knowing that it would result in a firestorm of criticism that would ignite the field of anthropology, and become an international news story.

 **Elizabeth Weiss** @eweissunburied · Sep 18, 2021       ···
So happy to be back with some old friends @SJSU #anthrotwitter #archaeotwitter

◯ 117          ↻ 77          ♡ 76          ᏂᏗ          ⬆

*Figure 5: Skullgate Tweet*

The media, from *The Mercury News* to UK's *Daily Mail* included worries from Indians, such as Val Lopez, the chairman of one of the Bay Area tribes, that human remains need to be reburied "for their spirits to return to 'the other side.'" In each of the interviews, I stuck with secular arguments – supporting science and the ability of images to ignite wonder. For instance, to the *Daily Mail* journalist, I said:

A skull is just a natural part of the skeleton. It holds no magic power. I have angered no spirits. No gods, devils, angels, or demons are upset -- because, there are no such things.

And, again, there was no initial reaction to the tweet, but around a week later, all hell broke loose. On September 27th, I noticed that the first tweet about my *Mercury News* op-ed had garnered hundreds of negative comments. It topped out at around 1,200 comments. My skull photo tweet got around 300 comments. For both tweets, the comments, which were mostly negative, but lacking in any substantive criticism, were piling up. (Many of the comments are now deleted and, thus, the numbers now are lower than previously.)

Why the lag in outrage? I think that perhaps one or two social media users with a high number of followers stoked this twitterstorm. And, as I mentioned, nearly all the comments were exceedingly nasty. For instance, "this is fucking ghoulish," "Racist POS," "grave robbing freak," and "You're a fuckin terrible anthropologist and a perfect example of the field's colonial legacy. Go to hell and take your racist grave robbing bullshit with you."

There was a smattering of supportive tweets too, like "...she loves doing her work. If my remains are dug up in a distant future, I'd love to have a friend like this, who is interested in humans living in a long forgotten past." This was one of the very few comments that addressed the actual issue, and it was from someone who clearly had a genuine understanding of – and love for – anthropology.

My chair Roberto Gonzalez and I also received emails from some of my haters, including one with the subject line: "Why hasn't this racist waste of space been fired?" She went on to call me a "narcissistic cunt." It's always a joy to see an erudite critic engage the issue in a calm and civil manner!

A few days before my tweets went viral, SJSU's provost Vincent del Casino wrote a letter supporting academic freedom, where he wrote:

> I am not naïve. I know the playing field is not an even one. I understand the histories that have created this uneven field. At the same time, I cannot demand nor can I make demands on my colleagues who choose to write certain opinions or publish certain papers that I, or others, might find politically, ethically, or morally problematic. Regardless of job title or level, we must respect everyone's right to free speech, and it is incumbent on our leaders

to give colleagues' work — whether they personally align with it or not — the space to be shared and viewed by others.

And, he ended the letter with:

If we don't protect these rights, universities will lose one of their core functions, which is to develop theories, ideas, and practices that help advance the well-being of others and take up the very real and, sometimes, scary challenges that lie ahead.

I am nearly certain that he wrote this in response to my op-ed. Later that the same day the College of Social Science Twitter account posted the link to my op-ed, since I had urged them to treat my achievements in the same manner as other professors' achievements – and getting an op-ed in a mainstream daily newspaper is considered a considerable achievement in academia.

Vincent's email was about as supportive of free speech as one could hope for coming from a university administrator. Perhaps it would be smooth sailing from here on? Not so fast – Vincent would do a U-turn on his position with regard to my second tweet just a few days later!

On September 27th, 2021, I received an email from Twitter that a complaint had been filed:

Twitter is required by German law to provide notice to users who are reported by people from Germany via the Network Enforcement Act reporting flow.

We have received a complaint regarding your account, @eweissunburied, for the following content:

Tweet ID: 1432792224270483461

Tweet Text: The skeletal collection I curate @SJSU is in danger of being reburied -- as are all California Native American collections! Here's my @mercnews & @eastbaytimes op-ed on this issue, championing science over religion. #NAGPRA #anthrotwitter @SJSUNewsroom [url]

We have investigated the reported content and have found that it is not subject to removal under the Twitter Rules (https://support.twitter.com/articles/18311) or German law.

Accordingly, we have not taken any action as a result of this specific report.

This complaint arose from my op-ed tweet, not the skull photo! Although a few years later, my Twitter account was temporarily frozen due to a skull photo in my profile – another attempt at censorship that I fought against and won.

The investigation concluded that my tweet was not hate speech – a category of speech that we don't legally have in the US, although if you go to Washington DC's Museum of American History it ironically states that "hate speech" will not be tolerated! Yet, for some individuals, this message and the ensuing investigation may be enough to scare them into silence. And, I'd love to know what's being done with these complaints. How can we forget that after the fall of the Berlin Wall, millions of files existed on ordinary citizens of East Germany? Everyone was being watched, investigated, and – therefore – controlled!

It still baffles me as to what or who actually set off the twitterstorm. Obviously these two posts were being shared, but although it was the op-ed tweet that received the majority of comments, it would be the photo tweet that caused the greatest havoc!

On September 29th, 2021, Vincent del Casino posted a long letter to the University community condemning my photo; in it he wrote:

> This image has evoked shock and disgust from our Native and Indigenous community on campus and from many people within and outside of SJSU.

He further stated that:

> While there are scientific issues at stake, there are also many things in the image itself that do not align with the values of SJSU or of academic inquiry. For example, in what context is it ever ethically appropriate for an academic to handle remains while smiling with ungloved hands while calling these remains "friends?" I doubt many colleagues in the fields of Forensic Science or Physical Anthropology would find this palatable. Moreover, it is very important to ask: Does the research "value"

implied in the image really outweigh the risk of harm and trauma to Native American and Indigenous peoples such an image evokes? Based on my reading of the ethical guidelines of the social science disciplines that govern such practices and laws such as AB 275 – which requires SJSU to consult affiliated California Indian tribes on protocols including the need to "minimize handling" of such remains – the answer is no.

He also added that:

I can say that SJSU does not condone or endorse the practice of posing with the human remains of others – be that Native American or any other human remains.

Vincent's previously-expressed commitment to free speech and academic freedom had suddenly evaporated.

The night before – actually at 2 AM that same day – Kimberly Robertson, a professor at California State University, Long Beach, wrote to the Native American Heritage Commission noting that she was "absolutely horrified and appalled" by the image and that it "gleefully and mockingly perpetuates and enacts ongoing violence" against Native Americans. Further, she stated that the tweet "blatantly causes continuing physical, emotional, and spiritual trauma to Native Nations and their citizens." She ended her letter by calling for me to be removed from my post and wrote that I shouldn't be allowed access to human remains.

Perhaps this email also spurred Vincent's response.

Thus, I felt it necessary once again to correct misinformed university administrators. Vincent hadn't reached out to me to discuss this issue; had he done so, I'd have explained the recent history of the University's use of imagery – including skeletal remains – to ignite interest in various fields. I'd have shown him that in the very halls of SJSU, just two floors down from his office, such images were used in abundance. I'd have explained to him that none of the tribes who had been consulted ever prohibited photography before – even as late as September 15th, no issues regarding photography came up in consultations with tribes. Charlotte Sunseri, the NAGPRA coordinator, kept notes, which revealed that photos only became 'taboo' starting September 29th, 2021 – a few days after my tweets went viral! And, a full 11 days after I posted the image. Perhaps, I should have been flattered that my views were – apparently – causing Native American spiritual beliefs to suddenly and mysteriously change! I guess this makes me an influencer!

Upon reading Vincent's letter, I reached out to him and suggested that we meet, respond together and work things out. He initially agreed to meet, but one day prior to the meeting his executive assistant rescinded his acceptance, and we never did get to engage in that conversation – which I think would have been fruitful.

So I wrote a response correcting the fundamental errors and misunderstandings about anthropological best practices contained in Vincent's September 29th email, and I asked Vincent to send it out to all those who received his letter. And, in fairness to Vincent, he did send out the letter on September 30th, 2021. I addressed the false belief that gloves should be worn when handling remains:

> Handling remains with gloves is only necessary if these remains have always been treated with gloved hands and other sterile conditions. By the time I arrived at SJSU, in 2004, the collection had already been handled for many years, by many people without gloves. Putting gloves on now would just be theater. When those interested in DNA studies have reached out to me, I made it clear that these remains have been handled for literally decades before my arrival without gloves and, thus, the DNA would need to be gotten through unbroken teeth.

I explained that the photo did not entail extra handling since it was done during my curational duties:

> The photo was taken during my curational duties. Throughout the years, I have boxed, reboxed, and taken care of these remains. In this case, I hadn't been in the curation facility since COVID-19 ended my ability to work with students on the collection, so yes, I was genuinely happy to be back with the collection.

I explained that the University (and the anthropological community more generally) often uses such images in its promotional materials:

We have a culture of promoting the anthropology department and the collection; this culture has revolved around interesting images. I have even gotten funding for this and helped promote human diversity by introducing people to the concept of skeletal diversity. There have been promotional posters in which I have a similar pose. This has never been against university, college or departmental protocol. Not long ago, as recently as 2019, this was celebrated (such as when I won the Warburton Award for excellence in scholarly activities in relation to my work on the collection). It instills a love of evolutionary anatomy, a love of anthropology, and a promotion of university resources.

And:

This university curates one of the finest (and last) teaching and research collections of skeletal remains in the US. We should be celebrating and utilizing this resource, before it's gone forever. I use the collection to instill a love of bones in my students, and in - hopefully - the next generation of anthropologists and osteologists. The photo you refer to is entirely consistent with this love of bones, and with the spirit of inquiry I foster (for example, in the 2015 Smithsonian traveling exhibition "What Does it Mean to be Human?," which I helped bring to the Bay Area).

Finally, I ended my response with these paragraphs:

We have no way of telling what the individuals whose remains we curate would think about this issue, but when one looks at the Egyptian mummies, Otzi the iceman, or the bog bodies of northern Europe, public display celebrates these individuals, telling their stories in a respectful way that gives them a voice they never had in life. The same is true of our collection, and we should be celebrating the lives of these first occupants of Silicon Valley - not allowing their voices to be silenced by a vociferous campaign orchestrated by woke activists whose strategy is to try to shut down debate, and promote superstition over science.

Now, to the heart of the issue. I have been the target of a constant cancellation attack for the last 10 months. It started with attacking and trying to get my book banned (an effort that half of my colleagues encouraged), then it moved to deplatforming my Society for American Archaeology talk. Recently, it involved over 1,200 comments on Twitter regarding my op-ed in *The Mercury News*. I was reported to Twitter and investigated in Germany due to the tweet regarding my op-ed. Finally, it's an attack on a genuine photo that celebrates our collection, my admiration for the collection, and my joy at being able to do my job. After your strong statement regarding academic freedom, I am disappointed that you were not courageous enough – as those reporting on me – to talk to me first, to have a rational discussion about these occurrences.

Perhaps he and others would see the absurdity of claims that this photo caused harm and was evidence of violence!

All these claims of me being disrespectful are, of course, utter nonsense too. My op-ed and photo revealed my respect for what skeletal remains can teach us and the knowledge they hold which can only be revealed through studying them. Research on bones and curation of collections are not funerals; they are times to celebrate our ability to tell the story of the past – a past when people didn't leave a written record.

The term "friends" or even "old friends" can only be thought of as disrespectful by those willingly misconstruing the term. We have many examples of using such terms, such as "Friends of the Library," "Friends of the Forest," and "Friends of America's Past;" and, in each of these cases that I can think of, disrespect never arises. Quite the opposite.

On October 5th, 2021, *The Mercury News* gave my tweet front page attention. The article was a classic hit piece, which brought up my marriage to Phil Rushton. The journalist wrote that "Weiss takes issue with each jab, calling her former marriage "irrelevant" and defending her right to her opinions." My marriage to Phil was irrelevant in this case. And, perhaps, most outrageous is that the journalist equated the attempt to ban my book, *Repatriation and Erasing the Past*, with the scandal of the athletic trainer, Scott Shaw, who sexually abused athletes. This wouldn't be the last time that this scandal was minimized, while my perspective on the importance of studying skeletal remains was scandalized!

One day later, a presidential directive with new protocols to gain access to collections was implemented.

Before I address those protocols, I'll mention that I received many supportive emails from people around the world. Colleagues at SJSU reached out to me; I had lunch with fellow professors that I had never met before. And, I was introduced to a whole new audience who wanted to learn about the past. This simple photo – one of pure joy – may have caused much trouble, but also achieved much in the form of bringing anthropology to the forefront of people's minds and alerting them to the real dangers that 'progressive' policies have on free speech, academic freedom, and our ability to conduct research.

Also, it's interesting that this photo still reverberates both negatively and positively. In her opening remarks, the new president of SJSU, Cynthia Teniente-Matson, held a meeting in April 2023 related to campus climate, which is exceedingly poor due to concerns of retaliation, and the strategic recalibration of the University's mission statement. During this meeting, she showed an antiquated image of a white women with bones. Then, she said:

> You might be wondering why this is important. Well, let me share with you a quick side note. [...] Like many places, we have challenges. Our campus has a history of narratives that might be based in historical inequities and discrimination, and from time to time these actions lead to hurtful and dismissive behaviors and the sense that some people feel unseen and unheard.

In other words, the poor campus climate related to my photo and tweet rather than the sex scandal, which was also mentioned in *The Mercury News*. In short, the poor campus climate, as assessed by the Western Association of Schools and Colleges accreditation report, revolved mainly around faculty fears concerning retaliatory action. These problems were more likely associated with the criminal actions of former director of sports medicine Scott Shaw, who sexually abused dozens of female student athletes. Many of these students came forward right away. Then, there were the subsequent retaliatory actions against whistleblower coach Sage Hopkins by the then-director of athletics Marie Tuite. Plus, there was neglectful inaction by former president Mary Papazian. Papazian and Tuite basically allowed Shaw to continue his abuse. Papazian resigned after this scandal, which started before her arrival, spanned more than a decade, and ended with an FBI investigation and Shaw's arrest! But – no! – the campus climate problem was apparently related to my photo! It was all my fault! What a crazy and mixed-up world we live in when a university president can seriously suggest that morale problems on campus relate not to a decades-long sexual abuse scandal, but to a photo of an anthropologist holding a skull – which in my field is as common and iconic an image as a medical doctor with a white coat and a stethoscope!

On the plus side, this photo has also led me to be invited to talk on TV and radio shows, on podcasts, and led to numerous writing opportunities – in each of these interviews I've been able to spread the message about anthropology's importance and the attacks on knowledge from the 'progressive' woke warriors!

Sometimes I wonder whether the same vitriol and actions against me would have taken place had I been pro-repatriation. After all, at the time, photos such as mine could be found on many university and museum social media pages. Individual anthropologists, too, posted such photos regularly. When preparing for my lawsuit against SJSU, my lawyers and I found an abundance of such images. I also had four affidavits from highly qualified and esteemed anthropologists who held academic positions that enabled them to work with collections for decades; they refuted the provost's claims about gloves, photos, and smiling.

Marshall Becker, a retired professor of anthropology at West Chester University who has published about 150 articles and has conducted research on remains from all around the world, and Native American remains from Ohio, Pennsylvania, and New Jersey, wrote:

> [G]love use is still rarely required; this rarity of glove use in the study of human remains can be seen as well with the lack of glove requirements when training students in osteology classes. Professor Elizabeth Weiss's lack of gloves is in no way a breach of standard practice.

Professor Elizabeth Weiss's promotion of the field of anthropology and the availability to study skeletal collections through the use of photos is also not objectionable. Many field schools, training classes, museum exhibits, and university promotions use similar photos...It is surprising that the SJSU would take such a drastic position on this type of photography related to our field of study; such a decision is not based on the norms of the fields of anthropology and archaeology.

Bruce Bourque, who received his graduate training at Harvard University and spent 45 years teaching at Bates College, wrote:

I have reviewed Professor Weiss's September 18, 2021, photograph and tweet. The claim that she handled the remains disrespectfully is baseless. She was photographed holding human remains while smiling which is not disrespectful or contrary to the norms of my profession.

Images such as those of Professor Weiss...have long been utilized by anthropologists to generate excitement about the study of skeletal remains and have been featured prominently in articles covering the developments in the field of anthropology.

And:

I also read provost Del Casino's critique of Professor Weiss's tweet. In that missive he posed the highly accusatory rhetorical question "In what context is it ever ethically appropriate for an academic to handle remains while smiling with ungloved hands while calling these remains 'friends'?...I offer the following response: Professor Weiss's conduct was appropriate at ANY time teaching about, or conducting research upon, ancient human remains. These are not mournful funerary events. Rather they celebrate the value of these ancient remains in allowing us to learn very important things about human history.

Bruce ended with:

Recent attempts by members of the SJSU community to thwart or even to prevent Professor Weiss's continued success as an educator do not reflect concerns about the professional norms of the field of Anthropology and instead reflect either a politically motivated effort to shut down scientific research by anti-scientific activists or mob-following cowardice. I celebrate Professor Weiss's courage and temerity in facing the attacks on her and standing firm.

Della Cook, who managed Native American skeletal collections from 1973 to 2021 at Indiana University, noted that "Workers and visitors were never asked to wear gloves during excavation, curational activities, or research." She also lists all of the places in which she conducted research and was never asked to wear gloves: Cornell University, University of Chicago, Peabody Museum at Harvard, and many others. Finally, in perhaps my favorite lines, she wrote:

> Photographs of researchers measuring or otherwise doing observations on bones, ancient and modern, are routine in our field, and many anthropologists smile in such photographs. There are several such photos of me in circulation, and in most of them I am smiling.

> Surely none of these smiles were meant as disrespect, and it seems bizarre to me that anyone would interpret them as such.

Douglas Owsley, who works at the Smithsonian and was the subject matter of the book *No Bone Unturned: The Adventures of a Top Smithsonian Forensic Scientist and the Legal Battle for America's Oldest Skeletons* by Jeff Benedict, has worked on cases from the Waco Texas catastrophe to early New Englanders who resorted to cannibalism in Jamestown. He was also key in the fight to prevent Kennewick Man from early reburial. Douglas wrote:

> For many years I have worked with many large and prestigious universities and museums to help them with the inventory process of NAGPRA to determine tribal affiliations and relationships. While completing that work, I have never had curators or

collections management staff tell me that I needed to use gloves to handle remains.

He also noted that photography was common and that he even often travels with a science photographer. Then, he noted:

During my experience working with universities and museums, I have not experienced objections to the taking of photographs or x-rays.

He ended his statement with:

Based on my professional experience, there was nothing improper about Professor Weiss's tweet. Professor Weiss held the skull with two hands, which is the proper protocol to ensure safe handling. Professor Weiss was handling ancient skeletal remains that have been frequently handled by others. Her holding the remains without gloves did not damage these remains.

These four eminent anthropologists, with years of research and scholarship, understand the field, the beauty of learning from remains, and the politics behind attempts to stop our ability to learn about the past!

On October 6th, 2021, my chair Roberto Gonzalez informed the department that a new presidential directive on the curation facility access was about to drop. And, if we had any questions, we should let him know. The president's directive laid out that only the NAGPRA coordinator, Charlotte Sunseri, and the tribal liaison, Alisha Ragland, and students chosen by them could enter the curation facility. Furthermore, the directive set out that any access to collections would require written approval from Charlotte and Alisha. And:

Audio, video, or photographic devices are prohibited in the curation spaces, as is taking photo images or videos of human remains, funerary objects, or the boxes in which these materials are held.

I guarantee you that both Charlotte and Alisha (as well as any of their student assistants) did not follow these protocols – nearly every cellphone now has the ability to take photos, videos, and sound recordings. I doubt that anyone left their phone outside of the curation facility! And, yet, at the time, I didn't have a cellphone and, ironically, was likely the only one who would have been following the protocols!

The locks were changed, literally overnight, and cameras were set up to monitor the area outside of the curation facility – as if they were worried that I'd break in!

Upon reading this directive I reached out to Roberto and President Papazian, who never responded to me, to let them both know of the many non-NAGPRA/non-CalNAGPRA items in the facility: a skeletal collection from Carthage, Tunisia dating between the 6$^{th}$ to 7$^{th}$ centuries AD; boxes of data on chimpanzee behavior; faunal remains from around the Ryan Mound that were not funerary items; and x-rays of bones. Both the x-rays and faunal remains would become hotly-contested items. I asked for access to all these materials, especially the Carthage Collection. Instead of immediately remedying this issue and providing access, Charlotte, Alisha, Roberto, and others at SJSU looked for ways to keep me from studying non-Native American materials as well.

One might ask why I didn't push back against my being barred from the Native American collection of human remains that I'd been hired to curate, and which I researched – without objections – for 17 years. The answer goes back to what I said about CalNAGPRA being "NAGPRA on steroids." Once the Muwekma Ohlone had decided (even if they'd been put up to it by activists, and even though my actions had never previously been an issue) that I was *persona non grata*, that was it. Under CalNAGPRA, the Native Americans (including tribes that aren't federally recognized) can halt all access to and research on Native American human remains collections during the consultation and repatriation processes. They, however, shouldn't have been able to dictate access to non-Native American remains, x-rays, non-funerary objects, or faunal remains – these were still worth fighting for!

The University's tactics to keep me from collections may have also been aided by the Native American Heritage Commission, who wrote to President Papazian that due to my photo where I was "grinning enthusiastically" while "handling the skull without gloves," coupled with my failure to consult with tribes (even though the consultations that had taken place up to nearly two weeks after the tweet placed no restrictions on photos), I should be "disciplined" and "receive cultural sensitivity training regarding California Indian culture and history." Keep in mind that the Muwekma Ohlone, who had been working with SJSU anthropologists for years, and who were at the time considered the most likely descendants of the Ryan Mound people, never mentioned anything about photos; they had even signed a memorandum of understanding in which they said that they supported all nondestructive research, and raised no issues about gloves or photos in relation to the procedures we had presented to them. The Commission's attempt to force me into re-education, however, did not work. The University's response to the Commission about me was:

> While we acknowledge the Commission's request in this regard, respectfully, due to confidentiality obligations including under the Collective Bargaining Agreement with our faculty union, we are unable to discuss personnel matters related to an individual faculty member or to make any comment regarding disciplinary action.

As a result of the University president's directive, the president, Roberto, my dean Walt Jacobs, and the provost all received a letter from my lawyers, on October 26th, 2021, that highlighted the overreach of the president's actions. The letter noted that:

> The new policy also overreaches substantially. SJSU houses both Native American remains and materials that are not subject to NAGPRA protections. While the University has removed some non-Native American skeletal remains to another area where Professor Weiss might be able to access them, there are other bones and bone-related materials pertinent to her research that remain inaccessible. These include many x-rays and non-human animal remains relevant to Professor Weiss's work. But the new policy appears to apply to these non-NAGPRA materials as well and puts the NAGPRA coordinator in charge of access to them. And in its haste to punish Professor Weiss it appears that the University put no thought into access to these materials.

They requested a reply within 21 days. Within that time period, the University responded that retaliation had not occurred and denied that I was being kept from non-NAGPRA collections. One day before the University responded (which was also one day before the 21-day deadline imposed by my attorneys), the President wrote to Roberto and Charlotte:

> If there are any collections remaining…that are not related to our campus effort to comply with NAGPRA, CalNAGPRA, and AB275, please begin to move those to a new, secure location.

My lawyers' letter stymied their obvious intentions to keep me from *all* research collections. And, actions related to trying to remove me from my position as collections coordinator were also halted. Roberto and other department members actively tried to take away my role as collections coordinator; this role was listed in my hiring contract. And, yet, Roberto wanted to vote on whether it should be rotating and what the role should entail. I pushed back against these changes and reminded him of what my hiring contract stated. This role was not under the purview of departmental votes, and the move to vote on this issue was tabled. The issue was eventually dropped altogether – again, I believe this was a direct result of my lawyers' letter.

During the meeting in which this occurred, tensions rose as I fought to protect my job. One of the department members, a cultural anthropologist, got exceedingly upset when I made the argument that the role of collections coordinator was in my hiring contract and, thus, not up for a vote. He had compared this to another position in the department that we had voted on, that was in *his* contract, but was a general departmental service. I had actually supported his perspective that when something is in your contract, then it shouldn't be voted on, unless it states that the position is up for votes by the department explicitly. Nevertheless, he got so flustered with this comparison, that he blurted out "With respect, respect when other people are participating in this conversation. Thank you very much!" and then went on to claim that I "seem to be enjoying this." Finally, he stormed out of the room; yet, we were on Zoom (COVID nervousness – or maybe just laziness – meant that in-person meetings weren't happening; even in 2024 they still haven't been reinstated!) and so he was storming out of his own living room, only to have to slink back a few moments later, tail between his legs.

But, it was not a smooth road to access to any of the materials. Initially, Roberto had stated that whether I got access to the Carthage Collection was "their decision" – where "their" meant Charlotte and Alisha! Furthermore, Charlotte wrote that if we wanted non-NAGPRA materials, we needed to ask her and Alisha directly. Why would the NAGPRA coordinator and the tribal liaison have any right to determine access to materials from Africa?

A week later, Roberto wrote to tell me that he'd communicated with Charlotte and Alisha about the Carthage Collection and "since it's a non-Native American collection, they've suggested that they're probably not authorized to assess your request." And, he then mentioned that he'd reach out to the Office of Research for guidance – the Office of Research deals with living human subjects, hazardous materials, and animals, not bones! At least, not prior to the cancel culture attacks on my work!

But even this wasn't the true story. Alisha Ragland, the tribal liaison, was adamant that I shouldn't get access to *any* materials. In an email she wrote to Roberto and Charlotte, Alisha stated:

I am not comfortable being responsible for allowing her permission to study another colonized population without direct support from descendant communities. This would be difficult as she seems fundamentally opposed to working collaboratively with descendant communities. Furthermore, her history of involvement in the modern eugenics movement, recent scientifically racist publications, as well as her blatant disregard for the respect of the dead disqualifies her in my professional opinion from working independently with human remains. Allowing her access to study ancestors from another colonized population once again puts the reputation of the Anthropology Department and the University – and as Kathy said, potentially the entire CSU system – in yet another vulnerable situation whereby her academic freedom and protected status as a tenured professor are used to advance narratives of racism.

Upon receiving this ridiculous, libelous, and full-on woke email, Roberto changed his perspective and perhaps realized that having the tribal liaison and NAGPRA coordinator make these decisions could be problematic, especially in view of a pending lawsuit. So, he wrote to Alisha and Charlotte:

> After thinking about this further, it's clear to me that Elizabeth Weiss's request should not be reviewed by you (since it's a request for non-NAGPRA related materials) – I think it's probably more appropriate for someone at the University's Office of Research (probably Jessica Trask, Director of Research Compliance) to grant permission. There may be international (for example, UN or UNESCO) guidelines on cultural patrimony, or Jessica may want to reach out to the Tunisian Consulate in San Francisco about this. (Incidentally, she has a PhD in anthropology!)
>
> Let me reach out to Jessica about this request – in the meantime, there's no need for you to reply to Elizabeth right now.

In other words, Roberto realized that having the tribal liaison and NAGPRA coordinator make decisions on non-Native American materials might be a bridge too far – and legally untenable – but he was nonetheless looking for another avenue to exclude me from research material access. Once he contacted the Office of Research, they directed him to Academic Affairs. Although it likely didn't have the intended consequences he had hoped for, the University would later place human remains in the category of "research compliant" work, but in an infinite loop, the Office of Research would tell me to work with my chair and vice versa. I will return to this issue of compliance in the next chapter. Thus, in the end, Roberto granted me access to the Carthage Collection; but not without a fight from me, and extensive virtue-signaling from him and others.

All throughout this time, Roberto kept trying to assure me that he was in favor of getting me access to the Carthage Collection and that he supported my requests to conduct research on the Carthage Collection – but I knew better. Roberto figured that he could halt my access until new protocols about human remains were put into place. And, thus, we held a meeting on November 5th, 2021 about these new protocols. The intention was to tie my hands and prevent me from photographing any human remains.

The old protocols that I wrote were quite clear and were about keeping the collection intact, well-cared for, and available to researchers quickly. There were no limitations on photography at all. Yet, Roberto dug out the one time that I had a no photo rule, which I explained was because I had 17 student volunteers that semester and I had wanted to ensure they were paying attention to data collection, not being distracted by taking pictures. After our data collection was completed, we even spent a few days taking photos, which were used in posters for the Southwestern Anthropological Association conference – two of these students won student research prizes, in large part due to the images they captured with their mobile phone cameras on those days after data collection.

The new protocol that Roberto was pushing included:

No photography of skeletal remains is allowed. No videos or other recordings of skeletal remains is [sic] allowed. No social media posting of skeletal remains is allowed.

And, it ended with:

These protocols are intended to ensure that human skeletal materials are handled with dignity and respect at all times, and to preserve the quality of the collections. Failure to handle the specimens professionally may lead to a prohibition on access to the collections. It may also result in disciplinary actions.

On that Friday, November 5th, 2021, I fought against any such prohibition on photography. I noted that photos have been used in research, teaching, information dissemination, and promotion of the field of anthropology. And, I stated that we must be wary of moving goalposts – first we cannot take photos of Native American remains; then we cannot take photos of non-Native American remains; next, we'll be prohibited from taking photos of casts!

Some of my colleagues, like Charlotte Sunseri, lamented that the images of bones may offend Native Americans, even if the bones are not from Native American collections – this is the exact type of moving goalposts that I was referring to!

Others, such as one of the cultural anthropologists, talked of the use of permission slips or consent forms, adding that she uses those in her research. Of course, she works with living people – in such a case I too would get permission from the individuals! This was like comparing apples to oranges. Nevertheless, she continued, after claiming ignorance about the collection – even though she knew it was from Carthage, which fell to the Muslim invaders and becomes Tunis in the 8th century AD. She lamented:

> Did they before they died voluntarily sign their remains over for the use of science to be put in collections? And, did they say they were okay with photographs being used of their remains? If the answer to those two questions are no, then we're again in ethical territory, which is – like – a much broader ethical discussion around it that we would have to make the decision collectively as a department…if those two questions are yes, they voluntarily donated their remains to science and they agreed to have photos taken, then it's an easy answer, but if those questions are no, then it's an ethical discussion that we need to have.

Of course, these people died hundreds of years before the camera was invented! One of my most supportive colleagues in the department then quipped: "Would that apply to Neanderthals?"

Unfortunately, SJSU was leading the pack of censorship woke warriors, and now this issue of photography seems to be creeping into all areas of anthropology. For example, now the Smithsonian won't display human remains or photos of human remains without consent if those remains are 300 years old or younger – this basically encompasses all remains from the beginning of photography. While the first consent forms probably came two hundred years later!

Our departmental debate about photography went round and round. No consensus was to be reached, but it was clear that this policy would mainly affect me – a point that I made to Roberto. Thus, I asked if he would meet with me to help draft the statement before sending it out for a vote. He angrily said: "I don't think it only affects you"! I once again needed to correct a university administrator and repeated that:

> I did not say it only affects me. I said it mainly affects me. It does mainly affect me. I'm the one who looks at skeletal remains. I'm the one who's been taking photographs for my work, both academic, public, and teaching. So, I do think it mainly affects me.

Furthermore, Roberto had made it clear that this protocol would not apply in the field – the other anthropologist who may have taken such photos would have likely been doing so only in the field!

Roberto claimed that he wanted to be supportive and that he had no plans to write up something that would have negative repercussions! Yet, I'd heard him talk about "support" before – and, then, go behind my back trying to finagle ways to hinder my work! And, I couldn't forget his promise to the CCAS to take me out of the classroom if I assigned my book, or his musings that he'd planned to give me a poor review, calling me incompetent, in my next evaluation.

In the end, Roberto agreed to meet with me, but then "forgot" about the meeting and sent out two options – one that I had provided in case he wouldn't meet with me – for vote in an email where he wrote:

> Here is a revised protocol regarding photography of non-NAGPRA collections in the care of our department – it incorporates a mechanism (Department Chair approval after consultation with the Standing Committee and Dean) by which a researcher might obtain permission to photograph skeletal remains for certain purposes, such as illustrations in academic journal articles:
>
> *(A) Photographing skeletal remains from the collections is not allowed without written approval from the Department Chair, in consultation with the Standing Committee and the Dean. Video recordings of skeletal remains from the collections are not allowed, nor are social media posts.*

Late last week after our Friday meeting, Elizabeth emailed a proposed alternative protocol, which would not require Department Chair or Standing Committee approval:

*(B) Photography and videography should not be undertaken for personal use, and should only be used for purposes of teaching, scientific research and publication, public outreach, and the promotion of anthropology.*

My proposal was a clear, practical, commonsense policy. His was the epitome of a bureaucratic mess.

Thus, in his proposed protocol, I would need the chair's approval, which would be in consultation with the standing committee (which is composed of all the tenure-track and tenured professors in the department) and the dean! No one else's research would be subject to approval from the dean, chair, and standing committee! I would not stand for that, and so I let him know:

I find the proposed policy requiring me to always get written permission from the Chair and Dean (in consultation with the Standing Committee) to take pictures to be very vague and troubling. Do I have to seek permission for each photo, each session, each bone? Also, what are the guidelines that prevent permission from being granted? And, finally, is there any sort of timeline associated with this permission? I am worried that without clear guidelines and standards my research will be censored or significantly delayed.

He acquiesced, perhaps knowing that this was an unwinnable battle, that I would not capitulate, and that my lawsuit against SJSU was looming. So, even now, there is no prohibition on photos of non-Native American human remains at SJSU!

This doesn't mean that I got quick access to the Carthage Collection; it would stay in a place where students sat and therefore could not be accessed Mondays through Thursdays, all day. I was physically kept from the remains for months more!

While waiting for access to the Carthage Collection and other materials, like x-rays and non-human animal bones, the department chair coupled with Charlotte and Alisha, kept up their antics, including putting out the "Statement on Handling Human Remains" on the anthropology webpage that was voted on by the department. This included an apology from the department for the photo posted on Twitter, for which they were "sorry for the pain it caused." It went on to state that they "strongly disapprove of the post and do not condone such practices." Finally, they continued to falsely claim that I was being disrespectful. I responded:

> Photography in anthropology has been a valuable tool to ignite curiosity, display human variation respectfully, and teach about the past fruitfully. As the Asian proverb states: Better to see something once than to hear about it a thousand times.
>
> The statement includes the sentence: "All human remains should be treated with dignity and respect." Skeletal remains – both human and nonhuman – should be treated with respect. Respect's definition, from Merriam-Webster dictionary, is "a feeling of admiring someone or something that is good, valuable, important, etc." There is no evidence that I have done otherwise; I continuously show respect and dignity for skeletal remains because I know how much can be learned from them.
>
> Holding a skull and taking a photo is not about a lack of respect, but rather a demonstration that I hold these remains in high value, that I admire what we can learn from them, and that I know the serious science that can be deduced from their study.
>
> I have no reason to apologize. I have done nothing wrong. I will continue to fight for science over sensitivity, religion, and superstition. And, I am happy to work with anyone who values truth and objectivity. And, thus, regarding this Statement on Handling Human Remains I choose to quote Ruth Bader Ginsburg, "I dissent"!

And, at the University level, on November 17th, 2021, new protocols for the Native American collections were sent out. They read like a list of everything I hate and included a "menstrual taboo." Other regulations included "no spitting, swearing, inebriation or otherwise inappropriate decorum or dress will be permitted" – who was this aimed at: drunken Indians?

They added that "gloves and face masks will be worn at all times. Should gloves rip or tear they are to be replaced immediately?" Masks? Really? Are they afraid that their long dead 'ancestors' would get COVID?

And, of course, "menstruating personnel will not be permitted to handle ancestors" – they couldn't even bring themselves to say "women," because among the social justice warriors, not only women menstruate!

The ridiculous, sexist, and highly offensive menstrual taboo was removed after my lawyers notified the University that I'd be filing a Title IX complaint, which relates to the 1972 law that "protects people from discrimination based on sex in education programs or activities that receive federal financial assistance." This resulted in the taboo being lifted, and Charlotte having to write a declaration about this change, including attesting that the protocols had never been applied to any individual. It was a small victory, but one that I still celebrate!

Yet, I still had no access to x-rays, faunal remains, and even the Carthage Collection was in an inaccessible location.

Even with the protocols put into place and the new restrictions on access, the Natives were still restless. On November 30th, 2021, in a letter written by the California State University East Bay Indigenous Acknowledgement Collective, the authors wrote that my actions were "prime examples of colonial violence," with comparisons to state-funded bounties for Native American scalps, and called for keeping me away from remains and any related materials!

The holidays arrived, and with them some unpleasant news for the University. The highest level of administration had been found guilty of neglecting their duties to protect female athletes from the sexually predatory behavior of Scott Shaw. There was also a discovery that President Papazian had been warned of this issue before taking office, but yet had done only a cursory investigation of these claims. The athletics director had also been found to have retaliated against the whistleblower Sage Hopkins. And, in the middle of all this fallout, President Papazian resigned!

The new semester started with a new interim president Steve Perez. Shortly after taking office, he re-sent out the "presidential protocol for curational spaces." It would be just days later when Pacific Legal Foundation would file the suit. They highlighted the many ways SJSU retaliated against me, including keeping funds away from me for webinars, preventing me from accessing the Carthage Collection, keeping the x-rays and nonhuman remains away from me, and more. It's here also that I was able to obtain the affidavits that I mentioned earlier – there is no way that I can fully express my gratitude to Marshall Becker, Della Cook, Bruce Bourque, and Douglas Owsley! In a hostile climate where it's no longer the norm, they took a stand for truth and for science.

Once again, with the filing of my lawsuit, I was front page news! But, also, because of the discovery process, the lawsuit enabled me to read emails between Charlotte, Alisha and Roberto, which clearly showed their intentions to keep me from all skeletal remains. The materials also revealed, once and for all, that no tribe had ever mentioned photography issues prior to September 27th, 2021! And, Charlotte revealed her true thoughts when she declared:

> I am very concerned that, were SJSU required to give Professor Weiss access to our NAGPRA and CalNAGPRA collections and allow her to do research on and photograph the human remains and cultural items, it would have serious harmful consequences for SJSU and the culturally affiliated Tribes. Those could include delays in completion of the repatriation of human remains and cultural items; damage, both physical and spiritual, to the human remains and cultural items; and undermining of our relationships of trust and collaboration with the Tribes."

It was also Charlotte who claimed that x-rays were "spiritually damaging" to the Muwekma Ohlone and, thus, would be burned upon repatriation:

> I know from communications with members of the Tribes that many consider taking and use of X-rays, like the taking and use of conventional photographs, to be disrespectful of and potentially damaging, in a spiritual sense, to their ancestors' remains. Tribes

have specifically requested that X-rays of the remains be repatriated to them along with the remains themselves. Tribes culturally affiliated with the CA-Ala-329 site, which is the only site which we have X-rays, have stated that they plan to ceremonially burn the X-rays and bury the ashes with the remains.

Upon hearing of this, Douglas Owsley noted in his affidavit that: "A request to destroy photographs or x-rays is highly unusual."

It's not clear whether this mumbo-jumbo about x-rays being spiritually dangerous genuinely came from the tribe, from Charlotte, or was born out of the back-and-forth between them; but, it was completely new, and had clearly been fabricated as a tactic to keep me from doing the scientific research that I'd been hired to do.

First, they came for the remains; then they came for the x-rays; what's next – book burning? And, if you think that's far-fetched, it isn't; as you'll find out later in relation to data.

It looked as if I wouldn't be getting the x-rays that I'd been requesting for months! The Muewkma Ohlone knew full-well that x-rays should not be considered sacred under the law, and don't belong to any of the categories of repatriation materials outlined in NAGPRA and CalNAGPRA. CalNAGPRA, like NAGPRA, defines sacred as "specific ceremonial objects which are needed by traditional Native American religious leaders for the practice of traditional Native American religions by their present day adherents."

On August, 25th, 2021, before I had requested the x-rays, the Muewkma Ohlone wrote that they would start repatriation as soon as possible and in that letter, they quote the law, and note that the materials that they'll be repatriating are human remains, associated funerary objects, unassociated funerary objects, sacred objects, and objects of cultural patrimony. This is what they're entitled to – not faunal remains that were refuse! Not x-rays!

The tribe is just making things up – in cahoots with SJSU – to retaliate against my anti-repatriation position. In one of my media articles, I quipped if the Muewkma Ohlone found that I had requested a pencil, they'd try to claim it was sacred. It's not about the photo; it's not about beliefs; it's about revenge!

As the wheels of justice slowly turned, I applied for one of the University's Research, Scholarship, and Creative Activity Grants, which would provide me with a lighter teaching load, to use for research purposes. My application, which was submitted in late February, included three research projects: one on iron-deficiency and growth; one on bone biology; and, one on the Carthage Collection. The first two required data that were previously collected on Native American remains and x-rays that were previously taken of these remains. Although I was explicit in my plans, my grant was approved. This, however, would turn out to be a hollow victory and perhaps even a trap! Worse was to come, and the dreaded DEI monster was about to rear its ugly head!

# Chapter 11:

# Pretendians: Mexicans by Any Other Name

On April 28th, 2022, we went in front of Judge Beth Labson. The wheels of justice may turn slowly, but my legal action against my University for their retaliatory actions had finally reached court. Due to the continuation of COVID practices, this was all still via Zoom! The pandemic may have died down, but the hysteria hadn't. I knew things weren't going to go well when the judge mentioned the standard, tired, old rhetorical questions – what if this was her grandmother's skull that I was holding? How would she feel? In actuality, this was no one's grandmother ever, as the skull that I had held belonged to a child. The individual died before puberty and, thus, could never have given birth. Repeatedly, she diminished my position, falsely claiming that substantive research that was of national interest could not come from SJSU; perhaps Berkeley or Stanford, but not SJSU. She was quite snobbish when it came to university positions and professors. In fact, SJSU has partnered with NASA; the anthropology department had worked with Jane Goodall on the ChimpanZoo project; and the University has played a key role in understanding wildfires throughout the US. I've had researchers from all over the world come to study the Ryan Mound Collection, including from prestigious universities such as Johns Hopkins University. I've collaborated with professors from the University of Witwatersrand in South Africa on research of forensic importance. She clearly didn't understand the importance of collaboration, collections, and sometimes the impact of a single individual. Ironically, sometimes the most liberal people are also the most elitist – this may or may not have been the case with the judge. Furthermore, she was downright chummy with the University's lawyer – not showing the neutrality that I expected from a judge. I get that people will know one another and, thus, friendly chitchat may commence, but I think that in these cases friendliness needs to be displayed to both sides, or a cool civility needs to be maintained for both sides.

At the end of this hearing, the judge sided with the University in their quest to get the case dismissed. She granted them a Motion-to-Dismiss based on Rule 19 – "the Necessary Party" rule. The judge wrote:

> The Court finds that the Muwekma Ohlone Tribe is a required party under Rule 19 to adjudication of Professor Weiss's claims about the Directive. Because the Tribe has sovereign immunity from suit and thus cannot be joined, Professor Weiss's claims regarding the Directive must be dismissed with prejudice.

In short, she stated that the tribe was an indispensable party to the case, but that the tribes – in California, even non-federally recognized tribes – were considered sovereign and, thus, can't be sued. Native American tribes, unbeknownst to many Americans, cannot be sued; they have immunity from suit – a privilege granted to no other Americans!

The same fate befell Tim White, from University California at Berkeley, and his colleagues who sued to gain access for research purposes to the La Jolla Paleoindian remains that I mentioned in Chapter 4. The La Jolla Remains were skeletons of two individuals dating to around 9,000-year-old that were found on the University of California, San Diego campus. They were repatriated and reburied before research could be conducted. Three anthropologists, led by Tim White of UC Berkeley, fought for access to the remains, but the judge decided to dismiss their case since the San Diego area tribe, the Kumeyaay Nation, was said to be essential and, yet, couldn't be sued, due to their sovereignty. This trapped Tim White and his colleagues in a Catch-22, just like I was trapped.

Those who wish to fight against repatriation laws will likely be fighting an uphill battle, even if it's on the basis of legitimate concerns over constitutional breaches, as in Jim Springer's and my concern regarding the fact that NAGPRA violates the First Amendment and, thus, causes erosion of the separation of church and state. The tribes are essential, but cannot be sued; so, to move forward, you need to add them to your list of defendants; but they cannot be added!

This Catch-22 applies to all issues that involve Native American tribes. Thus, with the Biden administration's new mandate to use "indigenous knowledge" (which is basically their animistic religious beliefs), scientists being funded by the many government agencies affected who want to move forward with objective reasoning, but are held back by Native American myths, cannot gain traction by suing the tribe – even if the tribe is obviously just being obstreperous.

Ironically, these Native American tribal members may be far less Indian than one thinks – more on this later!

Yet, Judge Labson gave us a Hail Mary Pass; she allowed us to amend our complaint within 30 days if we removed the request to study Native American remains. She wrote:

> The Court will, however, give Professor Weiss leave to amend her complaint as to her allegations of retaliation in the form of restricting access to and use of non-Native American remains and retaliation for her protected speech as it may pertain to her teaching and curation responsibilities.

In her explanatory remarks in the hearing, the judge said that she didn't like – in terms of natural justice – to give a plaintiff nowhere to go, essentially because of a technicality. We'd have to refile, stripping out all the Native American issues, and focusing only on the University's retaliation.

We would do so. In the amended complaint, we removed the request for access to Native American collections. Yet, we still had quite a long list of complaints related to retaliation against my speech. This included Roberto's directive to me that I should not attend or share my opinions at events such as the Native American Studies Center webinar; the University's refusal to support my efforts to hold a webinar on academic freedom; the efforts taken by the University that required me to seek extra approval for research; and Roberto's decision to place the Carthage Collection in an inaccessible location. We also mentioned Roberto's attempts to prevent me from taking photographs. Although he lost that battle temporarily, Roberto had mentioned that he'd like to re-address it at a later date – perhaps when the lawsuit was over? Roberto never retracted his threats to give me a poor evaluation if I taught from my writings. One of the issues that was brought up in our amended complaint was that the University decided to put "human remains research" in the strictest compliance sector, with a timeline for applying for access even earlier than for professors who are working with hazardous materials! All the previous issues that weren't related to the Native American skeletal collection were still included as well, such as Roberto's threats to take me out of the classroom. All of this, we argued, added to a loss of standing and put a dent in my scholarly reputation.

We also mentioned that the department took me off a thesis committee. Nearly half of the students who had me on their thesis committees received either college or university level awards – this is an outstanding record that illustrates the care and diligence that I put into my work, and which I in turn expect from my students. Yet, I had worked with a student for months just to find out through an email sent to all of the professors in the department that I would not be on her committee. Her research involved bones, and we had an informal agreement in the department – that both Charlotte Sunseri and Roberto Gonzalez endorsed – that I should sit on all thesis committees where bone research is involved. As the only physical anthropology professor in the department, this made sense. It came about in large part as a result of a previous student who had removed me from her committee because she thought I was being too hard on her. Well, her thesis project is now an embarrassment to the University. Although her committee consisted of a part-time forensic lecturer, one archaeologist, the Muwekma Ohlone's tribal historian who is also trained in archaeology, and the then chair of the anthropology department, it is riddled with errors. Perhaps the most embarrassing one was that the student repeatedly confused the words "muscle" and "mussel." For example, in this thesis project about a prehistoric shell mound, the student talks about "*Mytilus edilus*, the blue muscle," rather than the blue mussel! This error would not have gone undetected if I had been on the committee. I wonder whether any one of them on the committee had actually read the thesis project. Yet, the department decided that it was better to let students flounder than have them work with me!

Upon submitting our amended complaint, the University lawyer – a different one than the previous one who had moved on to become a judge – submitted an angry response to my amended complaint. He started with:

> She has inundated the Court with these scattered allegations (some of which are not even in the complaint) in an effort to frame a number of isolated past events as a "pattern" of retaliation.

He also wrote that:

> Plaintiff unbelievably accuses the Tribe of "manufactur[ing] an interest by requesting materials not contemplated by the statute's plain language," and comments that the Tribe's assertion of its position came "suspiciously soon after [Plaintiff] filed her [FAC]." Plaintiff's insulting implication is that the Tribe has nefarious motives for requesting to rebury photographs and X-rays of ancestors and faunal remains recovered from their burial ground. This is ridiculous and offensive.

But, of course, the concern for x-rays *was* manufactured, and x-rays, according to NAGPRA and CalNAGPRA, could *not* be considered sacred! Requests for x-rays, faunal remains and photos all arose out of the University and tribal collusions. He knew this, the University knew this, and the tribes knew this!

Furthermore, the lawyer claimed the fact that I hadn't identified any space other than the curation facility to place the Carthage Collection was a devious way to get back into the curation facility. In universities, space allocations are made through chairs, deans, and provosts. I had made the request through the proper channels, but Roberto, Walt, and Vincent were not willing to help me identify space. The space allocation office would not help me either, when I asked them for a list of available spaces. And, this all occurred during a time when space was abundant – there were rooms galore that sat empty as a result of the ongoing COVID panic, coupled with the drop in enrollment!

Perhaps most insultingly, the University lawyer accused me of lying. In regard to the phone call that Roberto made to me after the Native American Studies Center webinar, the lawyer called my statement that

Roberto told me that I shouldn't share my views because I may harm junior faculty a false allegation.

I think the attorney's angry and arrogant tone shocked the judge; and, in the second Zoom hearing held on October 13th, 2022, the judge reversed the Motion-to-Dismiss. The case could go forward. This was a victory – most Motions-to-Dismiss are not reversed – and although this wasn't the full case, there was vindication that the judge could see that the University was likely engaging in some retaliatory action against me for my speech and writings.

Unfortunately, she left Rule 19 in place, and we could not bring back any of the Native American remains issues. Also, both the NAGPRA coordinator, Charlotte Sunseri, and tribal liaison, Alisha Ragland, would be removed as defendants. According to the Judge, they were just following orders – where have we heard that before? Judge Labson didn't understand the egalitarian system of the university, where a colleague can easily become a chair, as Charlotte subsequently did. And, that individuals can play great roles in derailing careers because of the shared governance – even students can get a professor fired. But, more importantly, they weren't just following orders: they were making up rules and stoking the fires, while "collaborating" with the Indians. I can guarantee that no peace pipes were passed around during those meetings!

One example of such collusion between Alisha and the Native Americans came from an October 21st, 2021 email to Alisha, the tribal liaison, from Katherine Perez, who is a representative of the Northern Valley Yokuts, Bay Mewuk and Ohlone Tribes and Nototomne Cultural Preservation – a different tribe than the Muwekma Ohlone. In this email, it is clear that they're not just working to keep me away from the collections in the curation facility, but that they hope to prevent me from obtaining new collections:

> We would like to confirm that SJSU will not continue to accept any more Native American burials. In addition to insuring that EW is fully investigated regarding the CA-ALA-329 should there be anything missing. Since we were notified that EW will continue to deal with human remain that are from another non native collection unrelated to Native American. We want to insure that

EW will do her work in a different location from where CA-ALA-329 is being housed. [SIC]

I was going to put "sic" in brackets after each error, but I soon realized that there would be so many [sic]s that it would be unreadable. So, I've decided just to put a huge [sic] at the end of this illiterate rant!

A few months later, on June 10th, 2022, Perez requested that "all human remains and items of cultural patrimony and biological soil as well as photographs and x-rays which reproduce the likeness of our ancestors" be repatriated to the Nototomne Cultural Preservation group. What the heck is "biological soil?"

A prominent indication that Charlotte Sunseri would be as vindictive a chair as Roberto had been occurred during the election of the chair. During this election, a committee to count the votes is required. Usually, this vote-counting committee consists of one department faculty member, the associate dean, and one administrative secretary. Thus, I threw my hat in the ring to be part of this easy committee that would also count towards my departmental service credits. My offer was accepted by Roberto, but Charlotte asked for a second person from the department – sending a clear signal that she did not trust me to count the votes. This is absurd, since the votes are actually tallied through a computer program and there were two others who were also on the committee. Nevertheless, Roberto put a second full professor from the department on the committee. This resulted in the absurd situation where four people, three with PhDs, counted 19 votes that had already been tallied by the computer! Charlotte was signaling to others in the department that she didn't trust me and that neither should they! It was petty, and offensive.

As we put together the case and waited for the next steps in the procedure, I started to move ahead on research plans. My Research, Scholarship, and Creative Activity (RSCA) University Grant had been approved and I had been given a second course release (meaning that for the next two semesters I would be teaching three courses per semester, instead of the usual four courses per semester) for sorting out the Carthage Collection. Yet, these two course releases were attached to what looked like traps. For instance, in the leave paperwork that I was required to sign, there was a diversity, equity, and inclusion statement:

Faculty who received assigned time for these vital tasks are expected to be mindful of University, College, and department diversity, inclusion and equity goals and liaise with the chair, Dean's Office, and other units as necessary.

I asked Roberto if this had to be on the form, and he did have it removed – perhaps to avoid this being added to my lawsuit?

An additional problem arose when the letter approving my course release for research on the Carthage Collection stated that the work may fall under "research compliance work." I looked up what this meant – it was a phrase that hadn't been used in prior work with skeletal remains. And, I was shocked to find that the Office of Research website stated that:

> If your RSCA activities involve human remains (whole body or body portion), human bones/bone fragments, or hair, teeth, or nails from deceased individuals you must contact the Director of Research Compliance to confirm compliance with applicable regulations.

Although Jennifer Trask (who was the Director of Research Compliance) could not tell me when human remains were added to the research compliance list, using the WayBack Machine website, I found that this change must have been added just days before my RSCA Grant was approved. Perhaps the dean or the provost – at Roberto's urging – had made the suggestion to place human remains research on the compliance list.

To avoid running afoul of new regulations and having the Carthage Collection taken away from me, I ran the issue by both Roberto and Jennifer Trask.

No other institution in the California State University system had adopted a similar policy that required anthropologists to get approval from their offices of research compliance to conduct routine research on human remains. The addition of an approval process for human remains research was clearly adopted in retaliation and an attempt to control my research, just as Roberto had wished for in his October 2021 email to Charlotte and Alisha that I mentioned in the previous chapter.

Trask ended up just advising me to work with my chair; Roberto capitulated and just said that I should follow the 2008 protocols (which I had written). It was a bust for them since the point seemed to be to keep me from conducting research or catching me in a trap of non-compliance. Had I not filed a lawsuit against them or had the Motion-to-Dismiss stayed in place, I am certain that the University would have used this new compliance requirement to halt my work.

One more trap was in place; one that I couldn't overcome. My grant had been approved to complete three studies; two of which required x-rays from the Ryan Mound Collection. But, I was still not getting access to the x-rays. I had requested access through Charlotte, the NAGPRA coordinator, and Alisha, the tribal liaison; no access was granted. Furthermore, they reiterated that the Muwekma Ohlone planned to burn the x-rays, as I mentioned in the previous chapter.

The Muwekma Ohlone wrote in a June 28th, 2022 letter that:

[O]ur tribal council is submitting this formal request to repatriate any and all of our ancestral human remains and associated grave regalis and objects, including x-rays, photographs and reports (for our archive) under control of SJSU.

According to court documents, the Muwekma Ohlone Tribe had "identified *all* the materials currently located in the curation facility, including faunal remains and x-rays of the human remains, as funerary and sacred objects and items of cultural patrimony."

These new 'beliefs' were clearly conjured up as a result of collusion between SJSU and the tribe, aimed at preventing me from doing the job that I'd been hired to do.

Nevertheless, I carried on asking for permission for access to x-rays. I wrote to Vincent that:

I want to point out again that NAGPRA and CalNAGPRA are not intended to regulate materials other than human remains and cultural items. These laws do not include animal remains that were not buried with human remains (i.e., are not associated with burials), and are not artifacts (unlike the bird bone whistles that were buried with remains and were obvious grave goods) and do not include previously-collected data, such as x-rays, photographs, and data collection sheets.

Vincent's response was:

We are looking into the questions you raise about whether certain materials are or are not subject to CalNAGPRA. I hope to have more on that question soon.

I never heard back from him on the issue!

On September 19th, 2022, I suggested to Vincent that the x-rays could be scanned and provided to me as electronic files. Then, these could be retained for future researchers too. But, his response was:

I cannot provide what you request. The Tribes require that all materials associated with CA-ALA-329, including images and X-Rays, be included in what is repatriated. They also require that no further research be conducted on the collection.

In order to clarify matters, I asked Vincent two important questions:

1) When you say no research on the collection, does that even mean research on data that is already collected?
2) Did you ask the tribes specifically about scanning the x-rays?

Nearly a week later, on September 28th, 2022, he responded:

1) Yes, the Tribes have stated that no further [research] be conducted on any materials related to the collection.
2) No, I did not because they have already stated that they want no further research completed.

I cannot count the number of times people have suggested to me that I should just scan and return the bones, often even suggesting 3D scanning of bones and keeping the casts. These often well-meaning people think that this is a resolution for repatriation disagreements. The Native Americans receive the human remains and can engage in reburial; the scientists can continue to conduct meaningful research and teaching. What these individuals don't understand is that it isn't about the human remains; the Native Americans want control, so that no facts that contradict their myths become known. They also want revenge, especially against those who don't defer to Native American "wisdom" or alleged superiority. And, in my case, I believe it was coupled with a personal vendetta for my anti-repatriation views.

NAGPRA and CalNAGPRA were never meant to include previously-collected data, but I was being barred from such material too. I'm literally talking about measurements of bones, data collection sheets with pathologies, and so forth. This action could only affect me. The University could not control what others who had collected such data did with it. But, if they saw me using my data, then they could punish me with removal of access to the Carthage Collection, docking pay, or even firing me!

Although Vincent's response could only affect me, that is not to say that there isn't a lot of other foul play surrounding repatriation issues. I wrote for *History Reclaimed* about some of the funny business that occurred at University of California, Berkeley's Phoebe Hearst Museum of Anthropology. The museum repatriated to the Graton Rancheria Tribe a 16th century Spanish breastplate, Ming dynasty ceramics, and a bottle of Hires root beer! Furthermore, on their website, you'll find that they've removed the images from their e-catalog and replaced them with the message: "Image restricted due to its potentially sensitive nature." I was able to discover what images had been declared sensitive by using the WayBack Machine website and I discovered that some of these included empty bottles and pieces of ceramics. What is sensitive about a broken Ming dynasty bowl or an empty early 1900 bottle of dandruff shampoo? And, why the heck were such items being repatriated to Native Americans anyway?

Yet, the absurdity doesn't end at Berkeley. NAGPRA was not meant for materials made for display at museums. Historian Ron McCoy wrote about "retroactive sacredness" in his 2018 article "Is NAGPRA Irretrievably Broken?"[1] He documented that when NAGPRA was passed, the Senate Committee addressed whether objects that Native American artisans or artists made for sale or display could be defined as sacred. There was concern that this would "adversely impact the trade in Native American artwork." The Senate Committee did not intend the definition of sacred to include objects created for sale or trade. Yet, as early as 2010, such a repatriation occurred. As McCoy wrote:

> The notice announced plans to transfer 184 "medicine faces" – False Face masks – from the Rochester (New York) Museum & Science Center to the Tonawanda Band of Seneca Indians of New York. Claimants characterized these pieces were both "sacred objects" and "objects of cultural patrimony." This, despite the fact Senecas carved the pieces *specifically* for public exhibition between 1935-1941 while working with the New Deal's Works Progress Administration.

Replicas were being classified as "sacred objects" even though they were made for display! As McCoy said:

> It says something deeply unsettling about NAGPRA that pieces created as *replicas* for educational exhibits during the Great Depression can be classified, nearly seven decades later, as "sacred objects" and "objects of cultural patrimony" subject to repatriation.

Ron McCoy wrote that he is "deeply uncomfortable with and increasingly skeptical about what appears to be an over-broad interpretation of the term "sacred objects" in applying NAGPRA" – this was six years ago! And, the situation has just gotten worse over time.

By not granting me access to x-rays, which I wrote that I needed to conduct research, I would surely be reprimanded when the review of my research progress would arise. The University could take away my grant and would surely give me a poor evaluation for not completing the tasks that I had said that I would do. It was yet another Catch-22 – to fulfill my research duties that I set out in the grant proposal, which was approved by university administrators, I needed access to x-rays; but they had no intention of helping me get access to these materials, even though they are clearly not within the purview of NAGPRA or CalNAGPRA.

While working unsuccessfully on ways to get access to the x-rays, I finally started to re-box, catalog, and study the Carthage Collection. It had taken Roberto and Charlotte 10 months from my initial request for the remains to the movement of the remains to a place where access was feasible, and organization was possible. The collection, unfortunately, was in horrendous condition – years of looting during the Muslim invasion of Carthage removed the bones from their coffins and into the sandy soils of Tunisia. Excavation was also sloppy – the last season was done in haste, and burial numbers were inconsistent. This makes work on this collection difficult. Yet, I was able to conduct two studies: one on leprosy[2] and one on a spinal pathology likely arising from horseback riding, called kissing spines.[3]

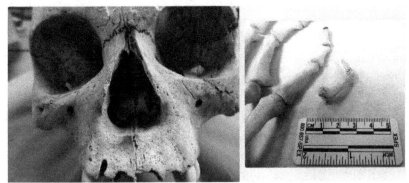

*Figure 6: Leprosy in Byzantine Carthage Collection*

The article on kissing spines was initially rejected from an anthropology journal. It's difficult to assess whether the rejection was based on who I was and my repatriation views, or due to the poor quality of data that I had to work with. I think it's likely that had I been another author, I would have received a revise and resubmit rather than a rejection. I've come to this belief – although not a firm conclusion – because I thanked the editor and acknowledged the article's shortcomings. Then, I noted that although I wouldn't be resubmitting the paper (since it was rejected), I would use the reviewers' comments to improve the paper and submit it elsewhere. I received no response from the editor, which is a bit odd in our field. Nevertheless, the medical journal *Spine* accepted the article and I'm glad that it's out there to read for others who are interested in these anatomical pathologies.

Returning to the issue of the Rule 19 decision, it seemed likely that this decision would prevent my success in gaining access to x-rays. Rule

19 was also preventing me from getting access to faunal remains – and I suppose the "biological soil" too, if I had wanted that dirt! I don't know why the Native Americans want dirt since – as you'll see later – there's more than enough dirt on them already. But, Rule 19 is even more absurd since the Muwekma Ohlone tribe are genetically indistinguishable from Mexicans living in the Los Angeles area. Yes, you read that right. Turns out these 'Native Americans' are more Mexican than Indian!

In April 2022, an article on the Muwekma Ohlone DNA compared to a dozen prehistoric skeletons, dating around 2,000 years ago, from the San Francisco Bay Area, came out in the prestigious *Proceedings of the National Academy of Sciences*.[4] The results were reported on by *The New York Times,* the *Smithsonian Magazine, USA Today*, and many other mainstream media sites. The news articles proclaimed that the DNA research proved that the Muwekma Ohlone were not extinct, as Alfred Kroeber, University of California, Berkeley's first anthropologist, noted in 1925. Kroeber said that the Costanoans, which was the name used for tribes of the area, were "extinct so far as all practical purposes are concerned." As I noted in my *American Conservative* article on the topic, Kroeber drew this conclusion because of the interbreeding, including extensive mixing with other tribes, Europeans, and Mexicans. He had also noted that the customs, such as female face tattoos, had been abandoned long ago. And, that the basketry showed European influences. Although Kroeber is depicted as having recanted his 1925 conclusion in the 1950s, he did not. In 1955, Kroeber noted that nearly all the remaining Costanoans were of mixed tribes.

Yet, the journalists reporting this story likely didn't read Kroeber and maybe hadn't even read the *Proceedings of the National Academy of Sciences* article. If they had, they certainly hadn't understood it. The authors of the DNA article acknowledge the extensive admixture of Europeans and Mexicans multiple times throughout the article. The data tables and figures clearly show that the Muwekma Ohlone are most similar to Mexicans in Los Angeles – a point ignored by the mainstream media, who just gushingly regurgitated the "we are still here" cliché.

Ancient remains from the San Francisco Bay Area and modern Muwekma Ohlone *do* share a little DNA, but these ancient remains are genetically more similar to other Indians, such as the Paleoindians from the Channel Islands. Most significantly, out of all the modern samples of DNA tested, none came from non-Muwekma Ohlone California Native Americans, and only a handful of other modern tribes were included: Aleut (from the Aleutian Islands off of Alaska), Canadian Pacific Northwest Indians, and some from the Sonoran Desert of the Southwest US. There is no way to say how closely related these skeletal remains are to the Muwekma Ohlone compared to other tribes in California; the DNA they share with these ancient remains could be from any of their admixed ancestry. And, of course, repatriation is supposed to be linked to the most likely descendant. In order to truly determine the relatedness between the ancient remains and the Muwekma Ohlone, we need to look at many more data points. More DNA samples must be added, but this won't occur since the Muwekma Ohlone got the results that they had hoped for. The article has the disclaimer that the Muwekma Ohlone retain "power over how the data is used" to "minimize harms." In a journal that prides itself on transparency and sharing data, this should not have been allowed.

The real reason that the Muwekma Ohlone celebrated this finding was that they used it to strengthen their case for federal recognition. If the Muwekma Ohlone get federal recognition, they may be in for a huge payday – a reservation on the Presidio of San Francisco, a casino at that site, and more! They would hit the jackpot!

When examining claims for tribal recognition, other tribes too question the Muwekma Ohlone legitimacy. As I mentioned in Chapter 2, the Muwekma Ohlone name seems to be a very recent construct. Relatives of Rosemary Cambra, the former Muwekma Ohlone tribal chair, have claimed that the Muwekma Ohlone isn't an ancient tribe at all. In a 2016 *Anthropology Now* article, written by Peter W. Colby, about the discovery of a 7,500-year-old skeleton in San Franciso, Ramona Garibay, who was serving as the Native American monitor at the construction site where the remains were found – although she wasn't there, because she thought it unlikely that human remains would be uncovered – mentioned that she and her family "by no means consider[ed] themselves to be Muwekma Ohlone."[5] Again, as I previously wrote, Colby reported that they suspected that Cambra "made the name 'Muwekma' up herself."

Andrew Galvan, who works at repatriating and reburying Native American remains on his family's Ohlone Cemetery, is related to both Garibay and Cambra. He describes himself as "Ohlone" but also does not consider himself "Muwekma Ohlone."

Unfortunately, as a result of the neo-tribal warfare, coupled with greed that resulted in Galvan not coming to an agreement about the excavation, research and care of this oldest San Franciscan, no one knows what happened to the remains. The Transbay Center's Management Construction Manager, whose project was disrupted by the discovery, noted that "the contract was never signed; the press release was never issued; and the analysis was never completed." Galvan refused to sign an agreement and the construction company ran out of options. Colby ends with this sad proclamation:

> What will become of the remains of the young San Franciscan is unclear. None of the documents produced by the agencies provide information on this. Perhaps they are being stored by Galvan — his guidelines for the construction crew specify that the remains will be removed by the MLD [most likely descendant]. Perhaps they have already been buried in the Fremont Ohlone Cemetery, as Galvan intended. Perhaps the remains lie beneath the massive rising towers of the new Transbay Center. For now, it is a mystery whether the young man's remains will be studied, be reburied or just languish in a jurisdictional limbo.

Now, eight years later, there are still no answers. This is what happens when greed replaces scientific and intellectual curiosity!

In their fight to gain federal recognition, the Muwekma Ohlone hired a consultant to put up a website called the San Francisco Inquirer, which looks like a news site, but is actually a propaganda machine for the Muwekma Ohlone. Most of their articles are anonymous, they have a few unaltered press releases, and they have what looks like corporate ads. Yet, an investigation by Shira Stein published in the *San Francisco Chronicle* on January 22nd, 2023, found that companies which were advertised on the site, such as Wells Fargo and Kaiser Permanente, were not aware of this site and had not authorized use of their logos. The main targets of the website are politicians who don't fully support the Muwekma Ohlone, alongside other Native Americans who may compete with the Muwekma Ohlone. For instance, there's a March 12th, 2024 article on the site about Greg Sarris, who is the Chairman of the Federated Indians of Graton Rancheria. The anonymous author claims that Sarris "doesn't have a trace of Indian heritage at all." They also claim that he "aims to genocide the Muwekma Tribe out of existence." They imply that Sarris is Jewish by mentioning "his unwed 16-year-old Jewish mother." Sarris, according to the article, has said that written records can be inconsistent and, thus, he relies on photos and oral tradition as proof of his Native American heritage. In an ironic twist – considering that Native Americans are often claiming that their oral traditions are as valid as historic documents, even over millennia – the article ends with the quote: "Oral tradition is nice, but documentation is better."

The thorny issue of Pretendians – those who fake their Native American heritage – can only be resolved by treating all people as equals. If there are rewards, especially material ones, to be had as a result of Native American identity, there will always be fakes – the Pretendians. Is Sarris one? I don't know and it really doesn't matter; what matters is that tribes will fight about these issues between them, but if anyone *else* raises the issue then they are called a racist and barred from research. Rules for thee, but not for me!

There are some well-known cases of Pretendians, such as Sacheen Littlefeather, who attended the Oscars for Marlon Brando's protest. Her sister came forward after Littlefeather's death to confirm that they were actually from Mexican heritage, and that the hard-luck story she spun was also untrue.

Another case is that of Canada's Mary Ellen Turpel-Lafond, who was a former judge and a professor at McGill Law School. She received the Order of Canada in 2021 and was considered the most accomplished indigenous scholar in Canada's history. Yet, in an October 2022 article in *Canadian Broadcasting Company* (CBC), investigative journalist Geoff Leo wrote about the evidence that she was not indigenous at all.[6] It appears that her time on reservations was the result of her white Canadian father's work as a medical doctor on the reservation. Not only does it appear that she's not an indigenous Canadian, but also she didn't live the life of poverty, abuse, and alcoholism that she claimed.

Geoff Leo also wrote about Carrie Bourassa, a professor at University of Saskatchewan, and Canada's leading indigenous health scholar, who self-identified as Metis, Anishinaabe, and Tlingit. She was also found to be a Pretendian. In a CBC report by Leo on this topic, the motivating factor in Canada is the many government grants that are provided to indigenous Canadians – this was usually based on the honor-system, but now stricter measures have been put into place.

And, in the US, a University of California, Riverside professor was accused of faking her Native American heritage. The case was covered in everything from *The Daily Beast* to *The New York Times*. She was compared to Rachel Dolezal – the white woman who claimed to be black and who worked for the National Association for the Advancement of Colored People (NAACP). Andrea Smith has written about her Cherokee roots, but under scrutiny these claims failed to hold up. As *The New York Times* reported, in August 2023, Smith posted: "I have always been, and will always be Cherokee."[7] It is particularly ironic that early on in her career she wrote a rant against white women culturally appropriating Native American spirituality.[8] Smith ended her article with:

> White feminists should know that as long as they take part in Indian spiritual abuse, either by being consumers of it or by refusing to take a stand on it, Indian women will consider white "feminists" to be nothing more than agents in the genocide of our people.

And, no discussion of Pretendians would be complete without mention of Elizabeth Warren's claim to be part-Native American, which led some to call her Fauxcahontas.

It's interesting that the Muwekma Ohlone could possibly gain federal recognition if they cede their right to a casino. In 2019, Congress recognized six new tribes in Virginia, but they were prohibited from running casinos. Even though the current chair Charlene Nijmeh – Rosemary Cambra's daughter – says she's against gambling, it is clear that they don't want to give up the possibility of a lucrative casino in the Bay

Area.[9] Furthermore, they had received financial support for their fight for federal recognition from a Florida real estate tycoon who has been associated with other tribal casinos.

While preparing the lab for the curation of the Carthage Collection, I came across records that revealed the Muwekma Ohlone's aggressive tactics in their archaeology firm, Ohlone Family Consulting Services. For instance, with regard to a request to sign a memorandum of agreement (MOA) to consult with the Federal Highway Administration during their work on the San Francisco Bay Bridge's seismic safety update, the Muwekma Ohlone wrote that they would not be signing the memorandum because it stated that the tribe was not federally recognized, which is just a factual statement. In this letter, Cambra also accuses a former chairwoman of the Amah Mutsun tribe of not being Native American. In other letters, similar sentiments arise. In a letter to the City Manager of Emeryville, about the possibility of some consulting and monitoring work involving the removal of toxic waste from a previously-excavated shell mound site, Rosemary Cambra wrote:

> Should any other individual Ohlone or group claim to be directly descended from the Huchiun Ohlones or descended from immediate neighboring aboriginal tribes from this region, please have them present their genealogical documentation.

All this was for naught, because they received a letter back indicating that they missed the deadline to be considered for the job by one day! The city had a lucky escape!

In another example of the Muwekma Ohlone tactics, the Barbaccia Management Company asked whether they could put some dirt on a part of the city land, and the city required Native American approval for this action. Nearly all construction, roadwork, and improvements in California require that an archaeologist be present, in case something is discovered, and the presence of the most likely descendant tribes in case human remains are found. Rosemary Cambra wrote up an estimate that included testing trenches, an archaeological report, a maximum of eight hours of monitoring, and 20 hours of writing at the cost of $30/hour – in 1999! Thus, to put a pile of dirt on a piece of land, they were estimating costs in the thousands. Nice work if you can get it! In response, the project manager wrote: "As I told you, we simply want permission from the City to allow us to stockpile dirt on the excavation occurring." In the end, the tribal historian, Alan Leventhal, received $540; what the Muwekma Ohlone received is unknown!

Some of their other endeavors brought them far more money – in 1994, they conducted a site excavation and were paid nearly $215,000. Yet, this archaeology money is small beer compared to the casino riches that await them!

Ironically, Bay Area tribes say that I should be watched, investigated, and that I'm not to be trusted. The current Muwekma Ohlone chair, Charlene Nijmeh, claims that myself and people like me "would continue to politically erase" tribes. Yet, they are the ones slinging mud, creating fake news sites, and engaging in "retroactive sacredness."

This goes beyond archaeology. Recently, the Muwekma Ohlone spiritual advisor Joey Iyolopixtil Torres, a face-tattooed thuggish-looking guy who is being courted by SJSU, has started to give blessings and land acknowledgements. At the investiture of SJSU's president Cynthia Teniente-Matson, he showed up wearing a hoody, but after his 'blessing,' Torres was wrapped in a blanket by the University's senior administrators, acting as if he had just undergone some spiritual awakening. Torres also recently said that the Muwekma Ohlone used marijuana as a spiritual practice: "We smoked, we exhaled spirit. It's a very sacred thing that you all bring it back and now we break that stigma, that colonized way of, it being 'poison' to us."[10] Yet, marijuana was brought over to the Americas by the Spanish – it is a colonial legacy!

Upon arrival at SJSU, I excavated with the Muwekma Ohlone. I was assured that the Muwekma Ohlone understood the value of research. I was told that they ran a legitimate archaeological consulting firm. In order for us, at SJSU, to curate the collections that they excavated, the Muwekma Ohlone signed a memorandum of understanding stating that they would support all non-destructive research on human remains. Yet, as soon as my opinion on repatriation because newsworthy, my access to collections was denied, effectively halting my research. In other words, they broke their treaty.

But, long before my battles, I found out about the Muwekma Ohlone's violent past from a 2007 article, three years after arriving in SJSU, and I felt that I could no longer work with them. In 1985, Rosemary Cambra attacked archaeologist William Roop with a shovel.[11] William Roop said that she tried to kill him. He needed stitches. Rosemary Cambra received a sentence of jail time during the weekends for one year, and three years probation. She also lost her nursing license. Yet, also, as a result of this attack, Rosemary Cambra became a hero in the Native American community. Now, her daughter Charlene Nijmeh, the current chairwoman, is showing similar aggressive tactics. These are people to stay away from – sometimes the noble savage is just a savage!

*Figure 7: Rosemary Cambra's Attack*
*on Archaeologist William Roop. Courtesy of History San Jose*

[1]McCoy, Ron. (2018, December 19). "Is NAGPRA Irretrievably Broken?" *Cultural Property News.* https://culturalpropertynews.org/is-nagpra-irretrievably-broken/
[2]Weiss, Elizabeth. 2023. "Leprosy in 7th Century Carthage: A unique Byzantine cemetery." *Southwestern Anthropological Association Proceedings.*

[3] Weiss, Elizabeth. 2023. "The Kissing Spines of Carthage." *Spine* 48(24): 1763-1766. https://doi.10.1097/BRS.0000000000004810

[4] Severson, A.L., Byrd, B.F., Mallott, E.K., Owings, A.C., DeGiorgio, M., De Flamingh, A., Nijmeh, C., Arellano, M.V., Leventhal, A., Rosenberg, N.A. and Malhi, R.S., 2022. "Ancient and modern genomics of the Ohlone Indigenous population of California." *Proceedings of the National Academy of Sciences*, *119*(13), p.e2111533119. https://doi.org/10.1073/pnas.2111533119

[5] Colby, Peter. (2016, April, 2016). "Remains of the Day: A Native American Burial Discovered in San Francisco is Shrouded in a Fog of Acrimony" *Anthropology Now.* *https://anthronow.com/print/remains-of-the-day-a-native-american-burial-discovered-in-san-francisco-is-shrouded-in-a-fog-of-acrimony*

[6] Leo, Geoff. (2022, October 12). "Disputed history." https://www.cbc.ca/news interactives/features/mary-ellen-turpel-lafond-indigenous-cree-claims

[7] Patel, Vimal. (2023, August 27). "Prominent Scholar Who Claimed to Be Native American Resigns." *The New York Times.* https://www.nytimes.com/2023/08/27/ us/uc-riverside-andrea-smith-resigns.html

[8] Smith, Andy. (1991). "For All Those Who Were Indian in a Former Life." https://www.yorku.ca/kdenning/+35102005-6/for_all_those_who_were_indian_in.htm

[9] Richardson, Valeria. (2023, March 1). Quest for federal recognition through Congress pits tribes against tribes." *The Washington Times.* https://www.washington times.com/news/2023/mar/1/quest-federal-recognition-through-congress-pits-tr/

[10] Olivares, Jovanna. (2021, April 21). "Activists oppose pot criminalization." SJSU News. https://sjsunews.com/article/activists-oppose-pot-criminalization-

[11] Staff writer. (2007, March 28). The Little Tribe that Could, *SF Weekly.* https://www.sfweekly.com/archives/the-little-tribe-that-could/article_c2a92470-2ed3-5182-8c69-5145d73fe558.html

# Chapter 12:

# New Beginnings

During the 2022-2023 academic year, which began in August 2022 and ended in May 2023, so much had happened. In the early part of the academic year, around October 2022, of course, the Motion-to-Dismiss was overturned and we began preparing for the court case. It was shortly after this court ruling that the University's lawyer reached out to offer me a settlement, which we didn't take. The offer was weighted in their favor to the extent that taking it would have been tantamount to my resigning. It was an insult and a joke.

I also collected data and conducted research on the Carthage Collection. My first presentation on the collection was at the American Anthropological Association annual meeting in Seattle, which was held from November 10th to 13th. This conference led me to further realize how far anthropology had strayed from being an academic and intellectual field. In my *Minding the Campus* article "Anthropology in Ruins," I wrote about some of the absurdity I witnessed. For instance, nearly 80 sessions used the word "decolonization." Even more ridiculously, over 70 sessions used the term "white supremacy" – none of these sessions featured talks that were actually about white supremacy; there were no ethnographic studies of white supremacy groups, like the KKK. Two session titles that demonstrated the field's direction were: "Pronouns, Bottoms, Cat-Ears And Cuerpes, Girl: For An Intersectional Trans Linguistic Anthropology" and "Unsettling Queer Anthropology: Critical Genealogies and Decolonizing Futures."

And, although everyone was vaccinated, and COVID was giving most people just a cold – if indeed it wasn't asymptomatic – you could ask for "comfort ribbons" that indicated whether you wanted to avoid all contact with people – maintaining the decidedly arbitrary six feet of distance between them and others; whether one was okay with elbow bumps; or you could give a greenlight for the ever-dangerous handshake! The left just couldn't let go of COVID; some of them *still* can't!

Many speakers started their talks by describing themselves. Speakers would describe their hair color, skin color, what they were wearing, how tall they were – and, of course, their pronouns. Why do they do this? The narrative is that it's for the sight-impaired, but in a sense, if you are providing information about other cultures that you study, what difference does it make if you're wearing a white shirt or a red shirt? The *real* reason for this performance is to ensure that you give proper deference to speakers from 'oppressed' groups – a person of color needs to be listened to; a person's pronouns signal their virtue and, thus, the importance of their opinion. Ironically, these personal descriptions were sometimes wrong (men tended to overstate their height, and some people got the color of their clothing wrong!), and at other times, these descriptions were the most interesting things these people had to say!

In a talk about children's bodily autonomy, a mother, whose anthropological research revolved around watching her child's behavior and interacting with a mother's group online (again, nice work, if you can get it!), spoke of her concern when her toddler did not want affection from black people – was she raising a little racist? The online mother's group tried to pacify the anthropologist's fears by stating that the child would outgrow this racist behavior!

Content warnings, land acknowledgements, and apologies for coming from a "settler-colonialist" background flowed through the convention halls. A talk about missing people in Mexico focused on the sounds of a rooster's crow and onions frying at the church where the searchers had gathered!

Yet, it was Ryan Harrod's talk that was most disappointing; I was a fan of Harrod's work on the bioarchaeology of violence. He had looked at big picture explanations of pre-contact violence in the Americas. In this talk, Harrod took a decidedly different approach; he apologized for his work, and for conducting research that Native American tribes did not approve of. Upon consulting with Native American tribal members, such as the Southwestern Zuni elders, Harrod learned that they do not want to know about past acts of violence; doubtless because it contradicts the schtick about peaceful, environmentally-conscious Native Americans. And, that the elders – for pay, of course – were more than willing to provide information on the remains without the use of scientific investigation. Harrod ended his talk by admitting that he may not be able to publish his new works, but, as he said, "I feel less guilty"! Harrod's approach – and any other anthropologist who takes this approach – saps anthropology of true facts about the past. The interesting stories that we can reconstruct are basically replaced with false tales provided by "elders," that don't have any bearing on past lives.

One talk tried to connect the "surreptitious burials" associated with the Residential Indian Schools in Kamloops, British Columbia (a topic I discuss at some length in Chapter 5) with current deaths and missing indigenous young adults in Canada. The Kamloops "clandestine graves" have never been excavated and are only assumed from ground penetrating radar (GPR) data. There is actually good evidence to suggest the blips from the GPR are actually a result of normal soil disturbances, such as plumbing systems and tree roots. Yet, at this meeting, the anthropologist argued that "the whole reason for residential schools was to destroy indigenous life;" he further added that GPR is a sacred tool imbued with ancestral knowledge that can show anthropologists where the graves are. Anthropologists are speaking to the dead through GPR! But, most offensively, he stated that asking for evidence of bodies plays to "right-wing pundits" and "skepticism is violence"!

"Anthropology in Ruins" was the top-read article of the year for *Minding the Campus*.

A stark opposite to the nonsense at this anthropology conference was the Stanford Academic Freedom Conference that was held just a week prior.

I had the honor to give a talk at the Stanford Academic Freedom Conference on a panel with Amy Wax, a law professor at University of Pennsylvania whose controversial, and yet well-researched, views on race differences in achievement have led her University to try to fire her; Frances Widdowson, who is currently trying to get her job back from Mount Royal University after having been fired for questioning the validity of the Kamloops Residential School clandestine graves; and, Joshua Katz who lost his job at Princeton due to his criticism of political-correctness and activist groups on campus who make everyone's life miserable. We also had an empty chair for Mike Adams, a criminology professor who had been at the center of a cancel culture attack for his outspoken views on Islam and modern identity politics. Adams left the university after a $500,000 settlement, but shortly afterward he committed suicide.

There were sessions about COVID and universities' hysterical overreactions to it, such as Stanford's own Jay Bhattacharya and Scott Atlas, both of whom viewed the shutdowns as deeply problematic and ineffectual. There were talks about the legal differences between academic freedom and free speech by law professors such as Eugene Volokh and former ACLU chair Nadine Strossen. There were sessions on best strategies, that ranged from suggestions on using the power of satire and mockery to battle cancel culture, to embracing those who oppose us to convince them that we are not bad people. Attendees debated the causes of cancel culture, and whether knowing this would enable us to fight this scourge in the universities.

Prior to the conference's start, there was an attempt to get it cancelled! As I wrote for *Academic Questions*:

> When reporters, bloggers, and other writers on social media started to write up negative stories about participants—such as accusing Amy Wax, the Robert Mundheim Professor of Law at the University of Pennsylvania, of being racist, trying to shame Steven Pinker, the Johnstone Family Professor in the Department of Psychology at Harvard University, for being acquainted with Jeffrey Epstein, or—my personal favorite—stating that I am "arguably the spiritual leader of this collection of white supremacists, racists and Trump-lovers"—even before the conference began, some junior faculty (perhaps worried that even listening to the speakers could threaten their careers) pulled out of attendance, a chilling reminder of how freedom to listen to other perspectives is being stifled.

What made the conference so worthwhile was that not everyone agreed with each other; there was genuine debate and a variety of opinions on every topic discussed. There could have been even more debate and more diversity in opinions if those from the 'progressive' left of academia had chosen to participate. The conference organizer John Cochrane had made an effort to reach out to people who criticized some of the speakers, but he got either no response, or refusals.

And, thus, with all this on my mind – the dismal state of anthropology, and the ongoing concerns with academic freedom – I had decided to start to look for an exit strategy.

I had decided long before *Repatriation and Erasing the Past* was published that if the skeletal remains that I curated and researched were repatriated, I would retire. In essence, this had happened: a virtual repatriation by allowing the tribes to claim everything – from x-rays to faunal remains – as sacred and, thus, off-limits.

Many colleges have skeletal collections in storage that have been kept away from researchers for years. Sometimes these collections are stored in the university facility for decades, but the tribes don't want to repatriate them because that may disempower them from trying to get land for a cemetery and, of course, a little casino next door! For years, students from California State University, Sacramento (my alma mater) would come to SJSU or travel as far as England to study remains, since the collections at Sacramento were no longer available for study – but the bones were still there!

I'd done all I could with the Carthage Collection. I'd sent out samples of bone for DNA and pathology analyses as requested by molecular anthropology researchers. And, I've left the collection in a better condition than I found it.

So, what was I to do? I thought of looking for other possible skeletal collections to study, and, thus, came upon Heterodox Academy's faculty fellowship call for their new Center for Academic Pluralism. Heterodox Academy is a non-profit organization whose mission is to foster diversity of opinions in universities; their motto is "Great minds don't always think alike." The Center is in New York City, which is the home to the American Museum of Natural History, not too far away from museums in

Philadelphia, and even only a three and a bit hour train ride from DC's Smithsonian's National Museum of Natural History. I decided to apply, and take a stab at understanding the culture of museums, making connections with curators, and learning how to access the remains housed in these institutions. After all, my PhD and post-doc were completed using data from human remains curated at the Canadian Museum of Civilization. Museums couldn't be more woke than universities. Could they?

I submitted my project, which would entail investigating museums for diversity of thought in their displays, explanations, and exhibits. I also proposed to Heterodox Academy that I would continue to do research, and write about the ways repatriation laws are violating the separation of church and state; perhaps being in New York City, I would have better luck at finding legal help to challenge this unconstitutional law.

I got an interview, and got the offer to spend an academic year – from September 2023 to May 2024 – at Heterodox Academy's Center for Academic Pluralism! I was thrilled. Now, I had to apply for a difference-in-pay leave, which is an off-year sabbatical. I needed the approval of my chair and dean to take the leave. If granted permission to take the fellowship, SJSU would reduce my salary by 50%; I would lose that year's retirement credit; and, upon the end of the fellowship, I would be required to return to SJSU for at least one more academic year. These are the standard conditions for leave at SJSU. Nevertheless, I thought it would be well worth doing. And, my chair, Roberto Gonzalez, and the rest of the University would likely be happy to see me leave for a year too!

Even though I'd gotten this prestigious faculty fellowship with a large stipend attached through Heterodox Academy, something that would normally have been celebrated at SJSU with an email announcement congratulating me, a formal announcement on the College of Social Science website, and an announcement at the department meeting, Roberto couldn't muster much enthusiasm for my plans. Remember, for my last leave to write *Repatriation and Erasing the Past*, Roberto wrote:

> [H]er new project is likely to spark lively discussions among various stakeholders. Consequently, her book might potentially boost the department's national reputation as a center that fosters creative and unorthodox viewpoints on important public issues.

Now, Roberto just wrote:

The proposed project might potentially provide Dr. Weiss with an expanded network of scholars whose writings and lectures relate to her assigned courses. Additionally, the project might result in new avenues for Dr. Weiss's work, such as museum research and opportunities for public scholarship.

Nevertheless, the leave was approved. I'd be heading to New York City!

It was also during this time that my lawyers from Pacific Legal Foundation and I started to discuss the possibility of a settlement. We had turned down two previous offers already, but now with New York City ahead of me and no desire to come back to SJSU afterwards, I thought that we might usefully enter into negotiations with the University's legal team.

As a side note, San José, the city, had also taken a turn for the worse and was a miserable place to live in the post-COVID era. When I initially moved to San José, the downtown was in a revitalization era, which brought to it movie theaters, a gourmet grocery store, a bookstore, lots of restaurants, events, and a good nightlife scene. It was also listed as the safest big city in the US. I used to head over to the Fairmont Hotel to listen to live bands and get some dancing in. I'd stroll over to the bookstore to pick up something to read, and I would enjoy walking the few blocks to the Farmer's Market on Friday afternoons. All this – and more – would disappear; the downfall of San José started before COVID, but COVID put the final nails in the coffin. At the time that I applied to the Heterodox Academy Faculty Fellowship, the movie theater had closed, there was no real grocery store downtown, the drugstore had shuttered, the bookstore was long gone, there were blocks of empty store fronts and shouting, angry homeless people roaming the streets. The Fairmont closed and then re-opened briefly as a Hilton – now it's student housing! I was happy to leave San José and SJSU!

We eventually hammered out an agreed-upon settlement that I think benefited both sides. For the University, they avoided a court case and would see me leave. For me, I would be getting full pay (instead of half pay) while I was in New York, I would get full retirement credit for that year too, and I was to retire when my year at Heterodox Academy ended – this would be after 20 years of working at SJSU. Any missing service credit, the University would pay for. Retirement differs from resignation; resignation would not provide me with the same benefits. I would also be granted emeritus status, a title not available to those who resign. Thus, I'll still be listed on their websites, retain my email address, have access to all the library resources, and, importantly, have a continued academic title that allows me to apply for grants, for access to collections, and to publish in academic journals. But, most importantly, it signals that I can and do hope to still study skeletal remains; and, if I ever get a lawyer to take up my claim that NAGPRA is unconstitutional, then I have a standing as a party of interest in such a case.

Furthermore, the agreement has no non-disclosure agreement, which is why I can write this book so freely!

Initially, I worried that I was letting a lot of people down; throwing in the towel; but I don't see it that way. Had I gone to court, maybe I would have won, but what would I have gotten? The Native American collections, including the x-rays and faunal remains, would still be off-limits to me. When one goes to court, one needs to have an "ask" – something that the court can actually do to remedy the situation. If there's no remedy, it's likely that the case will be tossed out. In the previous two and a half years, I fought hard, which is why I chose the title that I did for this book. I had racked up some victories – the removal of the "menstruating personnel" (an offensive phrase constructed to virtue-signal to the trans lobby) taboo in the protocols; preventing the University from prohibiting photos; and access to the Carthage Collection in a suitable location, without need for further permissions from the Institutional Research Office. I'd also hosted speakers, such as University of Alberta Professor Kathleen Lowrey, who spoke about the hierarchy in pre-contact Andean societies; and linguistic anthropologist Glynn Custred, who came to my class on mummies to speak about his testimony for the Spirit Cave Mummy court case, in which he revealed the utter uselessness of "oral history" after 500 years. Although the department chose not to fund my invited speakers, Roberto did provide honoraria from the chair's account (likely to avoid being called out on his lack of support during the lawsuit).

I also was never removed from my classroom and continued to assign my book. And, I brought national attention to repatriation and reburial laws and abuse of those laws!

I am certain that had I not filed suit against SJSU, I would have been fired. All the indicators for that were present! And, thus, while I didn't have the victory that I had hoped for, I had won many battles, and ultimately, the war is not over.

So, with the lawsuit settled, I headed to New York City. Nick and I chose a studio apartment a stone's throw from the Center for Academic Pluralism. And, my adventures started with giving the keynote address for the Center's opening night!

Shortly after my arrival in New York City, the American Anthropological Association cancelled the panel that I was to be on, which I discussed in chapters 2 and 5. The cancellation of a panel about the importance of *not* abandoning sex as a binary variable in anthropological research made headlines around the world. It was covered in *The New York Times* and I was able to stroll into the studio of *NewsMax* to do a live in-studio interview on the topic. Furthermore, Heterodox Academy saved the panel and we had it online. It seems to me that being in New York at the time of this cancellation was very fortuitous. But, there was to be a rude awakening.

It's hard for me to describe the absolute horror I felt upon discovering that the museum world is even more woke than universities! Much of this wokeness centers around kowtowing to superstitious indigenous myths. And, thus, much of my criticism of museums focuses on natural history museums and other similar science museums, like the Mütter Museum. Natural history museums and science museums should be criticized when they present mythical beliefs as facts. In art museums, I think artists' beliefs needn't face the same criticism – they're not passing themselves off as scientists. But, when science museums treat myths and superstitions as facts, something has gone horrendously wrong.

One of the very first museums that I visited was the American Museum of Natural History. I used to love this museum when I came here in the late 1990s and early 2000s. Yet, their most recently renovated exhibit, the Northwest Coast Hall, which they spent five years working on

– in collaboration with indigenous folk of the Northwest Coast region – and $19 million to complete, is an embarrassment. For instance, their description of totem poles (a term that one isn't supposed to use anymore) is: "Many figures on the wooden sculpture refer to family stories and supernatural beings who were encountered by their first Ancestors." Of course, no one actually encountered supernatural beings!

And, one of the collaborators on the exhibit said (as a detailed on a plaque by the display):

> What we have in the museum are not just works of art – they're spiritual beings. And when we see them, we know they're calling to us, 'We want to come home.' I'll always remember an Elder who went to a museum and she could see the mist of an object coming out of the drawer where it was contained. She said, 'We'll bring you back home.'

Other examples of pushing a Native American religious agenda include plaques that describe visits from "supernatural Thunderbirds" as historic events. And, most absurdly, the Northwest Coast Hall includes a case with a warning label that reads as follows:

> CAUTION: This display case contains items used in the practices of traditional Tlingit doctors. Some people may wish to avoid this area, as Tlingit tradition holds that such belongings contain powerful spirits.

There's no photography allowed of this case, due to the power held in the case! I, nonetheless, took some photos. I'm still waiting for the spirits to attack me for this egregious breech of protocol!

But, what visitors are not seeing is that such absurdity is abundant behind the scenes as well. Curators are following a set of protocols for "Objects of Power" that require ritualistic practices to prevent supernatural beings escaping from artifacts and drawers, and warn women to stay away from certain materials while pregnant! The protocols, introduced in 2021, include the need to "greet" the object and then "explain" to the object that permission has been granted from community representatives – I hope that these inanimate objects are paying close attention!

To prevent disturbing these objects, glass cabinets need to be covered with brown paper. And, to prevent spirits from escaping these confines, bundles of Devil's Club need to be hung in doorways and cabinets. Objects made with human hair are the "most dangerous," and museum staff shouldn't even handle these objects. Bird bone whistles can be deadly too – if someone were to inadvertently blow into the whistle it can set off intertribal warfare, due the supernatural beings that are summoned through the whistle!

As I wrote for *Reality's Last Stand*, the most insulting of all these protocols are the cautions:

> DO NOT APPROACH if you are feeling discomfort, i.e., if you are in a physically or emotionally vulnerable state (including menstruation and pregnancy).

Clearly, these warnings are sexist and imply that women, particularly during menstruation and pregnancy, are emotionally unstable and weak.

Natural history museums should not encourage these religious beliefs to be taken seriously in their place of science. I cannot believe that the curators and researchers actually believe any of these warnings, but they're playing along so that they can still conduct research and exhibit materials. In the end, it's a slippery slope – today the Native Americans bar the display of objects that contain human hair, tomorrow it may be the sacred artifacts made from stone that they'll want to hide away!

But it's not just the American Museum of Natural History; the Smithsonian's National Museum of Natural History contains some of this nonsense too! For instance, in the Smithsonian, shields used by the Plains Indians are said to offer protection from the "tough rawhide base and spiritual powers invoked by its painted cover." In 2019 the Smithsonian and indigenous collaborators replicated an ancient hat, and then repatriated the original to the Tlingit tribe; after these endeavors, they conducted a religious ceremony in Alaska to "put spirit into the new hat – making it a living sacred object (at.óow), just like the original."

It's one thing to describe these issues as beliefs that are culturally interesting and not fact-based; it is a completely different story to push it as real and part of science!

Another push into the supernatural comes from changes to NAGPRA, coupled with the Biden administration's mandate to include "indigenous knowledge" in decision-making across the span of government agencies. Museums are covering exhibits, removing materials, and consulting with spiritual leaders to determine what can and cannot be displayed, what tales are told in the exhibit halls, and what rituals need to be observed in curation facilities! We can expect far more superstitious nonsense to move into spaces designed and meant for science.

Why are science museums abandoning the objective reasoning that scientific explanations require? It goes back to the postmodern agenda – there's just the oppressor and the oppressed; nothing factual; and who tells the narrative is more important than its validity.

It's not just a US phenomenon. In a 2024 article, Lawrence Goldman wrote about England's famous Pitt Rivers Museum, which curates the anthropological collection that was gifted to Oxford University in 1883 by Augustus Henry Lane Fox; Fox was a soldier who fought in the Crimean War, a scholar, and a landed gentleman who was later known as General Pitt-Rivers.[1] General Pitt-Rivers displayed the material in a manner that highlighted progress, believing that cultures evolve. Thus, the materials were arranged in progression: simple to complex. For instance, a display case on weapons may start with simple stone arrowheads and end with firearms. This kind of display also, unfortunately, demonstrates that not all cultures reach the same "evolutionary" stage at the same time. General Pitt-Rivers believed that the more primitive cultures would progress and catch-up; and, thus, he was considered a progressive thinker during his lifetime.

Nevertheless, the new curators and museum administrators have decided that they must infuse the museum with postmodern ideology, including signs, such as those that say "Coloniality divides the world into 'the West and the rest' and assigns racial, intellectual and cultural superiority to the West." They even inserted concerns that Western colonial systems have imposed the "gender binary." By focusing on comments about the "black bodies," "gender," and "power," and in hand-wringing statements about stereotypes, they've lost the interesting story about how social evolution was a theory that all people progressed. It was a theory that was used by anti-slavery movements. And, cultural evolution married biological evolution with human development in a way that was supposed to humanize those who were once seen as less than human.

We can also see such issues played out in the decisions museums are making about not displaying human remains. The Smithsonian, the American Museum of Natural History, the Chicago Field Museum, the Penn Museum, and many more are deciding to stop showing human remains. The Penn Museum has said that wrapped mummified remains will still be on display, but these cases will contain warning signs! What type of warning signs would be needed – don't they know the curse of the mummy is fiction?

Museums like the Mütter Museum (the world's most famous anatomy museum, that features a wall of skulls and highlights diseases from birth defects to injuries) that revolve around displaying human remains, are struggling with this. They want to follow the woke herd of sheep, but they also know it'll be the death of them! So, instead, the Mütter Museum removed materials containing human remains from the internet; they've put up a big Black Lives Matter sign at the front door of their museum; and, they prohibit photography – although they still sell the postcards!

The display of human remains ignites the imagination; real bodies are far superior to any casts in their detail and individuality. The remains also show how cultures varied in how they treated the dead. For instance, in the American Museum of Natural History, there are artifacts from the Aztecs (from central Mexico) that are rattles used to make music, that have been created from human bones, like the shin bone. Obviously, then, the Aztecs didn't think that human bones were too sensitive to touch, carve, display, and utilize! But, curators are removing these artifacts too! Our ability to understand the past is being erased and replaced with a false narrative that all indigenous people buried human remains, saw them as sacred, and never would have allowed for such displays to occur!

But it's not just indigenous remains that are being removed. The Smithsonian's natural history museum has covered a display case that contains a mummy, because the photo *behind* the mummy contains images of the Terry Collection (a collection of skeletons dating from 1899 to 1941 that came mainly came from the St. Louis, Missouri area and consists of individuals whose bodies had not been claimed by relatives and, thus, were donated by the state to the medical school). And, they've drawn up a policy that states:

> Remains of persons who lived less than 300 years ago (12 25-year generations) will only be exhibited if NMNH has a written record of consent.

This, basically, is since the very beginning of photography. Furthermore, the policymakers are equating the display of human remains with the displaying of an image of human remains! Worse still, the Smithsonian has removed their "Written in Bone" website, which was an educational guide for teachers to talk about 17th century life in Chesapeake Bay. This guide introduced students to research on bones and how skeletal remains can be used to understand the past. It combined forensics with historic archaeology, and was a way to get students excited about learning. Now, when you go the website, you'll find a 4-page apology that includes these statements:

> In recent years, museums have been reckoning with the methods and means by which collections, including human remains, have been acquired. The Smithsonian National Museum of Natural History is no exception.
>
> We acknowledge that some of the practices of our past may not have been acceptable then and are certainly not acceptable today.
>
> We ask for your support in championing changes that reflect best practices in museums and research, understanding that all individuals and their represented human remains deserve dignity, respect, appropriate care, and stewardship.

Ironically, when it comes to Native American remains, the descendant communities have the say-so of what happens to their ancestors' remains. However, in this case, the Smithsonian acknowledged that "most of the individuals whose stories were featured…were shared with the consent and endorsement of family, descendant groups, and partner organizations serving as the communities of care." Yet, the museum's board members decided to overrule these people and "decided to refrain from making available this online content...."

And, in their archives, this type of material is now considered "harmful content" and comes with a trigger warning! It's a bizarre mix of wokeism, presentism, squeamishness, and superstition.

As I reached out to museum curators, their delayed responses – or sometimes complete lack of response – coupled with the new rules that are eliminating research possibilities for years to come, led me to believe that to continue anthropological research, I will need to continue to battle NAGPRA, even if the much-feared Rule 19 may thwart my efforts. I've reached out to attorneys in hopes of getting someone interested in overturning the law, especially through the use of the argument that NAGPRA breaches the separation of church and state, and the absurdities that NAGPRA has led to. So far, I've had no luck, but I will continue to write and speak out on the topic, and look for allies who want to save anthropology.

There's a saying: as California goes, so goes the Nation. We have definitely seen this happen on a variety of topics, and the new NAGPRA regulations are more similar to CalNAGPRA than to the original intent of NAGPRA. More problematically, California is going further downhill due to its lack of protection of science against woke warrior and indigenous beliefs. John Ramos, the state legislature who penned AB275, that was the topic of my *Mercury News* op-ed, penned more laws that Governor Gavin Newsom signed: AB226 and AB389. These laws will bury public university anthropology, as they require the University of California (AB226) and the California State University (AB389) systems to stop using skeletal collections (even when they cannot be affiliated with any living descendants) for research and teaching purposes. For instance, AB389 "prohibit[s] the use of any Native American human remains or cultural items for purposes of teaching or research at the California State University." And, in AB226, "[t]he University of California is strongly urged to prohibit use of any Native American human remains or cultural items for purposes of teaching or research."

As Jim Springer and I wrote for an article in *Skeptic Magazine*, teaching collections contain bones from a huge variety of sources.[2] SJSU's teaching collection predates not only my arrival, but also that of my predecessor. It contains remains from medical donations, remains likely purchased from India when it had a thriving skeletal trade, and remains likely from historical and archaeological sites. Many bones are marked UK, which doesn't stand for United Kingdom as some students have guessed, but for "unknown." Teaching collections also contain thousands of fragmented pieces, making it impossible to determine the number of individuals in the collection, and further making it impossible to determine the origin of those individuals. As Tim White said to me, in regards to the false allegations that he misused and hid Native American remains in UC Berkeley's teaching collection:

> There's nobody on this planet who can sit down and tell you what the cultural affiliation of this lower jaw is, or that lower jaw is. Nobody can do that.

NAGPRA was never meant to include teaching collections; CalNAGPRA was meant to mimic NAGPRA, except for allowing non-federally recognized tribes from California to repatriate remains. These reburial laws were meant to unite culturally affiliated skeletal remains with modern day tribes. Unaffiliated remains were to be left in the care of universities and museums. This compromise has broken down.

When it becomes impossible to determine what bones are Native American and which aren't, the reburial activists will just claim the entire collections. And, as teaching collections are buried, California universities will lose their ability to teach the next generation of forensic anthropologists, especially those who would be trained in disaster recovery efforts that require identification of human remains even when the bone is highly fragmented. Anthropologists have played key roles in helping identify victims of 9-11, the Waco Texas debacle, and those who have died in natural disasters. As I wrote for *California Globe*:

> When the collections are lost, we lose a tool to train the next generation who would bring justice to families of victims of terrorism, other crimes, and natural disasters. And, all we'll have left to offer these families is "thoughts and prayers," brought to you by the party of science.

At SJSU, the newest protocols, following the enactment of AB389, have led the University president to proclaim that the University will accept no new collections. Also, no audio, video, or photographic devices are allowed in the curation facility. And, data will be physically locked away! The protocols add that "associated documentation and photographs, and archival content" is now subject to this presidential directive. SJSU has buried anthropological research on the past!

For those who argued that 3D casts and sharing data are the way forward, their naiveté must be over. And, if one thinks that one can collaborate, still conduct real research, and draw sensible conclusions, a slew of papers illustrate otherwise. I've discussed the DNA research of the Muwekma Ohlone and ancient Native Californians in the previous chapter.

Yet, even other questions, like when did Native Americans start riding horses, are now being framed by oral myths instead of the data. Researchers who published in the prestigious journal *Science* argued that Native Americans rode and domesticated horses before coming into contact with Europeans.[3] The authors draw this conclusion because remains of horses, with DNA matching Spanish-introduced horses, were found in places where Spaniards had yet to meet with Native Americans. The researchers should have suggested that these domesticated horses escaped from the Spaniards and that the Native Americans then hunted and ate them, rather than rode them. There is evidence of butchering on the bones! And, there is no scientific evidence on the human bones of Native Americans of that time and location to support that the Native Americans rode the horses prior to European contact. But, this didn't prevent the researchers from concluding that the Native Americans were riding the horses – they drew their conclusion based on oral myths passed on by tribes! Part of the reason for this ties in with the woke agenda of eulogizing anything Native American – or indigenous more generally. Perish the thought that Native Americans hadn't figured something out! So, when the opportunity arose, the narrative changed: oh yes, Native Americans were domesticating and riding horses too! We'll see far more misinterpretations of data since including "indigenous knowledge" is now required for government funding.

And, in a stunning turnaround, the article "Extracting the practices of paleogenomics: A study of DNA labs and research in relation to Native American and Indigenous peoples," published online on February 17th, 2023, in the top physical anthropology journal – *American Journal of Biological Anthropology* – was retracted the very next day, presumably because the authors had second thoughts about sharing indigenous DNA data. The prevailing trend seemed to be that open-access to data was supposed to be decolonizing; but Native American activists have said that it actually perpetuates colonialism and that indigenous peoples must have control over the data, who it will benefit, and what information can be gleaned from it! Just when you think you've got away with it by being woke, it blows up in your face because you haven't been *quite* woke enough! It's tough being one of the wokerati these days!

The latest NAGPRA changes and the comments that were considered to make these changes reveal more bad news. I've attended NAGPRA information sessions on how these new rules change our ability to curate and research collections. Upon asking the question of "if consulting tribes do not respond and no repatriation is planned, at what time can collections be utilized for research?" The response was "never"! In other words, the tribes could ignore the museum and university outreach and stop all research!

I also queried:

> If an object has been declared as sacred, but was not previously considered sacred by the same tribe, can one use the previous statement from the tribe to support continued curation and research on the item?

The answer was "no" – they can change their minds at any time and no reason for this change of heart is needed. In the Biden administration's "indigenous knowledge" mandate, this ability for Native Americans to change what is sacred, especially when it comes to land, is also supported – tradition and sacredness seems to be contingent on benefit to the tribe!

But what's really scary is that many of the public comments – especially coming from tribes – want the regulations to be even *more* aggressive. They called for repatriation of soil, casts, records, photos, animals imbued with human spirits, and more! It's my advice to those studying skeletal remains to keep your data, photos, casts, and x-rays in your possession – not in university offices, labs, and curation facilities! These are now vulnerable places. And, of course, share the data in a manner that allows you not to lose them!

My time with Heterodox Academy's Center for Academic Pluralism is winding down. But, I'm not done yet!

---

[1]Goldman, Lawrence. (2024, January 30). A Breach of Trust in Oxford. The Pitt Rivers Museum and the Destruction of the Past. *History Reclaimed.* https://historyreclaimed.co.uk/a-breach-of-trust-in-oxford-the-pitt-rivers-museum-and-the-destruction-of-the-past/

[2]Weiss, Elizabeth and James W. Springer. 2023. Bone wars: How activists are targeting teaching. *Skeptic Magazine.* 28: 30-35. https://www.skeptic.com/reading_room/bone-wars-how-activists-are-targeting-teaching/

[3]Taylor, William Timothy Treal, Pablo Librado, Mila Hunska Tašunke Icu, Carlton Shield Chief Gover, Jimmy Arterberry, Anpetu Luta Wiŋ, Akil Nujipi et al., 2023. "Early Dispersal of Domestic Horses into the Great Plains and Northern Rockies," *Science* 379, no. 6639: 1316–23, https://doi.org/10.1126/science.adc9691

# Conclusions

When I first started to work on *Repatriation and Erasing the Past* in 2017, I couldn't have foreseen all the ways in which it would change my life. After all, I had written about the problems of repatriation laws and the ideology behind those laws for well over a decade by then. But now things are different; the tribes of academia have left their intellectual endeavors, and have fully embraced identity politics.

Postmodernism, although having started long ago (over a hundred years ago), took hold in universities in the 1960s and has been gaining traction ever since. At its apex now, postmodernism has led to an environment where reason is eschewed for the embracement of victim narratives. The world, according to the postmodern ideologues, is divided into oppressive agents – the West, whites, science, and objectivity – and oppressed agents – the indigenous, people of color (including Muslims, but not Jews, who are seen as oppressors), and superstition. Wokeism, with its obsession with race and racism, is the offspring of postmodernism. And, woke warriors are those who are constantly fighting against freedoms to battle the unending racism that they think lies within every 'white, colonial, settler's' heart – that is if they even have one – and within every Western institute.

This new academic world has split the people into tribes. Of course, there are the Native American tribes, some of which are as newly-created as the Muwekma Ohlone, but it's also about all the other tribes created by believed victimhood status – the Black Trowel Collective, the Queer Archaeology Interest Group, the Association of Latina/o and Latinx Anthropologists, Queers for Palestine, and the Trans Doe Task Force. Their reason for studying anthropology is to insert their identity into past populations, rather than trying to understand the past from an objective perspective.

Intersectionality of these identities also ensures that people can adopt multiple victimhood statuses, such as a nonbinary, Latinx, indigenous scholar. And, thus, in repatriation ideology – an offshoot of postmodernism – they too become "expert witnesses" who are not to be questioned. This leads to absurdities, such as demands not to identify the sex of skeletons (because we don't know how these past people identified; i.e., what their pronouns were!), or reconstructing the past through a "Queer lens." But, it also leads to a re-writing of the past, where concepts are recently introduced – like the 'two-spirit' concept in Native American culture, that was actually introduced in 1990 at the Third Annual Inter-tribal Native American, First Nations, Gay and Lesbian American Conference in Winnipeg.

Perhaps this tribal identity is why students and faculty are not concerned about the individual, and why attacks on one's appearance aren't considered inappropriate – that is, as long as it's an individual you are making fun of, rather than a tribal member!

But, throughout this time from when my publisher called to say they were in "crisis mode" to now, I've also made many new connections. My position as a National Association of Scholars board member has introduced me to many fine scholars; those who still read books and who care about saving liberal education. I've also made connections with fearless women, such as Amy Wax and Frances Widdowson, and courageous men, like Charles Negy, Bruce Gilley, and Glynn Custred – all of whom I am proud to call my friends and colleagues. These people, and many that I haven't mentioned, have intellect and humor. I'm grateful that my battles have led to these friendships and alliances.

I'm also thankful to organizations like Heterodox Academy, National Association of Scholars, the Society for Academic Freedom and Scholarship, the Babbling Beaver, and the Foundation for Individual Rights and Expression (FIRE) for all they're doing to help save academia. They have different purposes and different methods, but all are attempting to return academia to its intellectual origins by supporting free inquiry and fighting against censorious acts, like book bans and shouting down speakers.

Needless to say, I will be forever grateful to Pacific Legal Foundation, especially Daniel Ortner, Ethan Blevins, David Hoffa, and Wilson

Freeman. They took up my difficult case and fought with me, and for me.

Throughout these years of dealing with cancel culture attacks, I've shed many tears, but they were always tears of laughter. Because when absurdity strikes, there's no better response. I've never had a sleepless night, even when I was unsure of my job security. And, although I settled my case, I never apologized, and I never will. I have nothing to apologize for!

Even as I write these last lines, the internet is buzzing with personal insults as a result of the woke mob having heard about this book. The name-calling has returned: "ghoul," "grave robber," and "diggin' up grandma" have been resurrected! And, just the other day, I received an email in which the person called me an "ignorant racist cunt."

Due to my nuanced position on sex and gender, I've been called a TERF – an insult that stands for Trans-Exclusionary Radical Feminist – by the trans tribe, but I've also been called "nonbinary" and even a "man" or "trans" by the gender critical tribe!

But, it's not just social media that's still talking about my case and the now-infamous skull photo tweet. Mainstream media, like Newsweek – just this week, March 19th, 2024 – are still perpetuating the false narrative that I violated protocols by holding a skull with my bare hands. And, outrageously, comparing my acts to the murders of Native Americans in Osage County in the 1920s!

And, the new SJSU president Cynthia Teniente-Matson, who claims "we learn by taking the time to read and watch things that we disagree with," has decided to block me on her official university social media account, likely because I criticized her efforts to rework the University mission to focus on diversity and inclusion at the expense of freedom, truth, and knowledge.

As I head back to Tucson, I'm looking forward to my next adventures. The first of which will be to sort through the hundreds of x-rays of Native American bones that I have, start analyzing the data, and re-ignite my efforts to reconstruct the past!

Elizabeth Weiss

New York City, 3/22/2024

*Figure 8: X-rays Taken from Prehistoric Native American Collections*

# Further Reading

Benedict, Jeff. 2000. *Without Reservation : The Making of America's Most Powerful Indian Tribe and the World's Largest Casino.* 1st ed. New York: HarperCollins.

Benedict, Jeff. 2003. *No Bone Unturned : The Adventures of a Top Smithsonian Forensic Scientist and the Legal Battle for America's Oldest Skeletons.* 1st ed. New York N.Y: HarperCollinsPublishers.

Bondeson, Jan. 2001. *Buried Alive : The Terrifying History of Our Most Primal Fear.* New York: Norton.

Chacon, Richard J. and Rubén G. Mendoza. 2007. *North American Indigenous Warfare and Ritual Violence.* Tucson: University of Arizona Press.

Chagnon, Napoleon A. 2014. *Noble Savages: My Life Among Two Dangerous Tribes -- the Yanomamo and the Anthropologists.* New York: Simon & Schuster.

Champion, C. P. and Tom Flanagan. 2023. *Grave Error: How The Media Misled Us (and the Truth about Residential Schools).* Independently Published.

Flanagan, Thomas. 2019. *First Nations? Second Thoughts.* 3rd ed. Montreal: McGill-Queen's University Press.

Flynn, James R. 2020. *A Book Too Risky to Publish : Free Speech and Universities.* Washington DC: Academica Press.

Fynn-Paul, Jeff. 2023. *Not Stolen : The Truth About European Colonialism in the New World.* New York: Bombardier Books an imprint of Post Hill Press.

Gilley, Bruce. 2022. *The Case for Colonialism.* 1st ed. Nashville: New English Review Press.

Hooven, Carole. 2021. *T : The Story of Testosterone, the Hormone That Dominates and Divides Us.* 1st ed. New York: Henry Holt and Company.

Hunt, Morton M. 1999. *The New Know-Nothings : The Political Foes of the Scientific Study of Human Nature*. New Brunswick: Transaction.

Ives, Timothy H. 2021. *Stones of Contention*. 1st ed. Nashville: New English Review Press.

Lefkovitz, Mary R. 1997. *Not Out of Africa : How Afrocentrism Became an Excuse to Teach Myth As History*. Revised ed. New York: BasicBooks.

Lukianoff, Greg and Jonathan Haidt. 2018. *The Coddling of the American Mind : How Good Intentions and Bad Ideas Are Setting Up a Generation for Failure*. New York: Penguin Press.

Negy, Charles. 2020. *White Shaming : Bullying Based on Prejudice Virtue - Signaling and Ignorance*. Revised first ed. Dubuque: Kendall Hunt.

Owsley, Douglas W. and Richard L. Jantz. 2014. *Kennewick Man : The Scientific Investigation of an Ancient American Skeleton* (version First edition) First ed. College Station: Texas A & M University Press.

Quigley, Christine. 1998. *Modern Mummies : The Preservation of the Human Body in the Twentieth Century*. Jefferson: McFarland.

Saad, Gad. 2020. *The Parasitic Mind: How Infectious Ideas are Killing Common Sense*. Washington DC: Regnery Press.

Weiss, Elizabeth. 2015. *Paleopathology in Perspective : Bone Health and Disease through Time*. Lanham: Rowman & Littlefield.

Weiss, Elizabeth. 2017. *Reading the Bones : Activity Biology and Culture*. Gainesville: University Press of Florida.

Weiss, Elizabeth and James W. Springer. 2020. *Repatriation and Erasing the Past*. Gainesville: University of Florida Press.

Widdowson, Frances and Albert Howard. 2008. *Disrobing the Aboriginal Industry : The Deception Behind Indigenous Cultural Preservation*. Montreal Que: McGill-Queen's University Press.

# Index

# About the Author

Elizabeth Weiss is a retired physical anthropology professor, specializing in the analysis of human skeletal remains. For much of her career she was based at San José State University, where she curated one of the largest collections of skeletal remains in the US. She is the author of numerous books, including *Reading the Bones: Activity, Biology and Culture* and *Repatriation and Erasing the Past* (with James W. Springer), and articles in academic journals, such as the *American Journal of Physical Anthropology,* to popular science magazines, such as *Skeptic Magazine.* Weiss played an essential role in bringing the Smithsonian's traveling exhibition "What Does it Mean to be Human?" to the San Francisco Bay Area. She's been featured in *The New York Times, Science* and *USA Today*, and has been interviewed on Fox News and NewsMax.

Printed in the USA
CPSIA information can be obtained
at www.ICGtesting.com
JSHW060025230524
63641JS00007B/362

9 781680 533330